KU-573-870

QMC   652998 9

a30213 006529989b

WITHDRAWN
FROM STOCK
QMUL LIBRARY

ACCESS TO THE LAW

ACCESS TO THE LAW

A study conducted for the
LAW REFORM COMMISSION OF CANADA

by

M. L. FRIEDLAND
Dean, Faculty of Law
University of Toronto

in collaboration with
PETER E. S. JEWETT
and LINDA J. JEWETT

CARSWELL/METHUEN, Toronto.

180252
KF82. 60

Copyright © by Methuen Publications (A Division of the Carswell Company Limited)

All rights reserved. No part of this publication may be reproduced, stored in a retrieval system, or transmitted in any form or by any means, electronic, mechanical, photocopying, recording or otherwise, without the prior written permission of Methuen Publications, 2330 Midland Avenue, Agincourt, Ontario, Canada.

ISBN 0 458 91290 5

QUEEN MARY COLLEGE
LIBRARY
MILE END ROAD,
LONDON, E.1.

Printed and bound in Canada

1 2 3 4 5 6 7 8 9 AP 79 78 77 76 75

CONTENTS

Appendices

PREFACE

This study arose out of work that I began while a member of the Law Reform Commission of Canada. When I returned to the University of Toronto in the summer of 1972 the Law Reform Commission asked me to continue to explore the area. Throughout, the members of the Commission have supported and encouraged the study.

From its inception the Commission has been concerned about involving the public in law reform and making the law accessible to citizens. This was seen as part of the mandate set out in the Act establishing the Commission to develop "new approaches to and new concepts of the law in keeping with and responsive to the changing needs of modern Canadian society and of individual members of that society." In its first Annual Report in 1972 the Commission stated: "Law reform is not a matter for lawyers alone. In modern society there is virtually no individual life that is not affected, and often in very serious ways, by our laws. It is for this reason that we are determined to see to it that the general public, not merely the legal profession, should become involved in our efforts to modernize the law." The efforts by the Commission to involve the public in law reform are well known. In its second Annual Report in 1973 the Commission pointed out the need for "review, research and reform" of "the general form of statutory arrangement, drafting and interpretation." "It is essential," stated the Commission, "if the ordinary Canadian is ever to have any understanding of his law. It is essential if we are to have laws that are reasonably clear and intelligible and belong to us all. It is essential if we are ever to 'bring the laws of Canada home to the Canadian people.'" These themes were repeated in the third Annual Report in 1974. This study represents one attempt to explore in some detail access to the law.

I was fortunate to be able to work with Peter and Linda Jewett, both of whom have served full-time on the project for the eight-month period between March and November 1974. Peter is a recent graduate of the Faculty of Law, University of Toronto, on leave of absence from the law firm of Tory, Tory, DesLauriers & Binnington, and Linda is a librarian on leave from the Business Section of the Metropolitan Toronto Central Library. Their ability, dedication, and energy are reflected in all aspects of this study.

An Advisory Committee was appointed, consisting of Lyle Fairbairn, formerly the Assistant Provincial Director of Legal Aid and now counsel to the Ontario Law Reform Commission, Francess Halpenny, Dean of the Faculty of Library Science, Ian Montagnes, General Editor of the University of Toronto Press, Peter Russell, Principal of Innis College, and John Swan, from the Faculty of Law. They have assisted us greatly in formulating the conceptual framework for the study and in analysing our results.

We collected data on where people turn to for information about law and legal advice and the accuracy of the answers they receive. Visits were made to centres across Canada to study the various organizations from which citizens now obtain legal information and advice. Interviews were conducted with, and questionnaires completed by, persons from legal aid and assistance centres, government information offices, community information centres, libraries, and police departments.

All of those with whom we conducted interviews, who assisted us by filling out questionnaires, or who participated in our surveys co-operated with enthusiasm. A list of the organizations that assisted us is set out in Appendix 1 of this report at page 100. We are grateful to Patricia Myhal, a lawyer at the firm of Tory, Tory, DesLauriers & Binnington, for her assistance in the preparation of the French-language versions of our questionnaire and other materials.

Early in the study we held a one-day workshop at the University of Toronto to bring together a group of persons whose jobs regularly involved the handling of legal questions from the public. We found the discussions that took place at the workshop useful in defining the nature and scope of the problem we were studying. A list of the people who participated in the workshop is set out in Appendix 2 of this report at page 111.

In addition, we consulted a number of non-lawyers, who gave an interdisciplinary perspective to our work. Professor Anthony Doob from the Department of Psychology at the University of Toronto assisted us throughout the study, and Professor H.A. Gleason from the Centre for Linguistic Studies, Professor Paul A. Kolers from the Department of Psychology and Professors Brian Land, Katherine Packer and Anne Schabas from the Faculty of Library Science, all from the University of Toronto, and Alice Janisch, a librarian from Halifax, helped us with specific aspects of the study.

Our objective was to investigate whether any new delivery systems and print sources would improve access to the law. We asked a number of people to attempt to write the law in a form that could be read by non-lawyers. Extracts from the models they developed are set out in Appendix 11 at page 170. We would like to thank Jack Batten, Professor D.M. Beatty, Ray Chatelin, Professor T.E.J. McDonnell, Professor A.W. Mewett, Rick Salsberg, and Leslie M. Yager, all of whom prepared models for us.

We are also indebted to a number of persons for their helpful comments throughout the study. Many of these persons have already been referred to in this preface, but we would like to add the names of Rosalind Brooke, Robert Bruser, Richard Gathercole, Peter Gilchrist, Balfour Halévy, Larry Macdonald, Eric Miller, Diana Priestley, Robert Prichard, and Gaylord Watkins. In addition, we tested our ideas on a number of my colleagues in the Faculty of Law, to whom we are grateful.

During the summer we were ably assisted by Roselyn Zisman, who had just graduated from the Law School, and for shorter periods by Derek D'Oliveira, a second year student, and John Zinn, a third year student. Janelle Kingscott coped admirably as secretary to the project and also helped conduct some of the surveys. My own secretary, Patricia Dawson, helped us keep track of many of the administrative details involved in the project, and Julia Hall typed the final report.

We hope that this study will help bring about, as the title suggests, greater access to the law.

Faculty of Law   M.L.F.
University of Toronto
January 1975

Chapter 1
INTRODUCTION

The state has an obligation to ensure that its laws are available in an understandable fashion to laymen.

This proposition may appear self-evident; yet very little attention has been given to accomplishing this objective in Canada — or, indeed, in any common-law country. In fact, very little attention has been given to making our laws comprehensible even to lawyers. Governments have left the task of explaining the law largely to private enterprise, and in Canada the commercial publishers and the legal profession have done relatively little to assist the lawyer or the layman.

Over the past decade, much has been accomplished through our legal aid schemes to make the *courts* accessible; in the future, emphasis should also be placed on making the *law* accessible.

Why should citizens have access to the law? The simple answer is that good citizenship requires it. Citizens should be able easily to ascertain their rights and obligations. An increasing number of statutory and other provisions place positive obligations on members of the public, but a citizen cannot be expected to fulfil these obligations unless he knows of them. A basic assumption of our legal system is that the citizen knows the law; for example, section 19 of the Criminal Code provides that "ignorance of the law by a person who commits an offence is not an excuse for committing that offence." In an increasingly complex society, citizens also need to have access to the law in order to plan their affairs — financial and domestic, at home and at work.

Not only is it in the interest of the layman to have access to the law, but the legal system itself benefits from informed comment by the layman, comment which obviously cannot be informed without some knowledge of the law.

I. THE NATURE OF THE PROBLEM
Every citizen continually encounters situations and problems that involve law. To deal with these problems effectively the citizen must find out what the relevant law is and how it affects him. In serious and complex situations many citizens will rely on legal experts to advise them and recommend courses of action. But most of the situations and problems involving law which the citizen encounters involve reasonably simple questions that have reasonably simple answers. Most people who now seek legal information or advice do not go to a lawyer in

1

private practice. In fact, many people even when faced with serious legal difficulties are reluctant, or afraid, to approach a lawyer.

Most people attempt to get legal information from such sources as government offices, information centres, legal aid and assistance offices, public libraries and, somewhat surprisingly, the police. These information sources receive millions of questions of all types every year, and many of these involve the law. The police departments of 20 major cities in Canada, for example, receive a total of over 17 million telephone calls per year. As many as one-third of these inquiries require some legal knowledge to answer satisfactorily.

The 57 public libraries across the country that supplied us with figures indicated that they receive at least two and a quarter million reference inquiries each year. Of these, three to four percent are inquiries about law.

The legal aid offices and legal assistance clinics in Canada, obvious sources of information about law, receive over 800,000 requests from the public each year, and the number is increasing rapidly. Although almost all of these concern law, not even half of them involve legal questions or problems complex enough to require the services of a lawyer. At least 500,000 of these requests are simple information questions or straightforward problems that require only a few minutes of summary advice.

The community information centres across Canada handle over one million inquiries of all kinds each year. These centres vary a great deal in the services they provide; some reported that only three or four percent of their inquiries concern the law, while others indicated that virtually all their inquiries do. In total, these centres annually deal with at least 250,000 information questions or summary-advice problems involving the law.

Government offices, both the special information branches of the federal and provincial governments and the public offices of various specific departments, receive more information inquiries than all other sources combined. A vast number of the requests for information directed at the government pertain to the law, and to statutory and administrative law in particular. The Standing Senate Committee on National Finance estimated that in the fiscal year ending March 31, 1974 the total cost of all information dissemination within the departments and agencies of the federal government alone was as high as $200 million.[1]

Our tests, described in chapter 2, indicate that members of the public also approach a wide variety of other non-lawyer sources for this type of information and advice. The clergy, doctors, employers, trade union officials, the staffs of social service organizations, family members, and the like all receive such questions.

Unfortunately the major sources of information are not meeting the need as effectively as they are potentially able to do. We were surprised at the number of times they give incomplete, inadequate, or simply wrong answers to questions about the law.

The questions and problems received by these individuals and organizations vary considerably in scope and complexity. Many involve subtleties and technical problems that undoubtedly require a lawyer's expertise, and these should be directed to lawyers in private practice or in legal aid clinics. Nevertheless, the majority are simple and straightforward and can easily be solved once the inquirer learns a few particulars of the relevant law — often details of statutes or regulations.

The lawyers participating in the Hamilton Pilot Project of the Ontario Legal Aid Plan (involving the establishment of a legal aid clinic in the Victoria Park and Northwest Community Organization Centre) reported that 63 percent of the legal problems they encountered required only oral advice and a further 14 percent only summary legal assistance.[2]

Police departments receive many complaints and inquiries about all sorts of matters. Many of these result in police action and many deal with non-police matters, but a large number are direct inquiries about the law or require some knowledge of law by the officer handling the call. The following are examples of inquiries received by the London Police Force:[3]

1. How do I get an adjournment? Who can appear as an agent?
2. How do I get time to pay in the event of a conviction?
3. Can I get Legal Aid assistance for a Highway Traffic Act charge? How do I go about it?
4. What happens when I first appear in court on a charge?
5. If there are injuries, can a person recover all his damages or does the O.H.I.P. get their payments returned to them?
6. Does age make any difference in signing contracts?
7. Who enforces the Pollution Control Act?

They also receive questions about the point system under the Highway Traffic Act, about what constitutes a residence under the Liquor Control Act, about possessing firearms, and about what can be done legally with respect to complaints of noise. The London force reported that they even receive questions about liens on chattels and rights under the Mechanics' Lien Act.

Public libraries receive reference inquiries on virtually all subjects. Some examples of legal inquiries received by the Metropolitan Toronto Central Library are the following:

1. Do you have a copy of the Canada-Germany tax treaty?
2. Do you have any information about the Small Claims Court?
3. Can the police search a motor vehicle without a warrant?
4. What is the age limit for statutory rape?
5. Can an Ontario employer hold back an employee's first two week's pay until the end of the term of employment?
6. Is a disposition of the capital of an American mutual fund totally taxable in Canada, or only 50 percent taxable?
7. Do you have a copy of the Retail Sales Tax Act?
8. What is the minimum wage in Alberta?
9. Does an alderman have to resign if he is convicted of a criminal offence?

As mentioned above, government offices of various types receive more inquiries than all the other sources combined. The following are examples of questions received by the Citizens' Inquiry Branch, a special information branch of the Ontario Government:

1. How can I keep hunters off my property? They've even shot at my "no trespassing" sign.
2. Is it illegal to pick trilliums?
3. I want to ride my horse on the highway. Are there special traffic laws I should know about?
4. I want to bring my younger brother and sister from Hong Kong to live in Canada with me, but the Department of Immigration says the Province has to give approval. Is that true?
5. If I marry my non-Canadian boyfriend, who only has visitor status, will he be deported?

Some citizens with questions like these attempt to look up the law on their own; so also do members of the various information sources approached. Can the citizen or his non-lawyer advisor now look up the law successfully?

No doubt some of them succeed. But the legal cards are stacked against the non-lawyer. A simple experiment we conducted (described in chapter 2) shows how difficult it is for the layman to use existing legal materials.

Most people do not even know where to begin. They often do not know whether a particular matter is within federal or provincial jurisdiction or whether it is covered by legislation, by regulation, by municipal by-law, or by case law. Let us assume, however, that a situation is known to be covered by a federal statute. Where does the non-lawyer go to find the statutes? If a set of statutes is found, how does he or she know that there are not amendments to them, or relevant regulations, or cases that qualify the language of the statute, or other statutes that have a bearing on the question? If the relevant section is found, can it be easily understood? And when a matter is covered mainly by case law, the non-lawyer does not have a chance of discovering the law. There are relatively few legal texts produced in Canada to help even the lawyer; many important areas of the law are left uncovered. In these areas lawyers use English and American texts. Non-lawyers would obviously have great difficulty in applying a foreign text to Canada. In fact, a recent Department of Justice document, "Operation Compulex",[4] shows that lawyers themselves are not very comfortable doing legal research within the existing system.

II. RESEARCH OUTLINE

Relatively few citizens at present actually attempt to look up the law themselves. A member of the public faced with a simple legal problem often seeks assistance by contacting some information source. Although such inquiries are often referred to more appropriate sources of information and assistance, nevertheless, whether they are the first recourse or enter after one or more referrals, it is intermediaries who normally attempt to look up the law.

Lawyers, of course, are a special segment of the intermediary group. Ordinarily they handle the more complicated legal problems, and presumably they have more success in researching the law because of their expert knowledge, but the process is basically the same as for other intermediaries — they operate between the law and the public.

Access to the law is thus usually a two step process. To have effective access the public must be able easily to get in touch with an intermediary, who in turn can successfully find the relevant law. The purpose of our research was therefore to determine whether or not the public is able to obtain information about the law in this way, and, if not, why not.

We began by looking at the public in order to determine whether members of the public really do have difficulty in obtaining information about the law in Canada. We sought answers to the following questions: what do members of the general public do when faced with simple legal problems; and, if they seek information or advice, from whom do they seek it? and when they seek information or advice, do they receive accurate information and sound advice? To answer these questions we approached members of the general public in various areas of Toronto, Kitchener, and Lindsay and asked them what they would do if faced with each of a series of ten test problems. The problems were selected to be representative of the sort of simple legal questions and problems a citizen might be expected to encounter in his daily life.

Using the results obtained in the Toronto portion of the survey, and taking our cue from the Standing Senate Committee on National Finance, which, during the course of its examination of Information Canada, had researchers telephone Information Canada Enquiry Centres anonymously with test questions,[5] we telephoned the various information sources suggested by members of the sample and asked them for help with the problems.

The results of this surveying and testing of sources are described in chapter 2. Also contained in that chapter is a description of two further empirical tests carried out to complement the testing of information sources. The first of these involved telephoning various information sources and lawyers with two additional problems in an attempt to measure the success attained by lawyers, as compared to other sources, in providing information about the law. The second consisted of having members of the public attempt to find information in the statutes. The purpose of this test was to discover the success members of the public might be expected to have if they looked up law on their own, using existing legal materials.

Having found the answer to our two questions and having concluded, as chapter 2 will describe, that members of the public do have difficulty obtaining accurate information about law, we attempted to find out why access to the law is a problem. We did this by conducting an intensive study of the most important "intermediary" organizations to determine why they seem to be having difficulty handling legal questions and problems. We visited such organizations (legal aid offices and assistance clinics, government offices and information branches, community information centres, police departments, and public, academic, and law libraries) in 21 cities across the country.[6] In addition, we mailed questionnaires to organizations in areas we were unable to visit. In total, we conducted 184 interviews and mailed out 324 questionnaires, of which 133 were completed and returned. These organizations are listed in Appendix 1 at page 100.

The outcome of this study, a description of how each type of organization at present handles legal questions, is contained in chapter 3. Chapter 5 discusses some of the problems they encounter and suggests how their operations might be improved.

III. POSSIBLE SOLUTIONS

One obvious method of giving citizens access to the law is through lawyers. But even if it were practical to do so, it is surely wrong in principle to preserve the law in a form that only lawyers can find and interpret. We should not require high priests to keep the law.

Moreover, there probably are too few lawyers to go around. "Operation Compulex" showed that in 1971 there were only 13,200 lawyers in private practice in Canada.[7] There are more lawyers practising in the State of Ohio (with about half of Canada's population) than in all of Canada. Over the past several decades the number of lawyers in Canada has, of course, been increasing, but not in relation to the labour force and only slightly in relation to the population. During the same period there has been a vast increase in government legislation and regulations, and therefore in the number and variety of matters handled by lawyers.[8] While more lawyers are being trained, it is an expensive business. And, in any event, many persons avoid visiting lawyers for legal information or advice, even if they are available.

Instead, they approach a wide variety of people and organizations. To a large extent, the type of organization approached varies with the problem. The citizen expects and undoubtedly wishes to receive a different kind of response from different organizations. A person who goes to a public library is usually seeking information in a form different from that desired by a person who telephones the police or drops in to a community information centre. Inquiries about law involve a spectrum of questions and problems and what is needed is a spectrum of responses.

As described in more detail in chapter 5, we feel that a variety of measures are necessary to provide better access to the law in Canada. The public, in general, appears to know very little about law and the legal system. Increased education about the law and the legal process, both in schools and in adult education programs, would better enable people to recognize the legal aspects of day-to-day problems and to cope with them more effectively. In addition, the present systems of delivering legal information and advice could be improved by establishing more organized procedures for dealing with questions from the public and for training the staffs of various information sources in the handling of information in general and legal information in particular. Further, the expansion of legal aid into a large scale clinical operation should be seriously considered.

At present, attention is being given to providing the public with legal education and improving delivery systems. But no matter what progress may be made in those areas, the public will continue to experience significant difficulty in obtaining access to the law either directly or through others unless better legal reference materials are made available. Because we feel that such materials are fundamental to providing better access to the law, and because it is an area which has received far less attention than legal education, legal aid, and information delivery systems, we have given special attention in many parts of this study to the deficiencies of present legal materials and the need for new reference sources.

Chapter 4 contains a discussion of statutes and other existing legal materials and includes a number of suggestions aimed at improving the drafting and presentation of the law. Although improving the existing legal materials would help the citizen find the law, it does not appear to be enough. Not only will it be a long time before existing legal materials are written in a form in which they can be easily understood, but even then citizens or their non-lawyer advisors would still have difficulty finding the relevant provisions, integrating federal and provincial statutes and regulations, and discovering the relevant case law.

We know that many people have been turning for help to the popular legal handbooks available in bookstores. Unfortunately, these are inadequate; they are better than nothing, but no matter how well they are written they suffer from several major defects. For example, they cannot keep up with the changes in the law. And not designed to be used as quick reference tools, they tend to provide merely a general overview of an area of law rather than easily retrievable detailed information. Moreover, commercial publishers will concentrate only on major areas, like family law, and will not venture into other needed areas, such as workmen's compensation and mechanics' liens.

Other techniques of disseminating legal information, such as pamphlets, newspaper advertisements, television shows, and even "hot-line" programs, have a useful role to play. But they too are obviously not enough. What is needed is a reference tool that will give the citizen or his advisor specific information to deal with a particular question or problem at the time that it arises.

Section III of chapter 5 analyses and advocates a new legal reference tool for the citizen and his advisors: a multivolume legal encyclopedia, combining federal and provincial laws and regularly updated, which could be available to the various sources of information, and could also be available to members of the public, in public and school libraries and such places as government offices. Legal aid and assistance centres, Information Canada, provincial information offices, and community information centres clearly need a reliable source of legal information. The police, who are heavily involved in providing information on many matters, not just those relating to the criminal law, also clearly need assistance in this aspect of their work.

An important consequence of producing new legal materials is that lawyers in private practice might also find the volumes to be of help in looking up the law. And clients provided with copies of the relevant reference documents could more easily follow the steps their lawyers were taking.

Of course, many questions must be answered in relation to the preparation of such materials. Who should write them? At what level of sophistication should they be written? Should descriptive material be integrated with statutory material or should it be restricted to an introductory note? How should updating be systematized? How does one handle areas of law, such as contracts, that are primarily case law? Is it possible to include municipal by-laws? Should one go further than telling the layman merely what the law is and describe, for example, how to incorporate a company or draft a will or conduct one's own legal proceedings? At what point should the reader be warned that the area is complex and a lawyer should be consulted? What training should be given to non-lawyers responsible for using the materials? We explore these matters as well as questions of use, costs, subsidization, and implementation in detail in chapter 5.

The obligation of the government to promote the production of legal materials is overwhelming in a country like Canada, with a relatively small population, two major languages, eleven systems of law, and a complex and very sophisticated legal system. No doubt such an endeavour could not have been undertaken in the past, because it requires that enough of the law be in statutes to form a basis for intelligible exposition. But now many areas of Canadian law are almost wholly embodied in legislation or regulations: for example, unemployment insurance, workmen's compensation, landlord and tenant, income tax, copyright, criminal law, and labour law.

Surely it is time for the law to be available to those it is meant to govern.

NOTES

1. *Report of the Standing Senate Committee on National Finance on Information Canada*, Ottawa, Queen's Printer (1974), at 17.
2. Fairbairn, Lyle S., *Report on the Hamilton Pilot Project*, (October, 1973, mimeo.), at 6.
3. Taken from a series of reports by the heads of various branches of the London Police Force to the Chief of Police, Walter T. Johnson, and kindly supplied to us by the Chief.
4. Reprinted in (1972), 6 *Law Society of U. Can. Gaz.* 156.
5. *Report of the Standing Senate Committee on National Finance on Information Canada*, supra note, 1, at 26.
6. St. John's, Halifax, Charlottetown, Fredericton, Saint John, Quebec City, Montreal, Ottawa, Toronto, Hamilton, Kitchener, London, Windsor, Thunder Bay, Winnipeg, Regina, Saskatoon, Edmonton, Calgary, Victoria, and Vancouver.
7. It should be pointed out, however, that a number of knowledgeable persons with whom we spoke doubt the accuracy of this figure and feel that it is too low.
8. See the preliminary report prepared for the Committee of Ontario Law Deans by Meltz, "A Review of Historical Trends and Projections of the Number of Lawyers and Judges in the Ontario Labour Force" (1974), at 14, 21-3: between 1931 and 1971 the number of lawyers in private practice fell in relation to the total labour force, although it went up slightly in relation to the total population. Canadian figures up to 1950 can be found in Nelligan, "Lawyers in Canada: A Half-Century Count" (1950), 28 *Can. B. Rev.* 727, who notes at 729: "At the turn of the century, there were more lawyers in Canada in relation to the size of population than there have been at any time since." A similar pattern is found in the U.S. where the number of law professionals in relation to the labour force was approximately the same in 1970 as in 1900 (see Meltz, at 54).

Chapter 2

THE SEARCH FOR LEGAL INFORMATION

I. WHERE DO PEOPLE TURN FOR LEGAL INFORMATION?

Our examination of access to the law began by attempting to answer the
following questions: what do members of the general public do when
faced with simple legal problems, and, if they seek information or
advice, from whom do they seek it? To this end we undertook an
empirical study using samples drawn from the public in Toronto,
Kitchener, and Lindsay — a large, a medium-sized, and a small city in
Ontario. Each subject was presented with ten test problems and asked
what he or she would do in each case.[1]

The test questions and problems we used for this survey were the
following:

1. *Old Age Benefits*: You will be turning 65 years old in a few months
   and wish to apply for any old age benefits you are entitled to. What
   would you do?
2. *Leaking Roof*: You live in a rented house and your roof is leaking.
   What would you do if the landlord refused to fix it?
3. *Pregnancy Leave*: For 18 months, a woman has been working in an
   office which employs 26 other employees, and she becomes pre-
   gnant. If you were the woman, what would you do to find out what
   benefits you would be entitled to?
4. *Door-to-door Salesman*: You agree to buy an encyclopedia for $150
   from a door-to-door salesman to be paid in monthly instalments.
   The next day you change your mind. What would you do?
5. *Car Repair*: You took your car to a garage to have the starter repaired and paid $200. As it was not done properly you took it to
   another garage and were charged another $200. What would you do
   to get the $200 back from the first garage?
6. *Deserted Wife*: A man deserts his wife and children, leaving them
   with no money. If you were the wife, what would you do?
7. *Popular Song*: You have written the words and music for a song
   that you are sure will be extremely popular. What would you do?
8. *Speeding Ticket*: You receive a speeding ticket on which your licence number is incorrect. What would you do?
9. *Swimming Pool Fence*: Your neighbours built a fence around their
   pool and it doesn't look high enough to you. What would you do?

10. *Criminal Code*: What would you do if you wanted to know what section 195.1 of the Criminal Code says?

These problems were selected because they are the sorts of questions commonly received by information sources and are of varying degrees of seriousness and complexity. Some satisfactory solutions are set out in Appendix 4 at page 125. Problems 1, 3, and 10, dealing with old age benefits, pregnancy leave, and the Criminal Code, are straightforward information questions, although the pregnancy leave question is more complex than the other two. Problems 5 and 6, dealing with inadequate automobile repair and a deserted wife, are more serious legal problems involving a considerable amount of advice as well as some basic information. The other five problems, dealing with a leaking roof, a door-to-door salesman, a copyright question, a speeding ticket, and a swimming pool fence, are relatively simple everyday problems, the solutions to which are covered, or are affected, by law.

In total, 100 subjects were presented with the questions: 60 in Toronto, 20 in Kitchener, and 20 in Lindsay.[2] We used samples from a large, a medium-sized, and a small city in order to compare the responses from population centres of different sizes. One would expect the responses to vary with the difference in the number and types of information sources available. As well, it had occurred to us that since law offices are usually in more accessible locations in smaller centres, people there might be inclined to use lawyers more often, and that since there are fewer service organizations in smaller centres, people might be more inclined than in a large city to solve problems by acting without first seeking information or help.

The surveying was carried out mostly during business hours, with a few interviews being done in the evening. This resulted in approximately two-thirds of the total sample being women and a higher representation of people who do not work outside the home than the national average would warrant. Correction for these two factors might well affect our results.

In many cases a subject gave more than one answer to a problem. For example, a subject would say, in response to the old age benefits question, "I would call the Unemployment Insurance Office, but if they couldn't help me, I'd call the provincial government." We kept track of both answers in such cases and thus ended up with 1,369 responses rather than the 1,000 expected (100 subjects each responding to 10 questions).

The responses were divided into four categories for each question: A) those indicating that the subject would seek information or help; B) those indicating that the subject would contact a lawyer; C) those indicating that the subject would do nothing or would act on his own without seeking information or help; and D) those indicating that the subject did not know what he would do. Summaries of the responses are contained in Tables 1 to 14 of Appendix 3 at page 115. Tables 1 to 10 show the responses to each question broken down into the four categories mentioned above. They also show which individuals and organizations were suggested by the subjects as sources of information or help. Tables 11 to 14 provide summaries of Tables 1 to 10, so that the percentages of responses falling in each of the four categories for each of the ten questions may be easily compared.

One of the major characteristics of the responses was the wide variety of information or service sources suggested. An average of 12 different sources were indicated for each problem, and in only two cases were fewer than ten mentioned. Government sources were often suggested, but many others appeared too, such as the police, the Better Business Bureau, Star Probe (a newspaper column), a friend, an employer, a doctor, and even the telephone operator. Tables A and B show the frequency with which various sources were mentioned. Table B is a breakdown of the government sources which are shown in one combined entry in the first line of Table A.

Table A shows that approximately half of those who said that they would seek information or help would seek it from a government source.

TABLE A

Percentage of "Seek Information or Help" Responses Suggesting Various Sources of Information or Help (Including Lawyers in Private Practice)

Source	Sample		
	Toronto	Kitchener	Lindsay
1. Government	48.1	50.3	51.2
2. Police	5.1	7.0	9.8
3. Libraries	4.9	6.4	2.4
4. Star Probe	2.7	.6	3.2
5. Better Business Bureau	3.1	6.4	4.1
6. Other Individuals	6.4	8.9	11.4
7. Other Information Sources	6.7	5.7	3.2
8. Legal Aid	7.0	4.5	4.1
9. Lawyers in Private Practice	16.0	10.2	10.6
TOTAL	100.0	100.0	100.0

The frequency of government sources being suggested was similar for all three cities and Table B shows that all levels of government were thought of with approximately equal frequency in each city, even though there are fewer federal and provincial offices in Kitchener and

TABLE B

Source	Sample		
	Toronto	Kitchener	Lindsay
A. *Federal Government (TOTAL)*	14.9	12.1	21.1
1. General Inquiry	5.1	3.2	7.3
2. Specific Departments	9.6	8.9	13.8
3. Member of Parliament	.2	—	—
B. *Provincial Government (TOTAL)*	15.4	8.9	10.6
1. General Inquiry	5.4	3.2	2.4
2. Specific Departments	9.2	5.7	8.2
3. Member of Legislature	.8	—	—
C. *Municipal Government (TOTAL)*	17.8	29.3	19.5
1. General Inquiry	7.2	15.3	9.7
2. Specific Departments	9.0	11.5	8.2
3. Alderman or Mayor	1.6	2.5	1.6
TOTAL	48.1	50.3	51.2

Lindsay than in Toronto. Table A also indicates that subjects in smaller cities mentioned individuals as sources of information or help more frequently than service organizations. Perhaps this is because there are fewer information and service organizations in smaller cities. The frequency of legal aid being suggested decreased from Toronto to Kitchener to Lindsay, while the frequency of police being suggested increased.

In the tables in Appendix 3, lawyers are listed separately as a source of information and help. This was done because lawyers are obviously a special source of information and help and we felt that it would be worth emphasizing the results relating to them. The major point to note is that people do not go to lawyers very frequently with these sorts of questions. Table 12 on page 124 shows that, for each sample, less than 10 percent of the responses suggested contacting a lawyer in private practice. As one would expect, considerably more people would contact a lawyer with the two most serious legal problems — the inadequate automobile repair and the deserted wife. On the other hand, practically no one suggested asking a lawyer the three simple information questions — those dealing with old age benefits, pregnancy leave, and the Criminal Code. If the subjects were presented with legal problems of increasing seriousness and complexity, they would undoubtedly suggest contacting a lawyer with increasing frequency. However, for simple questions and problems members of the public apparently think of acting on their own or approaching non-lawyer sources for help. In fact, several subjects insisted that they would never contact a lawyer.

A further interesting aspect of Table 12 is that, contrary to our expectations, it indicates that the smaller the city the less likely people are to suggest contacting a lawyer.

We had expected that people in smaller cities would be more likely to act without first seeking information or help when faced with day-to-day problems. Tables 11 and 13 in Appendix 3 support this conclusion. Table 13 shows a regular increase in the percentage of those who would "act without first seeking information or help" from the Toronto to the Kitchener to the Lindsay sample. Table 11 shows a corresponding decrease in those who would "seek information or help." Only the responses to the problem of the swimming pool fence show an opposite pattern.

In general, then, it appears that people faced with simple legal problems frequently seek information or advice from some other person or organization. In seeking such information or advice, they approach a wide variety of sources, particularly government agencies. Lawyers in private practice are not approached with any regularity for help with such problems.

II.   HOW SUCCESSFUL IS THE PUBLIC IN OBTAINING INFORMATION?

The previous section gives some indication of the answer to our first question — where do members of the general public go, or whom do they call, to obtain legal information or advice? In order to obtain some data about our second question — wherever they go, do they receive accurate information and sound advice? — two researchers each telephoned the sources of information or help suggested by the members of the Toronto sample.[3] When telephoning a source, the researcher always spoke as a member of the public faced with the specific problem and asked for information.[4] In each case, it was noted whether the source gave a referral to another source, refused to answer the question and made no referral, or attempted to answer the question. If the source made a referral, the researcher followed it up by telephoning further and keeping track of the second source's response. If a source attempted to answer the question, a decision was made on whether the answer was correct, correct but incomplete, or incorrect.[5]

The results of these tests show that the public often does not receive accurate information or sound advice in relation to simple legal problems. Tables C and D show that an average of more than 25 percent of the sources called gave an incorrect answer or made a referral which led to an incorrect answer.[6] In addition, for Researcher X an average of six percent of the sources gave no answer and no referral, and an average of seven percent led to incomplete answers. For Researcher Y an average of three percent of the sources gave no answer and no referral, and an average of 19 percent led to incomplete answers. Thus,

TABLE C

Percentage of Sources Tested Which Gave Various Responses When Called

RESEARCHER X

Result of Inquiry	Question										
	Old Age Benefits	Leaking Roof	Pregnancy Leave	Door-to-Door Salesman	Car Repair	Deserted Wife	Popular Song	Speeding Ticket	Swimming Pool Fence	Criminal Code	Average
A. Correct answer given:											
1. By source called	26.7	—	12.5	42.9	25.0	7.7	25.0	50.0	44.4	41.7	27.6
2. After 1 referral	33.3	—	—	14.3	37.5	23.1	25.0	25.0	22.2	33.3	21.4
3. After 2 referrals	20.0	—	—	—	—	7.7	50.0	—	11.1	—	8.9
4. After 3 or more referrals	13.3	—	—	—	12.5	—	—	—	—	8.3	3.4
B. Incomplete answer given:											
1. By source called	—	—	6.3	—	12.5	23.1	—	—	—	—	4.2
2. After 1 referral	—	—	6.3	—	—	15.4	—	—	—	—	2.2
3. After 2 referrals	—	—	6.3	—	—	—	—	—	—	—	.6
4. After 3 or more referrals	—	—	—	—	—	—	—	—	—	—	—
C. Incorrect answer given:											
1. By source called	6.7	16.7	31.3	28.6	12.5	—	—	25.0	—	8.3	12.9
2. After 1 referral	—	16.7	12.5	—	—	—	—	—	22.2	—	5.1
3. After 2 referrals	—	66.7	12.5	—	—	—	—	—	—	—	7.9
4. After 3 or more referrals	—	—	—	—	—	—	—	—	—	—	—
D. No answer given:	—	—	12.5	14.3	—	23.0	—	—	—	8.3	5.8
TOTAL	100.0	100.0	100.0	100.0	100.0	100.0	100.0	100.0	100.0	100.0	100.0

15

TABLE D

Percentage of Sources Tested Which Gave Various Responses When Called

RESEARCHER Y

Result of Inquiry	Question										
	Old Age Benefits	Leaking Roof	Pregnancy Leave	Door-to-Door Salesman	Car Repair	Deserted Wife	Popular Song	Speeding Ticket	Swimming Pool Fence	Criminal Code	Average
A. *Correct answer given:*											
1. By source called	33.3	—	6.3	57.1	12.5	7.7	—	50.0	55.6	16.7	23.9
2. After 1 referral	26.7	—	25.0	—	12.5	15.4	25.0	25.0	22.2	8.3	16.0
3. After 2 referrals	33.3	—	6.3	—	—	—	25.0	—	—	—	6.5
4. After 3 or more referrals	6.7	—	6.3	—	12.5	—	25.0	—	—	—	5.1
B. *Incomplete answer given:*											
1. By source called	—	16.7	6.3	—	12.5	15.4	25.0	—	—	—	7.6
2. After 1 referral	—	50.0	—	—	—	15.4	—	—	—	—	6.5
3. After 2 referrals	—	25.0	—	—	—	23.1	—	—	—	—	4.8
4. After 3 or more referrals	—	—	—	—	—	—	—	—	—	—	—
C. *Incorrect answer given:*											
1. By source called	—	—	18.8	42.9	25.0	7.7	—	25.0	11.1	16.7	14.7
2. After 1 referral	—	—	25.0	—	12.5	15.4	—	—	11.1	25.0	8.9
3. After 2 referrals	—	—	—	—	12.5	—	—	—	—	8.3	2.1
4. After 3 or more referrals	—	—	—	—	—	—	—	—	—	8.3	.8
D. *No answer given:*	—	8.3	6.3	—	—	—	—	—	—	16.7	3.1
TOTAL	100.0	100.0	100.0	100.0	100.0	100.0	100.0	100.0	100.0	100.0	100.0

an average of only 61 percent of the sources when called by Researcher X, and 51 percent when called by Researcher Y, eventually led to correct answers. There was, of course, considerable variation in the success with which sources handled different questions. Some questions were dealt with very well, while in one case no source gave a correct answer.

Some of the incorrect answers given in response to the test questions were really quite startling. For example, when Researcher X telephoned the City Building Inspector with the leaking roof question, she was told that her only remedy was to lodge a complaint with the Inspector. However, she was warned that if she did so nothing could be done if her landlord gave her notice in retaliation. In fact, Section 107 of the Landlord and Tenant Act specifically protects a tenant who makes such a complaint.[7]

Two other specific responses to this question were also interesting. When Researcher X telephoned the York County Area Legal Aid Office she was told that the remedy to her problem depended on the wording of the lease. In fact, subsection 96(4) of the Landlord and Tenant Act states that the remedy mentioned in subsection 96(3) exists for all tenancies under agreements entered into on or after January 1, 1970. When Researcher Y telephoned Information Canada he was referred to a number at City Hall. When he telephoned that number it turned out to be the section of the Water Department which deals with burst water mains.

As mentioned above, in addition to many incorrect answers, many sources gave incomplete answers. For most legal problems an incomplete answer can be very misleading. The question about pregnancy leave, for example, involves a two part answer: 1) benefits under the Unemployment Insurance Act, a federal statute, and 2) job security under the Employment Standards Act, an Ontario statute (see Appendix 4 at page 125). Most of the sources called led, through one or more referrals, to the Unemployment Insurance Commission Office or the Employment Standards Branch. Each agency usually gave that half of the answer covered by the statute it administers but did not mention the other half, despite the fact that officials at one of them told us that an arrangement existed whereby each office would give out information about both types of benefits. In fact, after both researchers had been told by the Unemployment Insurance Commission Office that job security depended upon the individual employer, a third call was made to the Office. Again the researcher was told that job security depended upon the employer; when she said that she had been talking to the provincial government and had been informed that her job was protected by law for a period of 12 weeks, the Office told her that the provincial government was wrong.

Sometimes, however, receiving correct information or sound advice does not end an inquirer's problems in dealing with "intermediaries." In the case of the old age benefits question, for example, almost all of the sources led either directly or through one or more referrals to the correct answer. The advice given was usually for the inquirer to pick up an application form at the nearest Post Office. Although the Post Office had not been recommended as a source, our researchers called one of the postal stations in Toronto to inquire about forms. Researcher Y was told that the forms were at the Post Office and could be picked up at any time, but Researcher X was told that the Post Office did not have application forms and the employee answering the call was incredulous that she would telephone the Post Office with such a question.

In addition to the high number of incorrect and incomplete responses given, our tests showed a great deal of inconsistency in the answers obtained from the same source to the same question on different occasions. In total, 100 sources were tested by both researchers and 60 of them gave different responses to the same question. An extreme example of this inconsistency occurred in response to the leaking roof question. Many sources referred this matter to the Landlord and Tenant Bureau. Our researchers telephoned the Landlord and Tenant Bureau four different times with the question and received four different responses: call the City Building Inspector; call the Health Department; file a written complaint with the Bureau; and all that can be done is to file a complaint with the City Building Inspector. On none of the four occasions was the remedy under section 96 of the Landlord and Tenant Act mentioned.

Two additional problems faced by our researchers should be mentioned. Frequently it took an inordinate amount of time to reach a source, and the treatment our researchers received from some sources was sometimes disturbing. When the Ontario Community and Social Services office was called with the deserted wife question, it took 75 minutes of constant telephoning to get through to the office. One source deserves special mention. Several members of the Toronto sample said that they would contact the Better Business Bureau with the inadequate car repair problem. On both occasions when the Bureau was called, our researchers were told that nothing could be done and both repair bills would have to be paid. When our female researcher called the Bureau, the woman answering the question was highly abusive and suggested that the researcher should have her husband or boy friend look after the car.

So far our description has treated all the sources as being equally important. In fact, some are more important than others in the sense that more people faced with legal questions or problems think of them.

Although 16 sources were suggested by the Toronto sample as places people would turn to with the old age benefits question, in 42 out of a total of 65 instances the subject would resort to one of three sources. In considering the success of members of the public in obtaining accurate information or sound advice these "often recommended" sources obviously must be given more weight than the others. To do this we weighted the responses our researchers received by the frequency with which the various sources were suggested. Tables 2 and 3 of Appendix 4 on pages 128-9 show the weighted results for each researcher.[8] These tables show that, on the average, a high percentage of the responses recommended sources that gave incorrect or incomplete answers. An average of over 25 percent of the responses recommended sources that gave incorrect answers in the experience of both researchers, while an average of over 7 percent in Researcher X's experience, and over 26 percent in Researcher Y's experience recommended sources that gave incomplete answers. We have seen that an average of only 61 percent of the sources when called by Researcher X and 51 percent when called by Researcher Y eventually led to correct answers. Tables 2 and 3 show that on the average in Researcher X's experience 63 percent, and in Researcher Y's experience 44 percent of the responses recommended sources that eventually led to correct answers.

Our researchers felt that one of the reasons many sources gave incorrect or incomplete information was a failure by their staffs to look up the answers. However, one of the test questions indicated that looking up answers in existing legal materials involves its own problems. The Criminal Code question asked what section 195.1 of the Code says. Section 195.1 was added to the Code in 1972 by the Criminal Law Amendment Act of that year. This section was purposely chosen because to answer the question correctly a person would have to look at the annual volumes of the Statutes of Canada, not just the Revised Statutes, or would have to use a recent edition of one of the annotated Codes — the section appears in the 1972 edition of *Martin's Criminal Code* but not in the 1971 edition.

Many of the sources that attempted to answer this question quoted section 195(1) from a 1971, or earlier, edition of *Martin's Criminal Code*. In fact, one of the sources that quoted the wrong section from an out-of-date copy of the Code was the Metropolitan Toronto Police Department.

Many members of the sample and several sources recommended calling a public library with this question. Five libraries were called in the Toronto area, and all except the Metropolitan Toronto Central Library quoted the wrong section — one quoted from a 1972 edition of the Code, but quoted section 195(1) instead of 195.1, two quoted section 195(1) from a 1971 edition, and one from a 1964 edition.

TABLE E

Summary of Results Received from Various Sources of Information or Help Recommended by the Toronto Sample

Researcher X

Source	Number of Times Called	Result of Inquiry					
		Referral		No Answer or Referral	Information		
		Satisfactory	Unsatisfactory		Correct	Incomplete	Incorrect
1. Government	61	21	18	—	14	3	5
2. Police	6	2	1	—	1	—	2
3. Libraries	1	—	—	—	1	—	—
4. Star Probe	4	1	1	—	1	1	—
5. Better Business Bureau	3	—	—	—	1	—	2
6. Other Individuals	4	—	3	—	—	—	—
7. Other Information Sources	13	5	1	1	3	—	3
8. Legal Aid	5	—	—	3	1	—	1
9. Campus Legal Assistance Centre	3	—	—	—	2	1	—
TOTAL	100	29	24	5	24	5	13

TABLE F

Summary of Results Received from Various Sources of Information or Help Recommended by the Toronto Sample

Researcher Y

Source	Number of Times Called	Result of Inquiry					
		Referral		No Answer or Referral	Information		
		Satisfactory	Unsatisfactory		Correct	Incomplete	Incorrect
1. Government	61	22	18	—	11	2	8
2. Police	6	2	1	—	2	—	1
3. Libraries	1	—	—	—	—	—	1
4. Star Probe	4	2	—	—	1	1	—
5. Better Business Bureau	3	1	—	—	1	—	1
6. Other Individuals	4	1	2	1	—	—	—
7. Other Information Sources	13	5	1	—	2	3	2
8. Legal Aid	5	2	—	1	1	1	—
9. Campus Legal Assistance Centre	3	—	—	—	3	—	—
TOTAL	100	35	22	2	21	7	13

21

Up to this point we have been considering the results of the test in general terms, lumping together all the sources called. Tables E and F show a breakdown of the results, source by source.[9] The tables show how often various information sources made referrals, gave no answers and no referrals, or attempted to answer questions. When an answer was attempted it was rated as correct, correct but incomplete, or incorrect. The referrals are broken down into satisfactory referrals and unsatisfactory referrals. In doing this we defined a referral as satisfactory if it was to a source that attempted to answer the question (whether or not the answer actually given was correct, incomplete, or incorrect) and as unsatisfactory if it was to a source that merely made another referral.

A comparison of Tables E and F show that the experiences of the two researchers were remarkably similar. More than half the calls resulted in referrals, and close to half of all the referrals were unsatisfactory. In both cases just over half the attempted answers were correct, but still, a third of the attempted answers were not even partially correct.

The tests described in this section indicate that members of the public often do not receive accurate information or sound advice when they approach intermediaries for assistance with legal problems. Each of our researchers telephoned one hundred sources of information or help. As Tables E and F show, in the experience of one researcher only 24 calls resulted in correct information being given immediately, and only 29 more resulted in referrals to sources that attempted to answer the questions ("satisfactory" referrals). In the other researcher's experience, only 21 calls resulted in correct information being given immediately, and only 35 resulted in satisfactory referrals. In addition, sources showed a large measure of inconsistency when asked the same question on two different occasions.

III.   A FURTHER ASSESSMENT OF SOURCES OF INFORMATION

The previous section described the nature of the responses given to the ten test questions by the sources of information or help recommended by the members of the Toronto sample. That test was limited to the recommended sources. As a result, libraries and community information centres were not tested extensively, though we felt that these sources were sufficiently important to warrant further attention. In addition, the test was limited to asking the same type of source several different questions. A comparison of the results from various sources, as in Tables E and F, is therefore potentially misleading since the sources were often responding to different questions. We felt that a more accurate comparison could be obtained by examining the responses of several sources to the same question. We also wanted specifically to compare the quality of responses received from lawyers in private practice with those received from other information sources such as libraries and community information centres. We therefore decided another test was needed.

The next test used two new information problems. The first was as follows:

> X is living in a two bedroom apartment and is paying $225 per month rent but has no lease. When X moved in two years ago the landlord said that X could park her car behind the building for free. The landlord has now told X that he is going to start charging her $15 per month for parking. Can X's landlord do this?

This simple landlord and tenant problem was selected because it falls within an area of the law with which most sources of information have had some experience and because it is simple enough that one might expect most sources to attempt to answer it rather than to make a referral. (The answer is in the notes at the end of this chapter.)[10]

The second problem was:

> On June 9, 1973, X was charged with possession of .5 grams of marijuana. On December 20, 1973, he appeared in court, pleaded guilty to the charge, and received an absolute discharge. X has found out that criminal records can be expunged. Can X (in August, 1974) have his record expunged?

This problem dealing with criminal records is more difficult than the landlord and tenant question because it is of a type less frequently encountered and because its answer involves a relatively recent amendment to the Criminal Records Act. (Again the answer is in the notes.)[11] One would expect it to be referred elsewhere more frequently than the first question and that fewer sources would be able to answer it without research.

Forty sources in the Toronto area were telephoned with each question: ten lawyers in private practice, ten public libraries, ten neighbourhood information centres, and ten government and legal aid agencies.[12] The lawyers in private practice, the public libraries, and the information centres were selected at random, although some effort was made to spread the sample throughout the Metropolitan Toronto area and to select several large law firms located in the centre of the city as well as several lawyers practising on their own in suburban areas.

A summary of the responses received is set out in Tables G and H. The actual responses given are set out in Appendix 5 at page 132. Table G shows that, as we had expected, most of the sources were able to handle the landlord and tenant question successfully. Out of 40, 17

TABLE G

Summary of Responses to the Landlord and Tenant Problem Received from Various Types of Sources

Type of Source	Number of Sources Called	Referral			No Answer or Referral	Information		
		Satisfactory	Unsatisfactory	To a Lawyer		Correct	Incomplete	Incorrect
1. Lawyers	10	1	—	—	2	7	—	—
2. Public Libraries	10	5	—	2	2	1	—	—
3. Information Centres	10	6	—	—	—	4	—	—
4. Others	10	5	—	—	—	5	—	—

TABLE H

Summary of Responses to the Criminal Record Problem Received from Various Types of Sources

Type of Source	Number of Sources Called	Referral			No Answer or Referral	Information		
		Satisfactory	Unsatisfactory	To a Lawyer		Correct	Incomplete	Incorrect
1. Lawyers	10	2	1	—	3	—	2	2
2. Public Libraries	10	4	—	2	2	—	—	2
3. Information Centres	10	5	1	1	—	1	—	2
4. Others	10	7	—	—	—	—	—	3

24

gave the correct answer immediately and 17 more made a referral to a second source that gave the correct answer. Out of the remaining six cases the caller probably would have ended up with the correct answer on five occasions although after exerting more effort than is perhaps necessary for such a question. (Two were referrals to a lawyer, two advised coming to the library to look up the answer, and one advised making an appointment with the lawyer called.)

An important point is, however, that the information centres and the "other sources" handled this question just as well as the group of lawyers in private practice.

Table H shows that the sources tested did not handle the criminal record question nearly as successfully. Of the 40 sources tested only one gave the correct answer directly and 16 referred to a second source that gave the correct answer. No fewer than nine of the sources gave an incorrect answer, and four more referred to a second source that gave an incorrect answer. As predicted, fewer sources attempted to answer the second question directly than the first — 10 as compared to 17.

Not one of the lawyers in private practice gave the caller the correct answer directly — two told the caller to do nothing, two gave an incorrect answer, three said they did not practise criminal law, and three referred to a second source. It is true that all three referrals eventually led to the correct answer, but in two of these cases the referral was in fact made by the lawyer's secretary.

Again, the libraries and information centres handled the criminal record question as well as the group of lawyers in private practice, and the group of "other sources" performed best of all.

IV. CAN MEMBERS OF THE PUBLIC
LOOK UP LAW ON THEIR OWN?

So far we have been examining the intermediary organizations to which members of the general public turn for information or advice when faced with simple legal problems, and whether or not they give accurate information or sound advice. But some people in this situation attempt to look up the relevant law themselves. We therefore sought to determine how successful such an endeavour might be, using existing legal materials.

The test was conducted at the Ontario Science Centre where volunteers were requested from among the visitors to the Centre. Each subject entered a room containing two tables. On one table stood the Revised Statutes of Ontario 1970, the Statutes of Ontario, 1971-73, and the Revised Regulations of Ontario 1970; on the other table were the Revised Statutes of Canada 1970, and the Statutes of Canada, 1970-72. The subject was given a brief explanation of the meaning of "statute"

TABLE I

Results of Members of the Public Looking Up Information in Statutes

Response	Number of Subjects	Number Who Used Correct Procedure	Number Who Had Used Statutes Previously	Average Time Spent	Educational Background
1. Correct answer found	5	1	1	15 min.	5 — college students or graduates
2. Partially correct answer found	13	1	4	20 min.	7 — college students or graduates 6 — high school students or graduates
3. Wrong or no answer found	17	0	3	20 min.	7 — college students or graduates 10 — high school students or graduates
TOTAL	35	2	8		

26

and "regulation", a general description of the indexing of the statutes and regulations, and instructions on how to use the materials. Each subject was then given one of the questions listed in Appendix 6 at page 135 and asked to find the answer in the materials on the tables.

We selected statutes for the test because they are the most important source of law for the citizen and one the public should be able to use successfully. Citizens might, of course, attempt to use other sources, such as popular legal handbooks and legal textbooks. But in most areas statutes are the primary statement of the law and thus the most important source of information.

Table I summarizes the results of the test. Of the 35 subjects who participated, only five found the correct answer to a question. And of these five, only one used the statute volumes correctly; that is, after finding the answer in the revised statutes, he went on to check the annual volumes for amendments and to look for any regulations that might qualify the answer. In fact, all the subjects who found the correct answer were working on questions that did not involve amendments or regulations.

Table I shows that 13 of the subjects found a "partially correct answer." This means that they found the relevant statute but not the relevant section, or that they found the section but misunderstood it, or that they found only some of the statutes or sections that applied to the question. Again only one of these subjects used the volumes correctly.

This test indicates that members of the public do not at present have much hope of successfully looking up law on their own. Not only was this sample highly educated (54 percent were college students or graduates and the remainder were high school students or graduates), but also each subject had been given instructions on how to use the statutes immediately before attempting to find an answer. There are no similar instructions contained in the statute volumes themselves. It seems fair to assume that in a sample of the public with average education and having no prior instructions the results of the test would be even more dismal.

During the course of the test a few additional interesting observations were made. First, almost half of the subjects had no clear idea about which level of government had jurisdiction over the subject matter involved in a question, and many others simply guessed at it. Similarly, in a question involving dual jurisdiction none of the four subjects who attempted the question seemed to know that both levels of government could be involved in the same area of the law. Secondly, the subjects had far more success dealing with questions involving matters covered by subject references in the indexes to the statutes. And finally, subjects tended to stop once they had found what appeared to be a plausible answer. They made no further attempt to check for exceptions or more specific sections or to go on to see if there were any relevant amendments or regulations.

NOTES

1. It should be pointed out at the outset that this test, as well as the ones in the following sections, was done to determine in only a general way whether there is a problem and, if so, the nature of the problem. Because of the size of the sample and the way the subjects were selected, the results make it difficult to say anything definite about the total population.

2. In Metropolitan Toronto we originally used three samples of 20 subjects each and attempted to draw the samples from upper, middle, and lower income areas. In doing so we had hoped to obtain some indication whether people's responses varied according to socioeconomic levels. Essentially, no pattern of variance appeared (although we did notice that, as one would expect, the percentage of responses indicating that the subject would contact a lawyer decreases rapidly as one goes down the socioeconomic scale: an average of 12.4 percent of the responses from the upper income sample were that the person would contact a lawyer, while the percentages for the middle and lower income samples were 9.5 percent and 4.6 percent (respectively). We eventually decided to combine the three samples to form one sixty-subject sample for Toronto. This result should not, however, be taken as proof that people's responses do not vary with socioeconomic levels. Our upper, middle, and lower income samples were selected merely on the basis of a cursory examination of the physical appearance of various neighbourhoods. To say anything definite about the effect of income, occupation, and education levels, a far more extensive and scientific survey would be required.

3. Some suggested sources could not be tested; for example, a friend, a family member, or an employer. There are therefore slight discrepancies between the number of sources listed in the tables in Appendix 3 and the number of sources tested by telephone.

4. For several questions "Federal Government General Inquiry," "Provincial Government General Inquiry," and "Municipal Government General Inquiry" were listed as sources. In these cases our researchers telephoned Information Canada for the federal government and the Ontario government switchboard and the Metropolitan Toronto switchboard for the provincial and municipal governments since these seemed to be the most likely sources a person would telephone if he looked in the Toronto telephone book under "Government" for an information number.

5. In making these decisions the answers given in Table 1 of Appendix 4 at page 125 were taken as being satisfactory answers.

6. The results obtained by Researchers X and Y are presented in separate tables because it was felt that telephoning a source twice was not sufficient to make a general comment as to the quality of answers given by that source. Rather than combining the results and presenting them as an average of the percentage of sources, which would lead to various answers, we decided to present them separately and say nothing more than that this is what happened when two people called each source.

7. Under section 98 of the Landlord and Tenant Act, R.S.O. 1970, c. 236, a landlord may terminate a tenancy by giving the tenant proper notice, and under section 106 the landlord may apply for a writ of possession for the premises upon summary application to a County Court judge if the tenant does not move out after being

given notice. However, by section 107(2), the judge may refuse to grant a writ of possession and may declare the notice to quit invalid if it appears that (a) the notice to quit was given because of the tenant's complaint to any governmental authority of the landlord's violation of any statute or municipal by-law dealing with health or safety standards, including any housing standard law; or (b) the notice to quit was given because of the tenant's attempt to secure or enforce his legal rights.

8. Tables 2 and 3 in Appendix 4 look very similar to Tables C and D on pages 15 and 16. However, the figures in the two pairs of tables do not measure the same thing. The figures in Tables C and D are the percentage of sources tested that gave various responses, while the figures in Tables 2 and 3 are the percentage of responses from the samples of the public recommending sources that gave various responses. It is just coincidental that the figures are often almost the same.

9. Tables 4 and 5 in Appendix 4 are a detailed breakdown of the "Government" line in Tables E and F.

10. X has a month-to-month tenancy. Therefore, by sections 98 and 102 of the Landlord and Tenant Act, R.S.O. 1970, c. 236, X's landlord may terminate the tenancy by giving X one full month's notice. Thus X's landlord could charge X the $15 for parking and, if she did not pay, could give her notice. If X wants to stay in her apartment she will have to pay for the parking.

11. The answer to the problem is no; X must wait for one year from the date of the absolute discharge before applying to have his record expunged. There appears to be a slight paradox in the law in relation to this matter. Section 662.1(1) of the Criminal Code states that in certain circumstances "the court . . . may . . . instead of convicting the accused, by order direct that the accused be discharged absolutely or upon . . . conditions." Section 662.1(3) deems such a discharge not to be a conviction. This might well lead one to believe that since X received an absolute discharge, he was not convicted and thus does not have a criminal record. However, the Criminal Law Amendment Act of 1972 (S.C. 1972, c. 13) amended the Criminal Records Act to cover absolute and conditional discharges. Section 2(2) of the Criminal Records Act now states that a person who has been given an absolute discharge for a summary offence may apply one year after the date of the discharge to have his record expunged. One must assume, therefore, that there is some sort of record to be expunged. It is interesting to note that both a bonding company and the Metropolitan Toronto Police Department said that they consider someone who has received an absolute discharge to have been convicted and to have a record.

12. These ten sources were Information Canada, the Citizens' Inquiry Branch (Ontario government), the Toronto City Hall switchboard, the Metropolitan Toronto Police Department, the federal Department of Justice, the Ontario Attorney General's Department, the York County Area Legal Aid Office, Parkdale Community Legal Services, the Campus Legal Assistance Centre (University of Toronto), and the Community and Legal Aid Services Program (York University).

Chapter 3
HOW LEGAL INFORMATION IS DISSEMINATED AT PRESENT

We saw in the previous chapter that members of the general public faced with simple legal problems frequently obtain inaccurate or incomplete information when they seek assistance. In order to determine why it is difficult to obtain accurate information about the law we studied the most important sources of information — lawyers in private practice, legal aid offices and assistance clinics, government offices and information branches, community information centres, police departments, and public, academic and law libraries.[1] The present chapter describes how these sources at present handle questions about the law. The problems they experience with such questions and some possible ways to overcome them are discussed in Chapter 5.

I. LAWYERS IN PRIVATE PRACTICE
Lawyers in private practice are an obvious source of information. But they are not the most important in terms of the number of questions received. Many members of the public do think of calling a lawyer about simple problems, but we observed that only people who know lawyers personally or who have frequent dealings with them through their business activities generally consult them with this sort of question. Intimidated by the physical appearance of many law offices, by rumours of high fees, and by the lawyers themselves, it seems that most people do not resort to lawyers until a serious or complex legal situation leaves them no choice.

As Table 12 in Appendix 3 shows, less than 10 percent of the responses from the public survey described in chapter 2 indicated that a lawyer would be approached. A considerably higher percentage of those surveyed would contact a lawyer with the two more serious legal problems — the inadequate car repair and the deserted wife — but virtually no one suggested contacting a lawyer with the three straightforward information questions about old age benefits, pregnancy leave, and the traffic ticket. Nevertheless, lawyers in private practice do receive such information inquiries, although more frequently in some parts of the country than in others.

Lawyers are of course in a good position to handle such questions. Their expert knowledge allows them to establish the facts, to understand the potential implications of the questions and to consider laws bearing on the question that might be overlooked by a non-lawyer. They are accustomed to using legal reference materials and usually have more of them available than do other intermediaries. Many lawyers have sizable private libraries which they use in their practice and most have a court library close at hand. Of course, their experience with these materials does not mean lawyers do not have difficulty using them. Many lawyers we contacted complained of the same problems reported by other information sources — poor indexing, convoluted language, lack of sources covering certain areas of law, and difficulties with updating.

It is undoubtedly true that, in general, lawyers are more successful than other sources in dealing with these inquiries. Indeed, it would be amazing if they were not. However, the test described in section III of chapter 2 indicates that lawyers also on occasion give out inaccurate information. One suspects that the failure to give accurate answers usually results from a lawyer giving an instinctive answer off the top of his head without checking it. This may be because even they find existing legal materials troublesome and time-consuming to use. Lawyers are busy people, and for them to spend 15 to 20 minutes looking up information in response to a telephone inquiry is often an annoying interruption.

An additional problem with directing general information questions to lawyers is that many of them specialize in specific areas of law. They are naturally reluctant to deal with an inquiry relating to other areas of law, feeling uncomfortable dealing with matters they only infrequently consider and perhaps also feeling that spending the extra time necessary to look up law in areas to which they are not accustomed is a waste of effort. An example of this was observed in response to the criminal record question used in the tests described in section III of chapter 2. Three of the ten lawyers called said that they did not deal with criminal law and refused to answer the question.

Many people across the country also complained of this problem in connection with the lawyer-referral services set up by many local bar associations. Under these services a member of the public can call the bar association and be referred to a local lawyer who will give the person a half-hour appointment for a fee of $10. Usually, however, the lawyer's name given is merely the next on a long list of volunteers, with little effort made to refer the inquirer to a lawyer who specializes in the area of law his problem involves.

II. LEGAL AID AND ASSISTANCE

The various legal aid programs across Canada are of central importance to any analysis of the delivery of legal services and information to the general public.[2] One of the possible solutions to the problem of access to the law, and one that merits serious consideration, is the expansion of existing legal aid plans to include legal assistance clinics to which legal questions and problems of all kinds could be directed.

Every province now has some form of legal aid plan, although the plans vary a great deal in scope. Prince Edward Island has the simplest scheme, consisting of two full-time lawyers who act as Public Defenders, that is, they are available to defend anyone charged with a criminal offence who cannot afford his own counsel. Quebec, on the other hand, has the most elaborate program, consisting of 215 full-time lawyers operating out of 67 offices across the province.[3]

Newfoundland, New Brunswick, Ontario, Alberta, and British Columbia all have legal aid plans under which the legal aid offices are administrative only, and the actual legal services are performed by lawyers in private practice.[4] Manitoba and Saskatchewan have had similar legal aid plans but are now changing over to a clinical approach.[5] Finally, Nova Scotia has just finished a two-year trial of a program involving 27 full-time lawyers operating in nine offices throughout the province.

There are three basic types of legal aid offices: administration offices, legal aid law offices, and legal assistance clinics. While individual offices vary considerably in the method by which, and the extent to which, they handle simple legal questions and problems from the public, there are noticeable similarities among the offices within each general type.

(A)   Administration Offices

As indicated above, most of the provinces have, at least in part, legal aid schemes in which the actual legal services are performed by lawyers in private practice and the legal aid offices merely administer the scheme — usually by issuing legal aid certificates which authorize lawyers to do the work and bill the plan. Under such a plan a province is divided up into legal aid areas, each with an area office to administer the program. Except in the larger cities, the staff of a typical area office consists of an Area Director, usually a local lawyer in private practice who spends one or two afternoons a week in the area office, and one or two secretaries, who handle the administrative paper work and are usually in the area office full-time to take messages.

Technically, these area offices are strictly administrative and are not intended to perform any legal services themselves. Once an applicant has shown that he falls within the financial criteria of the relevant statute and that his problem falls within the scope of services provided by the plan, he will be given a legal aid certificate which he then takes to a lawyer in private practice who actually performs the services required and is paid by the plan. However, few members of the general public are aware of the exact nature of the legal aid program in their province, and many people telephone the local area office with simple questions and problems expecting to receive free summary advice from a lawyer. The extent to which this phenomenon is recognized and the method of handling such telephone calls really depends upon the individual Area Director.

These simple questions and problems are typically received by a secretary in the area office. Most of the problems are handled at that point, either by a referral to a more appropriate information source or by the secretary answering the question using personal knowledge built up through experience in dealing with similar questions. Some of the problems are passed on to the Area Director (the proportion depending on his or her willingness to deal with them) who normally responds with a referral or an answer from personal knowledge. Rarely is any research done on such a question. If research were necessary the caller would likely be told to come to the area office and apply for a certificate.

It was interesting to note that many Area Directors seem to be unaware that their offices receive such requests for information and summary advice. They stress their administrative functions and emphasize that they do not give summary advice but refer the few simple questions and problems that do reach their offices to other sources of information or to lawyers in private practice. The staff in many of these offices, by contrast, say that each office receives and handles several thousand such calls every year.

Some of the Area Directors have recognized this phenomenon occurring in their offices and have made some attempt to control it. The York County Area Office in Toronto, for example, initially instructed its staff to tell all callers with a legal problem to come to the area office and apply for a certificate. Normally when such application was made the applicant would be immediately interviewed by one of several staff lawyers in the area office. But the Area Director soon found that his office was being swamped by questions and problems that could have been handled easily and satisfactorily over the telephone. He therefore set up a system under which the switchboard operator, with the assistance of the staff lawyers, has created a card file of answers to simple questions and problems shown by experience to recur frequently. Now, when a caller asks one of these questions an answer is given immediately by the switchboard operator. Only people with more complex or unusual questions are told to come to the Area Office.

(B) Legal Aid Law Offices

In Quebec, and to a lesser extent in British Columbia, the legal aid plans have established offices that are largely indistinguishable from private law offices. In both provinces certificates are still being used, but an applicant can choose between taking the certificate to a lawyer in private practice or having his problem handled by one of the staff lawyers. The important difference from the straight certificate programs is that the legal aid offices actually perform legal services as well as administer the plan. As a result, the staff lawyers regard the giving of summary advice as a function that naturally falls within the scope of their job.

One problem for the person seeking simple information or summary advice from these offices is that they tend to have a policy against giving out information or advice over the telephone. Most of them operate on an appointment basis, and the majority of callers with anything but the simplest of questions and problems will be given an appointment with one of the lawyers. This means that many people with questions and problems that could be satisfactorily handled over the telephone must make a trip to the local office for an answer. Nevertheless, at the appointment they may receive free summary advice. One real advantage of such a legal aid scheme is that people with problems that can be solved through a 20- or 30-minute discussion with a lawyer have one available to them. The certificate legal aid schemes really do not provide that service except in the few areas that have duty counsel clinics.

One suspects that the secretaries in these offices play a role similar to that of the secretaries in certificate administration offices — referring callers to other information sources and handling simple questions on their own. However, the lawyer backup for such questions and problems is more readily available than in the certificate administration offices and is more willing to deal with such matters. Undoubtedly, a far larger proportion of such questions are passed on to a lawyer than would be passed to the Area Director in a certificate administration office.

(C)   Legal Assistance Clinics

The official legal aid schemes of Nova Scotia, Manitoba, and Saskatchewan involve the use of legal assistance clinics. In addition, as mentioned above, all the other provinces except Newfoundland and Prince Edward Island have some legal assistance clinics. These clinics are of two basic types: "appointment" clinics, operating for a few hours a week and staffed by duty counsel or law students, and "assistance" clinics, operating full-time and staffed by full-time legal aid lawyers or law students.[6] Of course, the clinics vary considerably from place to place, being geared to local needs and ideas; however, a certain amount of generalization is possible.

The "appointment" clinics do not handle large numbers of legal information questions. Such clinics ordinarily operate in conjunction with a community information centre and are open at fixed times one or two evenings a week. The majority of the clients have first approached the information centre (or in some cases the area legal aid office) and been given an appointment for or been referred to the clinic. Many simple questions and problems are therefore filtered out at the information-centre stage. Only more complex problems are referred to the clinic. Most of these can be dealt with there in a summary way in 15 or 20 minutes. If a problem turns out to require more extensive service the clinic will normally pass the person on to the official legal aid office or advise the person to contact a lawyer in private practice. Since the clinics really only deal in summary advice the majority of the questions or problems are handled from the lawyer's or student's personal knowledge; legal reference tools are rarely used.

The "assistance" clinics provide a wide range of legal services. An effort is made to transform them into community centres rather than places of business. Their atmosphere is very informal, and they usually gear their activities to a relatively small area in their city. People in the community are encouraged to approach the clinic with a wide variety of problems, and many clinics have established counselling and guidance services to complement their legal work. The clinics are purposely placed in accessible locations and try to be as unintimidating as possible.

Once "assistance" clinics become established and known in their community the number of simple legal questions and problems they receive increases rapidly. Such questions are generally first received by a secretary or receptionist, who refers some to more appropriate information sources, answers others from personal knowledge, and passes the rest on to one of the staff lawyers or students. Although these clinics do set up a schedule of appointments for clients with more complicated or continuing legal matters, they do not operate exclusively on an appointment basis. Thus there is usually a lawyer or student available to receive a telephone call or talk to an inquirer who has come to the clinic. These clinics generally do not have a policy against giving advice over the telephone. As a result, a higher percentage of legal information questions and simple advice problems end up being handled by someone with formal legal training than in other types of legal aid offices.

Again, the vast majority of these simple questions and problems are handled by the staff lawyers or students from their personal knowledge. Little use is made of legal reference tools, partly because the lawyers and students soon learn the answers to the majority of the questions and partly because there are very few reference tools dealing with the areas of law most commonly encountered by these clinics —

areas such as welfare, unemployment insurance, workmen's compensation, and immigration.

It is difficult to estimate the exact number of problems requiring summary advice and requests for information received by legal aid and assistance offices since most offices keep statistics only of actual files or of certificates issued. The wide range of questions handled makes it very difficult to draw a clear line between simple information requests and more complicated legal problems requiring the services of someone with legal training. But we estimate that all the legal aid offices and clinics across the country together receive at least 800,000 requests from the public per year, and the number appears to be increasing rapidly. Of these, perhaps 500,000 are simple information questions or summary advice problems.

The areas of law most frequently encountered are family law (especially separation and divorce problems and problems related to children and minors), criminal law, landlord and tenant law, consumer protection, debtor and creditor problems, motor vehicle problems, employment standards and unemployment insurance, and estates and wills.

The method of handling such questions and problems is substantially different in legal aid offices than in other information centres because of the presence of people with formal legal training. Many inquiries are straightforward enough that most lawyers would be able to handle them without doing any research other than checking the details of various statutes or regulations. As a result little use is made of existing legal reference aids, although office staffs expressed their need for a quick reference tool to look up details of law, especially in areas not covered by existing sources.

Most legal aid offices and clinics have copies of at least some provincial and federal statutes and several legal textbooks. Many also have some case reports and regulations. Statutes, case reports, and textbooks are used most frequently. When the lawyers and students in the legal aid offices do resort to these reference materials, they are less hampered by many of the problems faced by the staff of other information sources because they are familiar with the materials and the language used in them.

Because of the presence of people with formal legal training, legal aid offices in general undoubtedly have more success in handling legal inquiries than many other intermediary organizations. However, when these inquiries are handled by the non-legal staff without the supervision or knowledge of the legal staff, mistakes and bad referrals are made quite frequently. In addition, as in the case of lawyers in private practice, lawyers in legal aid offices sometimes make mistakes as a result of a failure to check answers in the reference materials they do have available.[7]

III. GOVERNMENT OFFICES

The majority of the legal and administrative problems that citizens encounter involve statutes and regulations. Many citizens look to the government for information about such law. As we saw in chapter 2, a large proportion of every sample suggested seeking information or help from a specific government department or from a general government office such as Information Canada or its provincial equivalents.

(A) Information Canada

Information Canada was established on April 1, 1970, following the recommendations of the Task Force on Government Information.[8] The Task Force felt that "the Government has an obligation to provide full, objective and timely information; and that the citizens have a right to such information"[9] Information Canada was seen as a vehicle for meeting this obligation through, amongst other things, a network of regional information offices. The Task Force also recommended an extensive 'outreach' program (which has been translated in practice into the establishment of Mobile Information Officers in Nova Scotia and Manitoba) and an information gathering function for the regional offices.[10]

A central Enquiry Centre was established at the Central Office in Ottawa both to handle questions from the public and to act as a supportive information source for Enquiry Centres at the Regional Offices in Halifax, Montreal, Toronto, Winnipeg, and Vancouver. In addition, Enquiry Centres have recently been opened in St. John's, Charlottetown, and Moncton in the Atlantic Region, and in Saskatoon and Edmonton in the Western Region. As mentioned above, Mobile Information Officer programs have been established in Nova Scotia and Manitoba.[11]

The entire system of 11 Enquiry Centres and two Mobile Officer programs at present receives between 350,000 and 400,000 inquiries each year.[12] Although some Centres estimated that as many as 65 to 70 percent of their inquiries dealt with law or statutes and regulations, it seems likely that an average of about 25 percent of the inquiries across the country involve legal questions and problems. Four Enquiry Centres kept an exact count of legal inquiries received during periods ranging from one to two weeks. These showed totals that were 26, 24, 5, and 13 percent of the average total number of inquiries received by those Centres over similar periods. Thus, it would appear that all the Centres together receive a total of about 100,000 legal questions per year, and one can expect this figure to increase as the total number of questions of all kinds increases.

The most frequent subject areas of legal inquiries are, as one would expect, areas covered by federal statutes: immigration, unemployment insurance, taxation, and copyright, trademark, and patents. However, the Centres receive some questions in all areas of law. Other common ones are minority and native rights, consumer protection, loans and debts, companies and business, children and minors, and motor vehicles. Interestingly enough, even though the Divorce Act is a federal statute and almost all the information sources we visited receive many inquiries about separation and divorce, the Enquiry Centres receive very few such questions.

The inquiries received by the Centres are handled by Enquiry Officers, These Officers undergo a two week training course and continuing instruction on the job aimed at ensuring that they can handle government telephones and the standard Enquiry Centre filing systems and equipment and can deal pleasantly and helpfully with inquirers. Most inquiries are answered with a referral to a specific government office or a more appropriate information source or with information taken from quick-answer information files. Frequently, the Enquiry Officers look up information in the many government pamphlets contained in the Centres, and sometimes such pamphlets are given or mailed to inquirers.

The Centres all have copies of the Revised Statutes of Canada, but that is essentially their only legal reference material. Many Enquiry Officers do not seem to know how to use the Revised Statutes. When the Officers do attempt to answer legal inquiries rather than referring them elsewhere (to other government offices, public libraries, lawyers in private practice, and legal aid offices), they use their quick-answer information file, government pamphlets, and only occasionally the statutes.

The majority of the Centres seemed to feel that they answer inquiries about law successfully. Centres generally refer such questions to what they consider more appropriate sources and their staffs regarded that as a successful method of handling these questions. The few doubts expressed reflected the staffs' concern that when they do attempt to give out information they are never sure that the information is complete and correct.

In the course of our tests of information sources described in chapter 2 we found that the Enquiry Centre in Toronto had more success in referring the test questions than in attempting actual answers. However, some of the referrals were wildly inappropriate. As can be seen from Tables 4 and 5 at pages 130-1 in Appendix 4, the Information Canada Enquiry Centre in Toronto ("Federal Government, General Inquiry") was called by each of our researchers eight times. Each caller was referred to another information source in six of the eight cases. Of these referrals, four for each caller were satisfactory and, in the case of one of the callers, two of the referrals were unsatisfactory in the sense that the sources referred to made a further referral, although they were sources one might expect the particular questions to be referred to — the city

Landlord and Tenant Bureau for a landlord and tenant question and the provincial general inquiry number for a question about a deserted wife. In the case of the other caller, however, one of the referrals was clearly inappropriate — the city water mains department for a landlord and tenant question. An attempt was made to supply actual answers to the inquiry in two cases for each caller. Of these four attempted answers, one was correct and three were incorrect.

(B) Provincial Government Information Branches

Over the last few years, several provinces have set up special information branches to deal with inquiries from the public. Some of these branches operate in much the same fashion as the Information Canada Enquiry Centres and appear to experience similar problems for similar reasons. Others operate more as government switchboards than as information sources.[13]

Nova Scotia, Quebec, and Saskatchewan have provincial information branches which operate in a way similar to Information Canada. The Nova Scotia Department of Communications operates the Nova Scotian Communications and Information Centre in Halifax, which is similar to an Information Canada Enquiry Centre. It has a staff of three officers and receives about 13,000 questions per year. Unlike the experience of other Centres, over half of these inquiries are received by mail and of these over half originate outside Nova Scotia.

The Quebec government has established Communication-Québec, which operates nine regional offices throughout the province staffed by a total of over 30 officers. These offices receive a total of 180,000 to 200,000 inquiries from the public each year, almost all of which are received by telephone and come from within Quebec.

In Saskatchewan the Provincial Inquiry Office has been set up in the Legislative Building in Regina. Its staff of four inquiry officers receives 25,000 to 30,000 inquiries per year, all by telephone. This office is connected to all parts of Saskatchewan by toll-free telephone lines and as many as 90 percent of its inquiries originate outside Regina.

All of these offices estimated that at least one-third of the inquiries they receive are questions involving law — especially statutes and regulations. They receive questions dealing with every area of law. Typically, the inquiries are received by an officer with a background and training similar to that of the inquiry officers at Information Canada. Most of the questions are answered from personal knowledge or from quick reference information files, although many are referred to more appropriate information sources. For example, questions dealing with the federal government are normally referred to Information Canada, and actual legal problems are often referred to lawyers in private practice or the local legal aid office. Little use is made of printed reference materials. If a question cannot be handled immediately with an answer from personal knowledge or a referral, the inquiry officer is more likely to telephone other sources, such as specific government departments, for information and call the inquirer back, rather than resort to reference books. Most centres have copies of at least some statutes, but they are seldom used.[14]

In Ontario the Citizens' Inquiry Branch is also somewhat similar to an Information Canada Enquiry Centre. However, rather than being a general inquiry centre for the public to call, it is regarded as a last resort for questions and problems that could not be handled elsewhere. The Branch's number is not listed in the telephone book, and almost all the inquiries it receives are referred to it from the general government switchboard or from a specific department. A member of the public calling the Ontario Government for information would normally call the switchboard, which would transfer the call to a specific department.

The Inquiry Branch is divided into two sections: an information and referral centre staffed by three officers who handle questions in much the same way as the staff in the centres described above, and the Special Inquiry Unit. The Special Inquiry Unit deals with problems that individual citizens are having with the provincial government. Its staff of five will investigate problems submitted to them to ensure that everything that can be done for the citizen is being done.

The information and referral section of the Inquiry Branch receives about 20,000 inquiries per year, and the Special Inquiry Unit deals with about 2,000 problems per year. The staff estimated that about one-third of these inquiries involve law.

The staff makes little use of reference materials. The Branch has a copy of the Ontario Statutes, but they are rarely used. The staff relies on their own knowledge, on obtaining information by calling contacts in specific departments, and on referring inquiries to other information sources. Many actual legal problems are referred to lawyers in private practice and to legal aid offices.

In Alberta the provincial government is in the process of establishing the Alberta Information Service, which will combine a government switchboard and an information source. When completed, it will consist of 35 telephone centres spread throughout the province, each of which will be connected to Edmonton by toll-free telephone lines. Citizens will be able to call the local centre with inquiries and receive basic information about government programs or a referral to a local source of assistance. More complicated questions about the government will be switched on the toll-free lines to specific departments in Edmonton. The staff of the telephone centres will use no reference materials other than a referral file of local sources of assistance and a set of summaries of government programs.

(C) Specific Government Departments

So far in this section we have been discussing information offices established by the various governments specifically to handle public inquiries. Many more inquiries are received by individual government departments. Many members of the public either know or guess which department has jurisdiction over the subject matter of an inquiry and call that department directly. As well, calls directed to the general government switchboard are often switched directly to a specific department.

Government departments handle a much larger number of inquiries than do other information sources. The Ontario Government switchboard receives well over three million telephone calls a year, and the Toronto City Hall switchboard receives over 600,000. Some examples of the numbers received by individual departments are: 600 calls a day (150,000 per year) by the British Columbia Rentalsman's Office; 15,000 calls a month (180,000 a year) by the Quebec Department of Labour; 70,000 calls a year by the Manitoba Rentalsman's Office in Winnipeg; and 65,000 calls a year by the Thunder Bay Regional Office of the Ontario Ministry of Natural Resources, Northern Affairs Branch.

Many inquiries received by specific government departments deal with administrative and government matters that a specific department is in the best position to handle. On the other hand, many are more general legal questions about matters that are related to a department's activities. For example, a Consumer Protection Bureau will receive complaints, which it will follow up, and questions about licences that it issues, but it will also receive a wide variety of questions about consumer and commercial law.[15]

Some departments have offices specifically designed to deal with the public. The Department of Manpower and Immigration, for example, operates offices across the country to deal with the people directly affected by labour and immigration statutes administered by the Department. Quite naturally, many thousands of information questions are received by these offices on all aspects of labour and immigration laws. The Department of National Revenue has established District Tax Offices to administer the Income Tax Act, and these offices receive many thousands of inquiries about details of tax law. Several provinces have set up a Rentalsman's Office. While the Rentalsman has specific powers to settle certain types of landlord and tenant disputes, his office inevitably receives thousands of inquiries about landlord and tenant law.[16] Other departments do not have "public offices" as such but still receive many inquiries from the public. An obvious example is the

Department of Justice or the provincial departments of the Attorney General, which receive inquiries on all areas of law.

Even though many of these departments deal with only a couple of statutes and many of the inquiries they receive concern those statutes, as Tables 4 and 5 on pages 130-1 in Appendix 4 indicate, government departments often give incorrect or incomplete answers to simple legal questions. Specific government departments were called on 31 occasions by each researcher and gave actual answers 17 times for Researcher X and 14 times for Researcher Y. Of those, four were incorrect for both X and Y, and three were incomplete for X and two for Y.

One problem observed was that the people handling these information inquiries in specific departments did not seem to know much about matters falling under the jurisdiction of other departments or other levels of government. This often resulted in incomplete answers being given. As noted in chapter 2, for example, in response to the question about pregnancy leave the Federal Unemployment Insurance Commission Office and the Ontario Labour Standards Branch each gave the part of the answer concerning matters dealt with by itself but failed to mention (presumably because the people answering the question did not know) that that was only part of the answer.

Another problem faced by an inquirer attempting to obtain information from specific government departments is that, especially in the larger cities, some departments are very difficult to reach on the telephone. For example, a researcher called the Landlord and Tenant Bureau and the Immigration Office in Toronto every 15 minutes beginning at 9 A.M. on a Monday morning late in May. It took two hours and fifteen minutes to get through to the Landlord and Tenant Bureau, and our researcher finally gave up trying to reach the Immigration Office on Thursday after listening to busy signals for three days.

IV.   COMMUNITY INFORMATION CENTRES

During the last five years a large number of community information centres have been established throughout Canada. Typically, these centres are set up on a very informal basis, often with the aid of a short-term federal government grant (such as L.I.P. and O.F.Y. grants), and serve a small local neighbourhood. Their stated purpose is to fill an "information gap" in the community by enabling the citizen to obtain, or to find the location of, the information he needs in order to carry on his daily life and deal effectively with government. Not surprisingly, these information centres receive a wide variety of types of questions, including legal questions.[17]

Again, it was difficult to estimate the number of legal inquiries these centres receive. Although most of them keep statistics of the total number of inquiries received, and many break these statistics down by subject area, the "legal" category is usually used as a miscellaneous one for inquiries that do not fit elsewhere. A question about Unemployment Insurance, for example, would be listed as a question about employment rather than about law. Nevertheless, the community information centres we contacted (perhaps a little over half of those in Canada) said that they receive a total of about 700,000 inquiries of all kinds from the public each year, and they estimated that a surprising 180,000 of these deal with law. While that is over 25 percent of the total inquiries, it should be pointed out that the proportion of legal inquiries varies a great deal from centre to centre.[18] It seems, therefore, that community information centres in Canada receive a total of between 1 million and 1¼ million inquiries annually, of which 250,000 to 333,000 deal with law.

There are three basic types of community information centres: information and referral centres, information branches of various service agencies, and lay advocacy centres. Each will be considered in turn.

(A)   Information and Referral Centres
Information and referral centres concentrate upon providing inquirers with information on a wide variety of topics or referring them to appropriate sources. Such centres come in numerous shapes and sizes, ranging from very informal, small centres set up under short term grants to fill a perceived local need[19] to larger, well established centres which not only give out information but also publish directories of social agencies and become involved in other community services.[20] The latter are often principally financed by the municipalities.

In spite of their differences, these centres nevertheless operate in much the same way. The bulk of the inquiries are received by telephone and are initially handled by a volunteer worker.[21] If the question is relatively simple this worker will attempt to answer the question or will refer the inquirer on to a more appropriate source. More complicated questions are passed on to a permanent staff member (usually the director or co-ordinator) who handles it in much the same way but with the benefit of more experience.

Such centres rarely use printed reference materials of any kind to find information. In many cases, a referral to a more appropriate information source is seen to be an adequate response to a question. Thus, little or no attempt is actually made to provide an answer to more complicated questions which would require the use of reference materials. Most centres put together a ready reference file of information sources and simple facts related to the most common questions. Files of this type become a centre's major information tool.

(B) Information Branches of Service Agencies

Many service agencies, such as the Edmonton Social Services for the Disabled or the Social Services Council of Saint John, receive many requests from the public for information and especially from the particular group they deal with in their social service functions. Many such agencies have found the number of inquiries to be so great that they have had to set up special information branches. These information branches operate in much the same way as the information and referral centres but even more informally, since they are merely a sideline of their organization's main function. Except in the case of inquiries related to the organization's activities, less attempt is made to supply actual information — the centres being satisfied with referring inquirers to other sources. Reference materials of any kind, except for a file of referral information, are used very seldom.

(C) Lay Advocacy Centres

A type of community information centre of special interest is what we have called a "lay advocacy" or "social action" centre. While most of these are found in the Metropolitan Toronto area,[22] a few exist in other areas of the country, such as the Council of Self-Help Groups in Winnipeg and the Victoria Park and Northwest Community Organization in Hamilton. These centres are specifically oriented towards solving legal and administrative problems. Not only do they provide inquirers with information about law and government but they also actively represent people in dealing with problems. The Council of Self-Help Groups, for example, will assist people in preparing the necessary papers for a divorce and will even accompany a person to court and assist in the actual proceedings. It is common for the staff of such centres to step in and deal on someone's behalf with a government office such as the Unemployment Insurance Office or the Immigration Office.

Because these centres specialize in legal and administrative problems, the bulk of the inquiries they receive fall in that category. Their staffs are usually composed of lay people who have learned the intricacies of certain areas of law through experience. In some cases this learning through experience process has been bolstered by paralegal law courses. For example, People and Law Research Foundation Incorporated in Toronto, in conjunction with a community college, runs a course on law aimed at members of the staffs of information centres. Participants are introduced to the structure of the law and the legal system and are shown what they can do without actually being members of the Bar. In several cases the centres also have law students present or available for advice.

While these centres take a very active role in handling legal questions and problems, and are more likely to attempt to deal with a problem themselves than to refer it elsewhere, the staffs generally impressed us with their awareness of their own limitations. They take seriously the possibility of misleading someone or of attempting to handle a problem too complicated for their knowledge. Problems falling beyond their range of competence are passed on, usually to legal aid.

While the staff of lay advocacy centres are more likely to attempt to research a point of law than the staffs of other information centres, they do not use existing legal materials a great deal. One problem is cost — staff members frequently resort to the materials in a public library — but, perhaps more important is the fact that many of the major areas of concern to these centres, such as welfare law and unemployment insurance, are largely ignored by existing materials. In any event, more reliance is placed on experience and verbal contacts than on printed sources.

Although community information centres vary considerably in the way they deal with inquiries, there is some consistency in the areas of law most frequently encountered. The most common areas are landlord and tenant, family law (especially separation and divorce), welfare, employment standards and unemployment insurance, and consumer protection. Other major areas are immigration law, taxation, and loans and debts.

For those inquiries referred elsewhere, the most common referral point is the local legal aid office or clinic, closely followed in frequency by government offices. Also, a significant number of inquiries are referred to social agencies of various types, lawyers in private practice, public libraries, and the police. An interesting point about referrals to public libraries is that, of 41 information centres contacted outside Ontario, 12 said they sometimes refer legal questions to public libraries, while of the 32 centres contacted within Ontario, 21 mentioned public libraries as a referral point.

We have seen that community information centres do not use reference materials a great deal; they rely on referrals, their own ready-reference files, and telephone contacts. In part, this is the result of their operations not being geared to book research, but also it is a result of the stringent budgets restricting most community centres. Reference books, especially legal reference books, no matter how useful, are just too expensive for them. As one might expect, the legal materials found in community information centres are most often popular handbooks of law for the layman, closely followed by desk copies of the most used provincial and federal statutes.

As described in chapter 2, our tests showed information centres to be fairly successful in giving referrals but to make frequent mistakes when they attempt actual answers. For example, Tables E and F (pages

20 and 21) show that "other information sources" (the majority of which were community information centres) made referrals in response to the test questions approximately half the time. Almost all these referrals proved to be satisfactory. However, the majority of actual answers given were incorrect or incomplete. Tables G and H (page 24) also support this conclusion: information centres made referrals in response to the two test questions more than half the time, and almost all the referrals were satisfactory; but on the occasions when an actual answer was attempted the answer was often incorrect.

This conclusion is not really very surprising. Information centres are, in general, geared to making referrals rather than to researching problems. They rarely have any printed reference sources other than their own ready-reference files. Most of their energy goes into building up a network of referral points.

(D)　Native Friendship Centres

Many special groups within our population have special informational needs and problems. To transmit information about laws to these people effectively, specialized information sources and delivery systems are necessary. Although we could not investigate all, or even a number of these special groups and the information sources available to them, we decided it would be worthwhile examining at least one of them in some detail. We chose the Native Friendship Centres because they are spread throughout Canada and because they supply information and services to a large minority group with pressing and unique legal difficulties — Canadian Native People.

Many Native People find themselves in a strange position with respect to Canadian law and society. Social and economic pressures are encouraging large numbers of them to migrate to the cities from reserves where, depending on one's point of view, they have been protected from or shut out of white man's society. The transition to urban life is a traumatic experience for many Native People. In an effort to help with the resulting problems and generally to assist all Native People in need of help with "modern" living, a network of Friendship Centres has been established across Canada.[23]

These places are much more than information centres. They provide social services, act as drop-in centres, and provide recreational facilities. But they receive many thousands of questions about urban life, a large proportion of which concern the law. It is very difficult to estimate the actual number of inquiries received by the Centres since they normally do not keep statistics of that sort, but all the ones contacted were aware of dealing with legal questions regularly, and the four Centres that kept statistics for us received a total of 261 legal inquiries in one week. (Based on that figure, the four Centres would receive about 13,500 legal inquiries in one year. If the experience of those four is typical, that would mean that the 54 Centres in Canada together receive about 180,000 legal inquiries every year.) Most of these fall into one of the following subject areas: welfare, landlord and tenant, criminal law, employment standards and unemployment insurance, family problems of all types, and minority and native rights.

The Friendship Centres vary a great deal from place to place as they undoubtedly must to meet local needs. However, none of those contacted had any sort of formal organization to deal with inquiries. Normally, a receptionist passes them on to a courtworker, a counsellor, or often the Centre's director. In almost all cases that person attempts to answer the question from personal knowledge or refers the inquirer to an outside information source, usually to legal aid offices, government offices, lawyers in private practice, the police, or various social agencies.[24]

One difficulty the Centres mentioned with referrals to other information sources is that with Native People there is a serious follow up problem — one of the reasons the inquirers are at the Friendship Centre at all is that they are intimidated and confused by government offices, lawyers, legal aid offices, and the like. Thus, rather than referring an inquirer to such a source the staff of a Centre will in many cases accompany the inquirer and help deal with a government office, for example, or find the information by calling the other sources themselves.

The Friendship Centres in general do not have or use printed sources of information. Few of them have even ready-reference files of referral information. A small number have a couple of desk copies of some statutes, and several said that they have and use popular handbooks on law; but most complained that legal materials were too expensive to have on hand. An additional problem, of course, is that there are very few printed materials of any kind in native languages.

One interesting aspect of the response to the Native People's special needs for legal information and advice has been the establishment in several provinces of native courtworker programs. These schemes basically consist of placing courtworkers in the lower courts to act as a liaison between a Native accused and the court. The courtworkers are usually Native People themselves with an ability to bridge the communication gap between the judicial system and the accused. Their function largely consists of ensuring that the accused understands what is happening and is aware of his or her rights.

While courtworker programs deal mainly with criminal law, they inevitably become broader in scope as they become more established. In Alberta, for example, the program is run by the Native Counselling Services of Alberta, a body that not only supervises the courtworkers but also carries on an Alcohol Education Program, Community Workshops about the law and courts, and research into matters such as sentencing practices.

The Native Counselling Services of Alberta handled 6,323 criminal law files in the 1973-4 fiscal year. In addition, however, the courtworkers received many legal questions and problems in other areas of law. The *1973-4 Annual Report* of the Native Counselling Services states:[25]

> "In many ways, it seems that Native people see the N.C.S.A. worker as a person to whom they can turn for advice on a variety of matters which generally fall within the scope of the Justice System. These inquiries are not limited to strictly criminal matters. N.C.S.A. workers are consulted with regard to statutes involving Child Welfare, Motor Vehicles, Highways, Liquor, Fish and Wildlife, City By-laws and Consumer Legislation, as well as a variety of administrative and procedural matters which affect the lives of Native people but which they often fail to fully understand."

The Counselling Services estimated that they receive as many as 22,000 such inquiries each year in addition to their actual files.

As in the case of Friendship Centre staffs, the courtworkers do not seem to rely heavily on printed materials. Most problems are handled by drawing on information learned through experience and on contacts built up on the job.

Regardless of whether or not the Friendship Centres are at present successful in dealing with these inquiries, they seem to be necessary as a special response to a special access problem. The gulf between Canada's Native People and the legal system is far wider than for the rest of the population and in fact includes a gulf between the Native People and the sources of information available to other citizens. To overcome these obstacles it has been necessary to establish a special information source.

V.   POLICE

When we began our investigation we were unaware of the extent of the role played by police departments in providing legal information to the public. Very few of the information sources we visited ever refer questions to the police. However, it seems that many people choose to call the police directly. There may be several reasons for this. The police telephone number is easily available in the front cover of local telephone books, and police departments operate 24 hours a day, so that an inquirer is not forced to find time to call during normal business hours. In the case of legal inquiries, a policeman is probably the only person many people directly associate with the law — in fact, to many people he is the law; it is not surprising then that he should be asked about the law.

Police departments receive a startling number of telephone calls from the public. During the course of the study we visited the police departments of 20 major cities, having a total population of approximately 8 million. The total number of telephone calls received by the police departments of these cities is about 17 million per year; the Metropolitan Toronto Police Department alone receives from 9 to 10 million calls per year. In addition, the R.C.M.P. receives a very large number of calls each year from people in rural areas.

The public call the police with a very wide variety of problems and questions, many of which require some legal knowledge on the part of the officer responding to them. Police departments do receive significant numbers of straight legal questions such as: Is there a by-law protecting people from being splashed by cars? Is it legal for me to own a semi-automatic rifle? or Can I burn leaves in my backyard? But many more of the calls are complaints that require some knowledge of law for a proper response. For example, when a caller complains about excessive noise outside his home, before a police officer can advise him as to what to do or can initiate police action he must know about the local noise by-laws and perhaps something about the law of nuisance.

We had difficulty estimating the number of calls that involve legal information received by the police departments visited. None of them keep statistics of that kind, and in most cases we spoke to senior personnel who have little direct contact with the people handling these calls. Because many of these requests are not phrased as straight legal questions, it was often difficult to make clear the sorts of calls that interested us. Nevertheless, it is fair to say that the 20 departments visited together receive several million legal inquiries per year. Of the annual total of 17 million telephone calls, the number of questions about the law would seem to be between three and six million.

These figures are based only on inquiries received by telephone. Officers on patrol are also asked about the law and, of course, meet situations demanding legal knowledge for an adequate response. Some questions are radioed or telephoned back to the department for solutions, but many are dealt with on the spot. We have made no attempt to estimate the number of those, but it must be very large.

As one might expect, the police receive many information inquiries on police-related matters, such as motor vehicles, criminal law, liquor control and licensing, firearms, and noise control. But they are also asked about many other areas of law — even mechanics' liens, taxation, and unemployment insurance. The most common questions, aside from motor vehicle and criminal law matters, concern separation and divorce, landlord and tenant, children and minors, and other family law problems.

Police departments usually have two telephone numbers for use by the general public: an emergency number, which is often used for all kinds of emergencies in a city, and an administration or complaints number. Not surprisingly, the majority of telephone calls, and almost all information inquiries, come in on the administration or complaints line.

Since a large percentage of the emergency line calls result in action by the police, the fire department, or the ambulance service, these calls are usually received at a special switchboard, often manned by experienced officers, from which requests for action can be quickly passed to an appropriate dispatcher. Calls on the administration line, however, are usually received at a normal switchboard or telephone-answering counter.

In approximately half the departments visited, the administration-line switchboard is manned by civilians, who ordinarily do not attempt to answer questions but merely transfer them on. Some inquiries are directed to information sources outside the department but the vast majority are transferred to a complaints desk, if the department has one, or to a specific section in the department. For example, a question about a traffic ticket would normally be switched to the traffic section. At the complaints desk or in a specific section the call will be handled by a police officer, who, in the case of information inquiries, may direct it to a more appropriate source outside the department or attempt to answer it himself.

In the other departments the administration line is answered by police officers, who transfer inquiries to specific sections or more senior personnel only if they cannot answer it themselves.

Thus, the majority of the inquiries received by the police are eventually handled by an officer with several years' experience. He will normally attempt to answer questions from personal knowledge accumulated at police college and through experience. Relatively often, though, he will refer questions to sources outside the department such as government offices, lawyers in private practice, or legal aid offices.[26]

Occasionally the officer handling an inquiry will attempt to find the answer in printed reference sources contained in the department. However, with a few exceptions, we found that police departments do not make extensive use of printed materials except for purposes of training. Most departments have a library of sorts, although often a small one largely consisting of police training manuals. As far as legal materials are concerned, all departments have at least some desk copies of federal and provincial statutes and regulations, most have copies of some of the local by-laws, and many have complete sets of revised statutes. A few also have statute citators, criminal case reports, criminal law periodicals, and legal dictionaries. Of these, statutes and by-laws are used most frequently.

The Calgary Police Department has established an interesting information centre to deal with inquiries from the public. The Department has three telephone lines: an emergency line, an administration line, and an information line. Calls on the information line are received in a special section consisting of six desks manned by experienced officers who spend their day responding to information requests. Each officer refers constantly to a file at his elbow consisting of the Calgary Police Manual, the Calgary Community Services Directory, and copies of several dozen federal and provincial statutes and municipal by-laws.

Police officers are in a sense paralegal personnel. They receive a considerable amount of legal training and know much of the law relating to 'police' subjects. Thus, in some areas of law at least, they are in a better position to answer legal inquiries than the staffs of some information sources. However, the officers answering the police telephones frequently show a tendency to give quick 'commonsense' answers. Most telephone calls to police departments are very short, lasting well under five minutes, and we suspect that the officers often do not attempt to understand a problem fully before reacting to it.

In the course of our tests of information sources, described in chapter 2, the two researchers each called the Metropolitan Toronto Police Department six times with six of the ten test problems, and each was referred to another information source for an answer in three of the six cases. Of the total of six attempted answers, three were correct and three were incorrect.

VI. LIBRARIES

Libraries are unique among the main sources of information and assistance in that they generally have large collections of reference materials. Many people telephone libraries seeking verbal information just as they might call other information sources. However, because libraries have reference books available for use they are also approached by members of the public who want to look up the law themselves or who are pursuing more academic questions. For example, many students approach libraries to do research into law.

We decided to visit and write to the sorts of libraries we expected would receive inquiries about law. Data was collected from public libraries, university libraries, university law libraries, and legislative libraries.[27]

(A) Public Libraries

During the course of the study public libraries were visited in all the major cities in Canada. These libraries, which were often the central reference facilities in urban library systems, were usually quite similar. Since we felt that many of these libraries' characteristics might be dependent upon their urban setting, we also sent questionnaires to all the rural public libraries in Alberta and New Brunswick to see whether they handled legal inquiries from the public differently than urban libraries. Metropolitan Toronto, with its vast network of public and specialized libraries, is in such a unique situation that we considered data from its libraries separately.

Fifty-seven public libraries supplied us with figures for both total inquiries on all subjects and legal inquiries. These libraries receive at least 2¼ million inquiries on all subjects each year and approximately 3½ percent of these concern law.[28] The number of inquiries varies a great deal between small rural libraries and large urban ones. Of the 26 rural libraries for which we had data in Alberta and New Brunswick, serving populations ranging from 800 to 20,000, eight reported that they receive no inquiries on any subject or receive some inquiries but none on law. The ten rural libraries that provided us with exact figures indicated an average of about 55 legal inquiries each per year. Urban libraries, serving much larger populations, naturally receive many more inquiries. The average of the population served by the 33 urban libraries surveyed outside Metropolitan Toronto is over one-quarter million, and each library receives an average minimum of about 1,800 legal questions annually.[29]

However, even though rural libraries receive few legal questions, those they do receive represent an average of 8½ inquiries annually per thousand population served. The urban libraries, on the other hand, receive 6½ legal inquiries annually per thousand population served. Thus the rural libraries that receive legal questions appear to be a comparatively more important source of legal information for the community than urban libraries. When the legal collection available in a typical rural library is considered (see Table J, p. 54) these figures assume increased significance.

People approach public libraries with questions on a wide range of legal topics, although some subjects are most often raised by students for academic purposes. The topics most commonly encountered are separation and divorce, landlord and tenant, and taxation. As well, about two-thirds of the libraries reported questions on company and business law, the law concerning motor vehicles and accidents, estates and wills, real estate, and immigration.

Among the organizations approached by the public for legal information, libraries are unique in their reliance on books and other reference tools to find answers, and a search for printed materials is the librarian's typical response to a legal question. Staff in rural libraries often find this search for material unsuccessful, and because of the limited staff size, there sometimes is no other librarian to be consulted. As a result, rural libraries typically refer inquiries about the law to other organizations and individuals, most frequently to government offices but also to other public libraries, university libraries, social agencies, or lawyers in private practice.[30]

Urban libraries usually have more staff members than rural ones, so that library staff other than librarians are often approached first by inquirers. In most cases a legal question would be referred immediately to a reference librarian, who would usually attempt to find useful material in the library's collection. Librarians in many urban libraries, unlike those in most rural libraries, tend to undertake a substantial search in statutes and other materials to find relevant information. This is sometimes done in consultation with a more senior librarian. Again, however, urban librarians are frequently unable to find books that will answer a particular question involving law and will then refer the inquirer to another organization. As in rural libraries, these referrals are most frequently to government departments and officials, but sometimes also to lawyers in private practice, to legal aid offices and clinics, and to law libraries, and, occasionally, to community information centres, social agencies, the police, other public libraries, and academic libraries.

Public libraries in Metropolitan Toronto differ somewhat from other urban libraries in their handling of legal inquiries. Despite the fact that several libraries in Toronto have librarians with some background in law librarianship, public libraries in Toronto immediately refer legal inquiries to outside organizations more often than libraries in other cities do, and Toronto librarians indicated that they are less likely than public librarians in other cities to do substantial research. More referrals to community information centres are made by Metropolitan Toronto public libraries than by libraries in other cities.

Thus an inquirer who approaches any public library with a legal question will usually be given relevant books or other material or, if the librarian is unable to locate useful publications, will be referred to another organization for information. Because librarians look first to books and other printed sources of law, these materials are fundamental to their handling of legal inquiries.

There is a wide variation between rural and urban libraries in terms of their legal collections. Table J shows the percentage of rural, urban, and Metropolitan Toronto libraries surveyed whose collections contain each category of legal publication. Several interesting aspects of the figures in this table should be pointed out. First, legal publications of any given category are held by no more than 40 percent of the rural libraries, and, except for popular legal handbooks and municipal by-laws, publications of any given category are held by no more than 25 percent of the rural libraries. Secondly, in both rural and urban libraries the most widely distributed category of printed legal material is the popular legal handbook aimed specifically at the lay reader.

TABLE J

Legal publications	26 Rural Libraries = 100%	40 Urban Libraries = 100%	13 Toronto Libraries = 100%
Revised Statutes of Canada	3 (11.5%)	36 all (90%) / 1 some (2.5%)	8 all (61.5%) / 4 some (30.8%)
Statutes for your own province	6 (23.1%)	37 all (92.5%) / 2 some (5%)	11 all (84.6%) / 2 some (15.4%)
Statutes for other provinces	0	4 all (10%) / 3 some (7.5%)	1 all (7.7%)
Statute Citators	0	9 all (22.5%)	4 (30.8%)
Regulations of Canada	1 (3.8%)	21 all (52.5%) / 2 some (5%)	3 all (23.1%)
Regulations for your own province	2 (7.7%)	29 all (72.5%) / 2 all (5%)	9 all (69.2%)
Regulations for other provinces	0	1 some (2.5%)	1 all (7.7%)
Canada Gazette	4 (15.4%)	33 all (82.5%)	8 (61.5%)
Gazette for your own province	2 (7.7%)	33 all (82.5%)	8 (61.5%)
Gazette for other provinces	0	2 all (5%) / 1 some (2.5%)	2 some (15.4%)
By-laws for your own municipality	7 (26.9%)	7 all (17.5%) / 19 some (47.5%)	1 all (7.7%) / 10 some (76.9%)
Popular legal handbooks	10 (38.5%)	39 all (97.5%)	13 (100%)
Legal Dictionary	2 (7.7%)	31 all (77.5%)	11 (84.6%)
Canadian case reports	0	18 (2 or 3 series) (45%)	4 (30.8%)
Legal Encyclopedias	0	4 (10%)	1 (7.7%)
The Canadian Abridgment	0	3 (7.5%)	0
Canadian looseleaf legal services	2 (7.7%)	20 (50%)	9 (69.2%)
Legal textbooks	6 (23.1%)	31 (77.5%)	12 (92.3%)
Legal periodicals	0	10 (1 or 2 titles) (25%)	1 (7.7%)
Indexes to legal periodicals	0	3 (7.5%)	2 (15.4%)

Thirdly, 22 libraries reported that they possess Canadian case reports. However, these are almost always limited to the two or three report series supplied automatically by the federal government to depository libraries; almost none of the libraries has actually chosen to order case reports. Finally, the legal publications held in Metropolitan Toronto public libraries reflect not only the reliance of branches on the main library in each borough for many reference materials but also the designated function of the Metropolitan Toronto Central Library as a back-up for the entire municipal system.

It can be seen that the legal collections held by public libraries are by no means complete. Rural libraries have small budgets and too few legal inquiries to justify the purchase of many law books on that basis alone. Larger legal collections are found in urban libraries, but the librarians point out that they purchase only the material suitable for use by non-lawyers and that gaps occur as a result.

Of the legal materials owned by public libraries, popular legal handbooks, statutes, municipal by-laws, and general government publications are the most frequently used in both rural and urban public libraries to answer questions about the law. Almost all urban libraries use statutes and by-laws as a source of legal information; slightly fewer use popular handbooks and general government publications. In contrast, fewer than half the rural libraries contacted use general government publications for this purpose, and only one-third of them use popular handbooks or statutes and by-laws.

One complication librarians face in connection with legal inquiries is the inability or the unwillingness of inquirers to explain their questions clearly. People who need information about law for school projects or term papers may have only a general idea of the kind of information wanted. Those who have legal questions caused by their personal situations are often more reluctant to ask for the specific information they need in a public library than they might be from other information sources.

Another complication is caused by the role public librarians have chosen for themselves in providing information about the law. With a few exceptions, public librarians will not explain or interpret statutes or other legal material. Librarians prefer to direct people wanting explanations or advice to other organizations. However, they sometimes find they are unable to do this because they do not know a suitable organization for library users to contact or because they lack specific information about the exact nature and functions of other organizations. Reference librarians usually have little opportunity during working time to make contact with these organizations in order to get this information.

As Tables G and H show, public libraries in Metropolitan Toronto referred the two test questions described in chapter 2 more than half the time — seven out of ten libraries referred the landlord and tenant question, and six referred the criminal record question. While these referrals were satisfactory, four of them were simply general referrals to a lawyer in private practice (something many inquirers are trying to avoid). Two out of the ten libraries tested responded to each question by asking the inquirer to come to the library to see what materials were there that could help him. On the three remaining occasions, actual answers were attempted over the telephone, and two of these were incorrect (both in response to the criminal record question).

(B) University Libraries
University libraries also act as sources of legal information for laymen, receiving many inquiries from students and faculty members as well as occasional questions from members of the public. If there is a law library on the campus, some questions are asked directly of the librarians, while others are referred to them by the reference and government documents departments of the main library. However, even in this situation the main library handles a certain number of legal inquiries without referring them to the law library; for example, it is often expected to deal with many law-related questions in fields like social work and business administration. Where there is no law library the university library deals with all law-related inquiries that arise. Librarians in reference and government documents sections of university libraries across Canada estimate that approximately eight percent of their combined inquiries concern the law.

Since most legal inquiries are course-related, the librarians find that the subjects vary throughout the year as new courses are taught and papers assigned. Legal subjects of current interest at many university libraries include criminal law, minority and native rights, taxation, labour law and employment, immigration, and constitutional law.

In these libraries a question about law is handled first in the reference or government documents sections by a librarian, a library assistant, or a clerk. In most libraries the inquirer is given statutes and other government publications relevant to his question and assisted in finding the exact information sought; he may also be referred to the senior reference or the government documents librarians for further help. These specialists would attempt to provide either more books and other material or specific information to answer the question before they suggested contacting specialized libraries on campus or referred it to non-university sources. The most frequent off-campus referral is to government departments, followed by non-university law libraries and lawyers in private practice. Often, of course, a referral of these questions is not really very helpful since most of them are for academic purposes.

Almost all Canadian university libraries have the Revised Statutes of Canada, the current statutes of their own province, the Canada Gazette, their own provincial gazette, a legal dictionary, and approximately a dozen looseleaf services. Most have current statutes for some other provinces and a few legal periodicals, while more than half have current federal regulations and popular legal handbooks.

(C) University Law Libraries

Each year law school libraries in Canada receive about 15 percent of their inquiries, or an average of about 850 questions per library, from people not connected with the law faculty. Most of these inquiries come from students and professors in other faculties, with very few from the public, and concern separation and divorce, criminal law, taxation, landlord and tenant law, and the law covering motor vehicles and accidents, although some law librarians report occasional questions on every legal topic. Usually the individual using a university law library would receive general assistance from clerical staff or law students before being referred to the reference librarian.

Most inquiries originating outside the law faculty are from students for their course work. Thus, although the types of materials they favour vary, most of the librarians would give the inquirer material they consider relevant to his question or do the necessary research to find useful information related to the specific inquiry rather than referring him to other individuals for a verbal explanation of an area of law or providing this explanation themselves. In about half of the university law libraries in Canada some of the librarians have taken one or more law courses and several law librarians have a law degree, although not always from a Canadian law school. They do not, however, provide interpretation of specific statutes or advice.

When interpretation or advice is the most appropriate response, the librarians in many law schools refer the inquirer to a student-run legal assistance clinic. They also refer inquirers to lawyers in private practice. Academic inquiries sometimes are referred to specific law faculty members or to other law libraries in the city that are not normally open to the public.

The print resources of Canadian law school libraries range from 37,000 to over 150,000 volumes. Almost all of them have more-or-less complete current collections of federal and provincial statutes, regulations, and case report series. Most law libraries have good retrospective collections as well. All of them have fairly good collections of texts and all buy some popular handbooks of Canadian law. Thus, the university law libraries' collections certainly do not lack any existing materials, and the majority of law librarians have experience in using these materials.

One reason law school libraries, like other university libraries, receive very few public inquiries may be that to the public they seem remote and intimidating. Many people think that these libraries can be used only by the students and faculty of the university. In fact, in most cases this is not so. Nevertheless, universities are unfamiliar and rather forbidding places to people who have never been to one, and it is not surprising that people outside do not approach them. Almost all the public inquiries received by these libraries come from former university students and graduates.

(D) Legislative Libraries

As well as their major collections of provincial materials of all kinds, legislative libraries have basic collections of current legal materials. Except for not having some current texts, case report series, digests, and legal encyclopedias they typically have the same Canadian legal materials as a university law library.

Their policies on public use vary from province to province, but legislative libraries usually allow public access, at least to their unique materials, and in some cases they offer staff assistance and unlimited use of their collections to anyone who requests it. Despite the often intimidating location of legislative libraries, their use by the public ranges from less than 10 percent to approximately half of their total inquiries. However, very few of these questions concern the law.

A reference librarian in a legislative library will normally try to locate useful material, or sometimes the specific information needed, to answer a legal question. Complicated questions may be referred to the senior librarian, who often has many years' experience with the legislative library collection. The staff of legislative libraries, as might be expected, also make use of their knowledge of and relationship with government departments to refer inquirers to people working in specific areas.

(E) Prison Libraries

Prison inmates are one group for whom access to legal information is much more restricted than for most of Canadian society, cut off as they are from many of the organizations citizens use for this purpose. Prison libraries, where they exist, are one of the few potential means of access now available to prisoners. Although prisoners are entitled to consult their lawyers, many inmates have a general interest in such matters as criminal law and family law which they would like to pursue on their own.

In the United States, the availability of law books in prison libraries has been established by litigation.[31] Inmate access to legal materials is a major issue for library associations in the United States. In Canada relatively little has been published about prison libraries, and almost nothing on the subject of inmates' access to law books. Edith Adamson's recent survey of prison libraries, described in an as yet unpublished article, reveals that in Canada only Ontario has any policy at all on law books for prisoners' use. Her own experience indicates that at present access is extremely limited. This is an area where an obvious need is not being met.

VII. OTHER SOURCES OF INFORMATION

This chapter has examined the major sources of information and advice available to the public, but it should be kept in mind that the clergy, doctors, employers, trade union officials, friends, family members, voluntary associations, special service organizations (such as civil liberties groups, senior citizens' associations, the Better Business Bureau, and so on), are all approached with inquiries about the law.[32] People often begin their search for assistance with legal problems by consulting someone they trust rather than someone with expert knowledge in the field.

It seems likely that these various groups and organizations handle questions about the law in the same way as other non-lawyers — the majority of questions are answered with a referral to another information source or with information taken from personal knowledge. For example, a minister or priest will often be consulted about family law problems. Over the course of time he will learn a considerable amount about family law through dealing with these problems and will build up contacts in the community with lawyers, family counsellors, and the like.

Most of these individuals and organizations do not use legal reference materials. While some of them might have popular handbooks dealing with areas of law they frequently encounter and a few might have copies of one or two statutes, they generally would not have any kind of comprehensive source of law. When they actually attempt to find specific information about the law rather than passing the inquirer on to another information source, they would be more likely to telephone personal contacts than to look up the law on their own.

One special source of assistance with legal and administration problems that should be mentioned is the office of the ombudsman that has been established in several provinces.[33] Each of these officials deals with several hundred complaints from members of the public each year, and most of these complaints involve the law. The majority of these complaints, however, are of a more complex nature than the kinds of questions and problems being examined in this study. The function of the ombudsmen is to investigate and mediate disputes between individuals and government departments, agencies, and officials; they are seldom approached with strictly informational inquiries.

NOTES

1. There are two very useful English studies on the provision of legal information and advice: Brooke, *Information and Advice Services*, Occasional Papers on Social Administration, No. 46, (1972); and Abel-Smith, Zander and Brooke, *Legal Problems and the Citizen: A Study in Three London Boroughs* (1973).

2. During the course of the study, we met with the provincial directors of the legal aid plans to discuss the nature of the existing plans and the role of legal aid in providing information and summary advice to the public. We also visited 25 legal aid offices and clinics and mailed questionnaires to 89 offices and clinics in more remote areas, of which 33 were completed and returned.

3. The Quebec plan also includes five legal assistance clinics which predated the official plan and have been loosely incorporated into it.

4. British Columbia has begun to establish legal aid offices not unlike those in Quebec. In addition, in all the provinces except Newfoundland there are legal assistance clinics, most of which were established by student legal aid societies at the law schools, and in Ontario the official Legal Aid Plan operates several evening clinics staffed by duty counsel who are lawyers in private practice. A Report by an Ontario Task Force on Legal Aid under the chairmanship of Mr. Justice Osler is to be released early in 1975.

5. By the summer of 1974 there were two clinics operating in Winnipeg, one in Regina and two in the Saskatoon area. At least six more clinics in each province are to open over the next two years.

6. Examples of the first type are the clinics operated by the Ontario Legal Aid Plan in Toronto, Hamilton, Ottawa, Kitchener, and Windsor, the clinics operated by the Student Legal Aid Society at the University of Toronto, the Student Legal Services clinics in Edmonton, and the clinics operated by the Vancouver Community Legal Assistance Society. Examples of the second type are the Dalhousie Legal Aid Service in Halifax, Saint John Legal Aid Inc., Community Legal Aid Services in Fredericton, Services Juridiques Communautaires Inc. in Montreal, the Campus Legal Assistance Centre and Parkdale Community Legal Services in Toronto, Legal Assistance of Windsor, the Isabel Street and Main Street Neighbourhood Law Centres in Winnipeg, the Saskatoon Legal Assistance Clinic, and the Valley Legal Assistance Clinic near Saskatoon.

7. Tables E and F (in chapter 2) show that the York County Legal Aid Office (one in which the information-giving function is supervised by the legal staff) responded to several of our test questions with correct answers or satisfactory referrals but gave incorrect or incomplete information on two out of ten occasions and refused to give information or a referral on four occasions.

8. See *To Know and Be Known; The Report of the Task Force on Government Information*, Ottawa, Queen's Printer (1969). See also the *Report of the Standing Senate Committee on National Finance on Information Canada*, Ottawa, Queen's Printer (1974).

9. Ibid., at 49.

10. Ibid., at 49-51; *cf.* the *Report of the Standing Senate Committee.*

11. During the course of the study we met with senior personnel from Information Canada in Ottawa, visited eight of the eleven Enquiry Centres (including all the Regional Centres), received a completed questionnaire from one other Enquiry Centre, and discussed the Mobile Officer program in Nova Scotia at some length with the staff of the Halifax Regional Office.

12. This estimate seems to be consistent with figures supplied to the Senate Committee on National Finance. Those figures indicated that the six Enquiry Centres existing at that time received a total of 196,193 inquiries during the fiscal year ending March 31, 1973. Not only are there now five new Centres but all Centres are experiencing a steady increase in inquiries as their presence becomes known.

13. During the course of the study we visited the provincial information branches in Alberta, Nova Scotia, Ontario, Quebec and Saskatchewan.

14. In Saskatchewan the Provincial Inquiry Office keeps copies of current Bills before the Legislature and receives many requests from the public for the exact wording of various sections. This type of question seems to be a Saskatchewan phenomenon; many other information sources in Saskatchewan also reported receiving inquiries about current Bills.

15. One interesting example of government offices dealing with information inquiries is found in the regional offices of the Northern Affairs Branch of the Ontario Ministry of Natural Resources. These offices are located in areas in which there are very few offices of other government departments. To facilitate administration, the Ontario Government has made the Northern Affairs Branch the agent in these areas for other departments. As well, several federal departments have asked the Branch to act as an information outlet for them. As a result, these regional offices receive questions on a wide variety of matters and operate in much the same way as general information offices like the Information Canada Enquiry Centres.

16. Barrie Clark, the Rentalsman in British Columbia, was quoted in the *Globe and Mail*, October 2, 1974, as saying: "Most of the calls are requests for information. People want to know what their rights are."

17. During the course of our study, we visited 48 information centres of various types. In addition, we sent questionnaires to 86 other centres including many in more remote areas of the country. Of these, 26 were completed and returned.

18. Some of the information and referral centres said that only three or four percent of their inquiries deal with law, while some of the lay advocacy centres said that all of their inquiries deal with law.

19. Examples of such centres are: Information Montreal, the North End Information Service in Hamilton, and Community Switchboard in Regina.

20. Examples of such centres are: the Community Information Centre of Metropolitan Toronto, the Information and Referral Centre of Greater Montreal, and the Advice, Information and Direction Centre in Calgary.

21. Many centres experience continual difficulty in obtaining and training volunteers. An interesting solution to this problem has been tried in Vancouver, which has a large network of over 20 Neighbourhood Information Centres. In that city people on welfare receive an extra amount if they work in a centre for a set number of hours per month. While several centres said that volunteers obtained in this way often lack basic skills, the scheme does provide the centres with a ready source of labour and appears to have a therapeutic effect on welfare recipients suffering from emotional problems connected to work and dealing with people.

22. Examples of such centres are People and Law Research Foundation Incorporated, the Action Service Contact Centre, and the New Welfare Action Centre.

23. There are at present 54 Friendship Centres in Canada. Of these, we visited six and mailed questionnaires to the other 48 from which nine completed questionnaires were returned.

24. One interesting factor in the data available to us was that every centre located in smaller cities or towns said that legal inquiries were frequently referred to the police, while the centres in Toronto, Winnipeg, Regina, Calgary, Edmonton, Vancouver, and Victoria, the only "big city" centres from which we have data, said that inquiries are never referred to the police.

25. *1973-74 Annual Report of the Native Counselling Services of Alberta*, at 10.

26. Inquiries about matters falling within the RCMP's jurisdiction, such as narcotics control, are often referred to them. As well, in a few cities the relationship between the police and legal aid seems to be one of hostility and distrust, and in those cities the police rarely refer an inquirer to a legal aid office.

27. We visited 37 public libraries and mailed questionnaires to a further 89 from which 56 completed questionnaires were returned. In addition, we visited 11 university

libraries, 14 university law libraries, and three legislative libraries and received completed questionnaires by mail from one university library and one university law library. County law libraries are usually reserved for lawyers and were not surveyed.

28. It may well be that these figures are low. Some public libraries are selective in recording daily inquiries and as a result the total inquiry figure is incomplete. Moreover, relatively few libraries could supply actual figures for legal questions except during the traditionally quiet summer period, although their figures for total inquiries were representative of the entire year's activity.

29. Of the over 75 public libraries in Metropolitan Toronto, we surveyed only 13. Thus the figures we have for numbers of inquiries received by libraries in Toronto are incomplete and have not been included in the figures in the text.

30. Rural libraries in Alberta reported that they refer legal inquiries to the police as frequently as to lawyers in private practice and social agencies; however, none of the rural libraries in New Brunswick indicated that they ever refer to the police.

31. See, e.g., *Gilmore v. Lynch* (1968) 400 F. 2d 228 (U.S.C.A., 9th Cir.), aff'd *Younger v. Gilmore* (1971) 404 U.S. 250.

32. See generally, Abel-Smith, Zander and Brooke, *Legal Problems and the Citizen: A Study in Three London Boroughs* (1973), at 55-60.

33. Six provinces have appointed ombudsmen: Alberta, Manitoba, New Brunswick, Nova Scotia, Quebec (Public Protector), and Saskatchewan. We received completed questionnaires by mail from the ombudsmen of Nova Scotia, New Brunswick, Saskatchewan, and Alberta.

Chapter 4
AN EXAMINATION OF EXISTING LEGAL MATERIALS

Many of the intermediaries approached by the public with information questions about law and legal problems attempt to look up answers in printed legal materials. Even though many questions are initially referred to other information sources, sooner or later someone will resort to reference materials for an answer. Even if the person providing the actual information does so from personal knowledge, at some time in the past he or she had looked up the answer or was told the answer by someone else who had done so. Adequate printed sources of legal information are thus fundamental to providing access to the law.

Almost all the information agencies we contacted that use printed legal materials complained that these sources are at present inadequate to provide non-lawyers with information about law. Librarians in Canadian law school libraries, for example, have most of the existing legal materials at hand, and some of them have legal training. Yet they experience difficulty in providing legal information. The central problem complained of is the existing legal materials. The available tools do not easily provide answers to specific questions. Even lawyers in private practice and in legal aid offices have difficulty with them.

We decided, therefore, to examine existing printed sources of law in an attempt to determine some of the reasons why their users find them to be inadequate. The legal materials most commonly used by non-lawyers are statutes and by-laws, popular legal handbooks, and government leaflets and pamphlets.

I. STATUTES

Almost all legal aid offices and clinics, government offices, police departments, urban public libraries, and law libraries have at least a few desk copies of specific provincial and federal statutes, and many have the complete revised editions. Because statutes are found in most of these information sources and are more authoritative sources of law than the other materials commonly used, most of this chapter is devoted to a discussion of the form of statutes in particular. Of course, much of what is said here about statutes is also true of other materials, such as by-laws, regulations, legal encyclopedias, and so on.

Statutes are not only the most commonly used source of law and probably the most available source of law, they are the most important source of law. They impose many positive obligations on citizens and regulate much of their daily lives. To respond to these obligations and regulations the citizen must be able to find out the contents of statutes.

Almost all the people we encountered at various information sources agreed that the major problems with the present form of statutes are their technical and convoluted language, the inadequate or non-existent indexing, their complex structure, and the difficulty in keeping track of recent amendments.

A simple experiment, described in section IV of chapter 2, was conducted to discover whether citizens can now use statutes and regulations. It will be recalled that volunteers from among people visiting the Ontario Science Centre in Toronto were each given a relatively simple question, provided with federal and provincial statutes and regulations, which were explained in general terms, and asked to find the answer. By the very nature of the way we conducted the experiment the persons that took part were, by and large, educated, inquisitive, and motivated. Nevertheless, they had very little success, although each person spent about twenty minutes searching for the answer. Less than half even came up with the right statute. Only five of the thirty-five volunteers (14.3 percent) could find the correct answer, and in all of these cases the questions did not involve amendments or regulations. In fact, only one of the five properly checked the amendments and regulations.

Statutes must also be understood by the officials who enforce the law and the legislators who enact it. We should aim, therefore, as the English Law Commission has stated,[1] "at ensuring that any statute can be understood, as readily as its subject matter allows, by all affected by it." To do otherwise would only contribute to "feelings of helplessness and frustration" caused by obscurely-worded government rules and regulations.[2]

The statutory draftsman can direct his statute to a number of audiences: to the reasonably intelligent layman, to members of the legislature, to those who have to enforce the law, to the lawyer who must use it, or to the judge who must interpret it. Ideally, he should keep all potential users in mind. Draftsmen currently concentrate too much on the judge who *might* be called upon to solve a dispute. But, of course, very few matters ever get to court, and most statutory provisions are not the subject of reported judgments.

Instead, legislation should be deliberately directed primarily at the non-lawyer. F.A.R. Bennion, an English legislative draftsman, puts the point well: "the product of the legislative machine should, like the products of most other machines, be designed for the consumer."[3] "Laws should be written," states an American academic, A.F. Conard, "with more emphasis on making readers understand what the law commands, and with less emphasis on controlling the judges by rigid grammatical constructions. Judges are more likely to be controlled by clear statements of purpose."[4]

Those who draft statutes are faced with the task of making the statute both certain and readable. These are potentially competing demands: in general, the more certain a document is, the less readable it is. At present, statutes tend to overemphasize certainty at the expense of readability, though most legislative draftsmen no doubt genuinely attempt to produce readable statutes. One easy solution is for the legislature to simplify the law by using general words such as "undue" or "reasonable" to cover a mass of detail. But one does not simplify by oversimplifying. The more general the legislation, the more the courts are called upon to give meaning to the words; and the more the courts are involved, the more non-lawyers are excluded from gaining an understanding of the law. Whether or not boards and commissions and administrative discretion should be used more widely as devices for fleshing out the law is outside the scope of this study. The present concern is to enable citizens to gain access to the law, whatever the vehicle chosen to enunciate it.

The task of making a legal document readable is, of course, not a simple one. The concepts dealt with are often very complex. The present Deputy Minister of Justice and one of the principal draftsmen of the Income Tax Act, D. S. Thorson, has responded to the criticism that our laws should be written in a simple style or, as some suggest, in the style of the Ten Commandments by stating,[5] "the fact is that Moses is not available for employment by the Department of Justice, and even if he were available, it would be interesting to see what Moses could hope to do with such concepts as 'tax-paid undistributed surplus on hand', 'control period earnings' and 'foreign accrual property income'." We are not convinced, however, that Mr. Thorson is correct in stating that the large number of difficult concepts in the tax law "creates complexities in the expression of the law that . . . doom any reasonable hope or expectation that the law can ever be written so as to be readily comprehensible to the non-expert."[6] In the model prepared for us entitled "The Tax Consequences of Selling Real Estate" (set out in Appendix 11 at page 179) T.E.J. McDonnell provides evidence to the contrary. The challenge is to simplify the manner of presentation, not necessarily to simplify the law itself.

In addition to complex sections resulting from complex concepts, statutes also contain occasional deliberately difficult or confusing sections brought about by political compromise,[7] and sections designed to change judge-made law without adequately explaining what the former common-law rules said.[8] Nor can one overlook the constant time pressure during the drafting process.[9]

Professor Elmer Driedger, the dean of Canadian legal draftsmen, has said that statutes are necessarily difficult to read and no one should be expected to read them without a great deal of effort.[10]

> "Anyone who wishes to understand a statute must be willing to spend a little time with it, reading it through, slowly and carefully, from beginning to end, and then re-reading it several times. Of course, the ordinary reader will not be able to grasp its full implications and he will have difficulty in applying the statute to an actual case. But that situation he must accept."

This is asking too much of the citizen or his non-legal advisor. Certainly he cannot expect to gain the meaning by skimming. But surely most statutes should be comprehensible with one careful reading. It is probably impossible to reach Bentham's goal of having the law written so that the ordinary citizen "may have presented to his mind an exact idea of the will of the legislator,"[11] but the legislature can produce better statutes than it now does.

We are not competent to say anything about the readability of the French version of our laws, but it is difficult to believe that they are more comprehensible than the English version. As Elmer Driedger acknowledges:[12] "ever since Confederation our federal statutes have been drafted in English by English-speaking common law lawyers, and then, when they were finished, translated hurriedly and badly into French. . . . It is also true that the Statutes of Canada have been written in terms of common law concepts, ignoring the civil law." Professor Driedger points out, however, that progress has been made to correct these deficiencies and that "we will eventually succeed in having two genuine versions of the same law." But even if future drafting is better, the bulk of the French versions of the statute law will remain in its present form for many years.

(A) Legal Language: The Need for More Interdisciplinary Studies

There have been some very good books by lawyers urging their fellow lawyers to improve their drafting.[13] But lawyers alone cannot achieve the objective of making statutes readable. They understand legal language too well. Lawyers have spent their lives reading legal material and probably are not aware of the real difficulties faced by the citizen.

We asked a linguist, Professor H. A. Gleason, and a psychologist, Professor Paul A. Kolers, to assist us in examining legal language. In addition, we surveyed some of the literature on linguistics. These forays into the non-legal world confirmed our initial view that there is much to be learned from interdisciplinary studies in the language and the form of the law. We hope that the impressionistic survey set out here will encourage others to study the field in greater depth.

We had hoped to carry out some "readability" tests on statutes.

However, we found that the standard tests are difficult to apply to legal language. This result was supported by Professor Kolers who expressed serious doubts about the value of such studies in the context of legal language. (His analysis is set out in Appendix 7 at page 136.) The difficulty faced by the citizen is not so much in the individual words used, but in the way legal language is constructed.

Legal language differs from other forms of English. An example of one of the differences is that lawyers often use more than one word when only one could be used. (This tends to occur in non-legislative documents to a greater extent than in legislation.) It is interesting to note that one of the reasons for this is historical: when legal language was starting to shift from French to English, those drafting documents used both the English and French words. For example, in the phrases "breaking and entering" and "goods and chattels" the first word is English, and the second is derived from the French.[14]

Another example of how legal language is different from other styles of English is that "adjectives and adverbs — extremely common elsewhere — are completely absent."[15] Moreover, common words are sometimes used in a particular way: for example, *shall* is "the obligatory consequence of a legal decision, and not simply . . . a marker of future tense, which is its main function in other varieties" of English usage.[16]

But it is the structure of legal sentences that probably causes the most difficulty. Legal language could be vastly improved if the order of the sentences simply followed more closely other forms of English writing.

Professor Kolers points out that English is a "right-branching" language, in which the qualifications and exceptions normally come after the verb. By contrast, legal language usually starts out with the qualifications and exceptions. This order makes it more difficult than it need be for a person who is not legally trained to understand the material because he must keep in his mind all the qualifications that come first. But perhaps more importantly, as Professor Kolers points out, "having grown accustomed to processing language in a right-branching fashion, the typical reader of English finds his comprehension retarded by left-branching construction."[17] Professor Gleason makes the point in this way:[18]

> "There is a principle of English style that can be stated somewhat as follows: If, in any two-part construction, there is an appreciable difference in length between the two, then it is usually preferable for the shorter one to precede. Note that this is expressed in terms of a preference. It is this feature that makes the rule one of style rather than of grammar. A convenient designation for a construction which runs counter to this preference is 'front-heavy'."

No doubt one could trace the history of this front-heavy legal "style." It may simply be a carryover from the time when legal documents were drafted in Latin, a language that often places the verb at the end of the sentence. But whatever the origin, the style was solidly fixed in legal drafting following George Coode's influential work, "On Legislative Expression," published in 1843.[19] Coode, an English barrister whose work is still regarded as a guide to good drafting,[20] broke down drafting into four components in which logical order took precedence over grammar.[21] Coode stated his rule as follows:[22]

> "The rule to be observed is of such simplicity as to make its utterance appear almost an absurdity; but simple as it is, it is the most frequently neglected of any rule of composition.
>
> It is, that wherever the law is intended to operate only in certain circumstances, those circumstances should be invariably described BEFORE any other part of the enactment is expressed."

Coode's approach can be illustrated with the following excerpt from a recent book, *Legal Drafting*, by Robert Dick:[23]

> "Thus the complete drafting order, as outlined by Coode, is: (1) case; (2) conditions; (3) legal subject; and (4) legal action. The following are modern legislative sentences that illustrate Coode's notion of correct order:
>
> | | | |
> |---|---|---|
> | 1. | Case | Where the number of directors of a corporation is more than six, |
> | 2. | Conditions | and if authorized by a special bylaw, |
> | 3. | Legal Subject | the directors |
> | 4. | Legal Action | may elect from among their number an executive committee. |
>
> | | | |
> |---|---|---|
> | 1. | Case | Where proceedings have been stayed, |
> | 2. | Conditions | and if default again occurs under the mortgage, upon application |
> | 3. | Legal Subject | the court |
> | 4. | Legal Action | may remove the stay. |
>
> It must be acknowledged that Coode was quite perceptive; his suggested approach will be found in many modern statutes and most documents that a lawyer peruses."

Both sections are obviously front-heavy. They would be more readable if the order of the sentences were reversed as follows:

> "The directors of a corporation may elect an executive committee from among their number where the number of directors of a corporation is more than six and if authorized by a special bylaw."[24]
>
> "The Court may, upon application, remove a stay of proceedings if default again occurs under the mortgage."

The difficulty in comprehension is accentuated by the lawyer's custom of "nesting" clauses within clauses. As the linguist P. K. Saha has observed, "the human mind can take only a limited amount of syntactic nesting because nesting forces the brain to keep track of the initial part of the construction until the nested item has been absorbed and the balance of the construction is revealed."[25]

Another obvious problem with legal sentences is that they are too long. Some sentences go on for pages. Indeed, although this is an extreme example, [26] the Income Tax legislation introduced in the spring of 1974 (and that led to the dissolution of Parliament) went on in one place for 31 pages without a period. Lawyers tend to try to put everything into a single sentence, rather than, as is usual in language, expressing a thought and then qualifying it or expanding on it in a later sentence. As Crystal and Davy state,[27]

> "legal sentences are usually self-contained units which convey all the sense that has to be conveyed at any particular point and do not need to be linked closely either to what follows or to what has gone before. It seems that many types of discourse — especially conversation — prefer to convey connected information in a series of short sentences which need linking devices to show their continuity, while legal English moves in the opposite direction by putting all such sequences into the form of very complex sentences capable of standing alone."

Surely sentences could be shortened.[28] The present practice of not having more than one sentence in a section or subsection[29] unnecessarily forces draftsmen to use long and complex sentences. As Lord Reid, a member of the House of Lords Appeal Court, stated to the English Society of Public Teachers of Law:[30] "If only lawyers would realize that no language is a precision tool and that short simple sentences, though they may look less precise, are really much more likely to have a clear meaning than the kind of jargon which is now fashionable."[31]

There are some statutes that do use a narrative form of presentation. The Rules of Evidence of the United States Federal Military Code is perhaps one of the best known examples.[32] For example, the rule relating to cross-examination (rule 149(b)(i)) has three paragraphs, the first of which states:

> "(1) *Cross-examination.* Cross-examination of a witness is a matter of right. It should, in general, be limited to the issues concerning which the witness has testified on direct examination and the question of his credibility. Counsel often cannot know in advance what pertinent facts may be brought out on cross-examination, and for that reason it is to some extent exploratory. Reasonable latitude should be given the cross-examiner, even if he is unable to state to the court what facts his cross-examination is intended to develop.

The cross-examination of a witness need not be restricted merely because it appears to be repetitious of the questioning or testimony of the witness on direct examination. Leading questions may be used freely on cross-examination."

(B)   Aids to Interpretation

In addition to using more readable language and improving sentence structure, other techniques could be tried to make the contents of statutes more understandable.[33] Comments and examples could be incorporated after each section.[34] We should also use formulas where appropriate instead of elaborate verbal formulations of rules.[35] Such aids as diagrams,[36] charts, and tables,[37] which increase the readability of the statute could be used far more often than they are.

The visual form of the statute could be improved by using different kinds of type for various parts of the legislation. For example, italics could be used for words that were defined earlier; or the main operative parts of the legislation might be distinguished by larger type from the technical operational parts. A substantial improvement was introduced in the most recent Revised Statutes of Canada when references to section numbers used symbols instead of words.

A problem frequently complained of by those we spoke to is the complex structure of most statutes. From a lawyer's point of view our statutes are set out in a logical manner: they usually begin with definitions and then move on to application sections, then to the operative part of the statute, and end with such things as administration, regulations, and penalties. This is obvious to a lawyer. Lawyers are able to skim statutes and pick out the key parts. Non-lawyers have difficulty. The marginal notes are helpful — and should, in fact, be considered an official part of the legislation to assist the courts, as they undoubtedly assist the lay reader,[38] in gathering the legislative intent[39] — but more assistance is needed for the non-lawyer by providing tables of contents which would show at a glance what is in the statute.[40] In addition, there should be a brief introduction to explain the object of the statute. English Statutory Instruments now provide such brief explanatory notes, although they are specifically stated not to be part of the document. As Professor Kolers observed, "Information-transfer is greatly facilitated when the reader knows what the information is about and what to look for."[41] Most scientific publications and many legal journals now provide abstracts of the key parts of articles. Similar abstracts would be just as useful for legislation. Such an introduction could supplement or perhaps take the place of preambles, which are still sometimes used,[42] although they are not liked by draftsmen.[43]

In addition to an introduction, a statute might have an explanatory memorandum that would be part of the legislation. Members of Parliament look at a Bill having had the assistance of the Minister's speech on the second reading of the Bill, as well as explanations and comments on each page opposite the draft of the Bill. Even the Minister has assistance in understanding the Bill: he has a Black Book specially prepared for him explaining each section of the Bill. But once the Bill is passed and becomes an Act of Parliament, all these explanations and comments are lost. They do not accompany the Act into the statute book. It is interesting that what is necessary for members of Parliament is not thought to be necessary for the private citizen.

An explanatory memorandum could be drafted as part of the Bill and could be based on the substance of the Minister's second reading speech. It would explain what the Bill was trying to do and how the various sections relate to each other and to the existing law.

A similar recommendation was made by the English and Scottish Law Commissions' study of the Interpretation of Statutes,[44] but it has met with considerable resistance, primarily because of concern that it would make it more difficult for the Legislature to get through its business. No doubt this is true, because not only must members of Parliament be concerned about the actual words in the legislation, but they would also be concerned about the explanatory memorandum. However, in our opinion the benefit of having such a memorandum would outweigh the disadvantages. One solution to prevent taking up too much additional Parliamentary time might be to prohibit amendments to the explanatory memorandum while the legislation was before Parliament; instead, a Parliamentary Committee could amend the memorandum following the passage of the legislation to make certain it was consistent with the Act, and the memorandum could then be laid before the Commons and the Senate.[45]

It has often been suggested that it would be desirable to change the present rule followed by the courts[46] and permit the debates in Hansard to be used to interpret legislation. But we think that the above proposals are far preferable. It is often very difficult to gather the intent of the Legislature from the speeches in Parliament. Moreover, copies of Hansard are not located in very many places, and their use would make the law even more inaccessible than it is now.[47]

The same considerations apply, although to a lesser extent, to the use of committee and commission reports as aids to interpretation. Without obtaining these documents the non-expert would be at a disadvantage in understanding the legislation. It would be better in appropriate cases to incorporate the explanation into the statute itself.

(C) Indexing

The other major criticism levelled at existing legal materials by those we contacted was the inadequacy and frequent absence of indexing. We felt this to be a problem of such importance that we asked Professors K. H. Packer and A. H. Schabas of the Faculty of Library Science at the University of Toronto and Alice Janisch, a librarian from Halifax, to examine and comment upon the existing indexes to statutes in Canada. Excerpts from their papers, from which the following comments have been selected, are set out in Appendices 8 and 9 at pages 139 and 145.

Professors Packer and Schabas concluded, in relation to the Index to the 1970 Revised Statutes of Canada, that

> ". . . the present index does not satisfy the criteria that have been generally accepted as the hallmarks of sound indexing practice regardless of its intended users, and it is woefully inadequate to meet the needs of the layman."

Alice Janisch described existing Canadian statute indexes as follows:

> "The federal and provincial statute indexes in Canada are all, upon close examination, found to be lists of Acts, with each Act indexed to some extent, and with some cross references for topics. If all of these 'Act analyses' were removed from the statute indexes (and perhaps placed at the top of chapters in the statutes) there would be very little left of the indexes."

In fact, Professors Packer and Schabas removed the "Act analyses" (which they call "mini-indexes") from the Index to the 1970 Revised Statutes of Canada and found that they were left with only 1550 different index terms. Of these, only 600 proved to be true subject entries.

Because there are so few subject entries, the user will rarely find a topic he is looking for in the Index to the Revised Statutes of Canada. There are no entries under terms such as 'children', 'deportation' and 'fingerprints'. The subject indexing now done just refers to other Acts, and does it on a very "hit or miss" basis. For example, under "Civil Liberties", the only reference is to the War Measures Act! In order to use the "Act analyses" one has to know the name of the relevant Act. But, as Alice Janisch points out: "The average person, without intimate knowledge of the law, doesn't say to himself, 'I wonder what the requirements of the X Act are concerning Y?' He is much more likely to say 'I need to know something about the law concerning Y'."

What is needed is a much more sophisticated indexing system. Indexing of individual Acts is useful and should be continued as part of the general index. Indeed, these indexes should be printed as part of the Act itself whenever an office consolidation of the Act is printed. But there should also be much more subject indexing done. After their detailed examination of existing indexes, Professors Packer and Schabas concluded that:

> ". . . the major improvement needed in the RSI [Index to the 1970 Revised Statutes of Canada] to make it useful to the layman is to provide more subject access, phrased in user (layman) vocabulary. Because different users approach information with different terms

in mind the index must provide for all reasonable alternatives: variant spellings, multiword phrases and inversions, synonyms and different levels of generality. . . . The importance of providing context with the index entry as a selection aid to the user has to be stressed, and further it is recommended that a systematic approach to this be adopted."

The use of subject indexing will, of course, substantially increase the size of the index and will require persons trained as indexers with a knowledge of law to be involved in the work.[48] The cost of the index will therefore increase; but the index will be far more useful than it now is.

Computers can play an important role in indexing, not just in producing word indexes, but also in producing a "key word in context" (KWIC) index that can tell the user the context in which each indexed word is used.[49] The Federal statutes are now in a machine-readable form, so that a computer can now easily be used for this type of indexing.

An index should be viewed as an integral part of the statutes and should appear at the same time as the statutes. In the case of the Revised Statutes of Canada of 1970, however, the index did not appear until late 1973.

(D) Arrangement of Statutes

Many people we spoke to said that they have difficulty in keeping track of amendments to statutes. We are fortunate in Canada in having revised statutes in all provinces as well as at the federal level.[50] Unfortunately, the revisions do not take place as frequently as they should. For example, federal revisions were done in 1927, in 1952, and in 1970. They should be much more frequent than this so that it would not be necessary to look through a great number of annual volumes to discover the present state of the law. Revisions should be carried out at least once every five years.

Indeed, the most sensible scheme is to maintain a continuous revision of the statutes, using pamphlets which can easily be replaced in a looseleaf binder. Federal Bill C-23, which was introduced in April 1974 and died with the dissolution of Parliament, but was re-introduced in the Fall of 1974 as Bill S-3, provides for an edition in looseleaf form as a way of keeping an up-to-date consolidation of the statutes and the regulations.[51]

The annual statutes are very difficult for a lay person to use. There is no explanation of how they operate or how they relate to the revised statutes. For example, the difference between public general and local and private Acts is not explained. There is an important table at the back of the annual volumes of the federal and most provincial statutes that lawyers find indispensable in tracing legislation, but a non-expert would have great difficulty in understanding how this table is to be used. In this connection a pamphlet describing the use of the Revised Statutes and the annual volumes could be issued by the Queen's Printer in each jurisdiction; such a pamphlet has been made available in England free of charge by the Statutory Publications Office.

Another problem faced by statute users is in finding Acts that have been passed but have not yet been published in the annual volume. An important step to correct this deficiency has been taken by the federal government which has announced that commencing in January, 1975, the Public Acts of each session of Parliament shall be published as a separate detachable part of The Canada Gazette as soon as practicable after receiving Royal Assent.

The federal government and most provinces now arrange their Acts alphabetically. From the standpoint of the user, it is probably preferable to arrange them according to subject matter, as is now being considered in Manitoba and Saskatchewan and is in the process of being done in England. The new English scheme, which will consist of over one hundred subject entries, looks very good in principle (certainly a vast improvement on the present chronological arrangement) and incorporates many good ideas, such as producing Acts in separate booklets to be incorporated in binders so that amended ones can easily be replaced. But whether the English scheme will in fact turn out to be a significant improvement will depend to a large extent on the way it is administered.[52]

II. OTHER SOURCES OF LAW

So far the discussion in this chapter has concentrated on an examination of statutes. Other sources of law must also be considered, especially popular handbooks and government pamphlets which are frequently used by non-lawyers.

(A) Regulations

It is often misleading to read legislation without the regulations. However, regulations are less accessible than legislation. They are consolidated less frequently than legislation and the consolidations are not properly indexed.[53] One advantage is that draftsmen do not take them quite as seriously as legislation, which allows more freedom in the way regulations are framed. Draftsmen do not feel the same compulsion to make them stylistically pure. This allows a greater use of formulas, tables, examples, and descriptive material. Indeed, one sometimes sees more than one sentence in a section!

In fact, regulations should be treated in the same way as legislation and should be integrated or at least set out with it, as is often done unofficially in office consolidations of Acts and regulations.

(B) Case Reports

Case reports are almost impossible for the non-lawyer to deal with. They are hard to find and to interpret and it is often difficult to assess the weight to be given to a particular case. The problem is difficult to overcome because there will continue to be cases interpreting sections of statutes and legal training will continue to be necessary to interpret the cases. But some improvements can be made.

Many judges are concerned about their style and have adopted certain techniques for making their writing clear. For example, some divide their judgments under headings — often indispensable for the reader. Indeed, the judges who produce the most readable judgments are the ones who sometimes use this technique (e.g., Lord Denning M.R. in England). Some introduce the facts of the case and the key issues in short, easily understood sentences. The judges themselves would concede that much could be done to improve the clarity of their writing, and at least one appellate court in Canada has had sessions with an expert on English style.

The appellate judges can assist by not making a virtue out of uncertainty. It is understandable and desirable that a number of separate judgments, both concurring and dissenting, will often be written. But the judges should not be laws unto themselves, each going his own way. A court should be under some obligation to sit down after all the judgments have been written and explain the meaning of the reasons for judgment — in other words for the court to write its own headnote. We feel that with comparatively little effort the writing of appellate judgments can be improved.

(C) Legal Textbooks and Encyclopedias

The existing legal textbooks, encyclopedias, and abridgments are also almost impossible for non-lawyers to use. Written for lawyers, they assume the reader has considerable knowledge about law and the legal system as well as access to a full law library. In addition, they are poorly indexed, particularly for the non-lawyer. Moreover, they are found in very few places where the public can go to find legal information.

(D) Popular Handbooks and Government Pamphlets

Many non-lawyers (and in fact some lawyers as well), perhaps frustrated by their attempts to look up law using the more traditional legal reference tools, turn to popular legal handbooks and government pamphlets and leaflets. Excerpts from some of these are set out in Appendix

10. However, these publications also pose problems for their users, even though they are steps in the right direction and are generally more readable than statutes, case reports, and legal textbooks.

One of the major problems with them is that they are not comprehensive either in their treatment of the specific topics they deal with or in their coverage of the whole body of law. Most of the government publications are not designed to give a great deal of specific information; they tend to give a general description of an area and encourage people having specific questions to contact specific government information sources.

The popular handbooks usually cover the topics they deal with in some detail, but because they are produced commercially, they cover only those topics in which enough people able and willing to purchase handbooks are actively interested. Thus they are available in such areas as motor vehicle law, family law, and tax law, but not mechanics' liens or welfare law. Moreover, in areas of provincial law, the handbooks published deal with the law only of the largest provinces, which of course provide the largest markets. There are many handbooks explaining the laws of Ontario and British Columbia but none dealing with those of Prince Edward Island or Newfoundland.

Another major problem with these materials is that they are seldom indexed. In fact, they are not really intended nor designed to be used as reference tools. Many of the people we contacted who have used popular handbooks said that they are useful in giving the reader some general knowledge about an area of law but for the most part cannot be used to find detailed information in answering specific inquiries.

These materials also quickly become out-of-date. By their very nature they cannot be updated — new information can be added only by publishing a new edition. And many of the government pamphlets and leaflets are not dated, which means that readers are not even warned that the information contained in them might no longer be correct.

Many pamphlets also suffer from oversimplification. They often use a question and answer format which includes only the most basic questions and of course only the questions the author thinks of. Many of the people working in information centres complained that the inquiries they receive always fall between the questions in the pamphlets, and the pamphlets never give any indication of what effect a few changes in the facts would make in the answers to the questions.

NOTES

1. *Report of the English and Scottish Law Commissions on The Interpretation of Statutes* (1969), at 3.
2. See the English paper on government regulations cited in Crystal and Davy, *Investigating English Style* (1969), at 6.
3. *Proceedings of the Ninth International Symposium on Comparative Law*, Ottawa (1972), 115, at 121.
4. "New Ways to Write Laws" (1947), 56 *Yale L.J.* 458 at 481.
5. Thorson, *Address to the Opening Plenary Session of the Canadian Tax Foundation Conference* (1972), at 13.
6. Ibid., at 13-14. By strictly construing tax statutes the courts have forced the draftsmen to try to achieve certainty by covering all possibilities and this, of course, results in complex legislation.
7. See Craies, *Statute Law* (7th ed., 1971), at 28; Reid, (1972) 12 *J.S.P.T.L.* 22 at 28.
8. See Bennion, supra note 3, at 125-6.
9. See Thorson, supra note 5, at 18; Driedger, *The Composition of Legislation* (1957), at xvi; Bennion, supra note 3 at 134-5.
10. Supra note 9, at xxii.
11. 3 Bentham 207 (Bowring edition).
12. *Proceedings of the Ninth International Symposium on Comparative Law*, Ottawa (1972), 71, at 76-7.
13. David Mellinkoff, *The Language of the Law* (1963), is an excellent historical analysis; see also the writings of Reed Dickerson: e.g., *The Fundamentals of Legal Drafting* (1965); of E. A. Driedger: e.g., *The Composition of Legislation* (1957); and the recent book by R. C. Dick, *Legal Drafting* (1972).
14. See Crystal and Davy, supra note 2, at 208; Mellinkoff, supra note 13, at 120-2. A good example of this phenomenon is found in Form 28 in the Criminal Code which uses the language: "made and levied of their several goods and chattels, lands and tenements".
15. Crystal and Davy, supra note 2, at 206.
16. Ibid., at 206-7.
17. See Appendix 7.
18. Gleason, *Linguistics and English Grammar* (1965), at 442.
19. See Coode, "Legislative Expression", extract from the introduction to the Appendix annexed to the *Report of the Poor Law Commissioners on Local Taxation* presented to Parliament in 1843, reprinted in Driedger, supra note 9, at 167.
20. See, e.g., Dick, supra note 13, at 56 *et seq.*
21. See Crystal and Davy, supra note 2, at 217.
22. Cited in Driedger, supra note 9, at 185.
23. Supra note 13, at 58-9.
24. Some members of the Faculty of Law with whom these redrafts were discussed expressed concern that by switching the order the "and" might be construed as an "or". This does not appear likely to us and, in any event, the problem could be handled by making the conjunctive meaning even clearer.
25. "A Modern View of Language" (1972) 23 *Case Western Res.L.Rev.* 318, at 351.
26. The example is admittedly extreme because the legislation was introduced as a Ways and Means motion.
27. Crystal and Davy, supra note 2, at 201.
28. See Bennion, supra note 3, at 148; see his evidence in the Report of the Statute Law Society, *Statute Law: The Key to Clarity* (1972), at 61, and in the *Second Report from*

the *Select Committee on Procedure* (1971), Q. 1129. For the historical background see Mellinkoff, supra note 13, at 152 *et seq.* and 366 *et seq.*

29. Driedger, supra note 9, at 101.

30. "The Judge as Law Maker" (1972), 12 *J.S.P.T.L.* 22, at 28.

31. Professor Clarence Smith has emphasised the point that long sentences are not found in legislation drafted by civil law lawyers: Clarence Smith, "Comparative Summing-Up" in *Proceedings of the Ninth International Symposium on Comparative Law*, Ottawa, (1972) 155, at 170.

32. *Manual for Courts-Martial* (1969), chapter XXVII.

33. See generally the Memorandum produced by the U.K. Society of Public Teachers of Law, *Preparation of Legislation* (1974), 13 *J.S.P.T.L.* 96.

34. For example, see the Indian Evidence Act, discussed in Craies, *Statute Law* (7th ed., 1971), at 226. See also the Committee Comments in the Code of Criminal Law and Procedure of Illinois in the Illinois Annotated Statutes, c. 38; and the Official Comments in, e.g., the Uniform Commercial Code, the Uniform Partnership Act, and the Uniform Consumer Credit Code.

35. See the Statute Law Society Report, *Statute Law Deficiencies* (1970), at 39-40. Thorson, supra note 5, at 19. For an example of a mathematical formula, see The Highway Traffic Act, R.S.O. 1970, c. 202, s. 74, relating to axle weights; see also the formulas in the Canada Shipping Act, R.S.C. 1952, c. 29, not repeated in R.S.C. 1970.

36. See, e.g., The Mining Act, R.S.O. 1970, c. 274, s. 56.

37. See The Highway Traffic Act, R.S.O. 1970, c. 202; The Assessment Act, R.S.O. 1970, c. 32; The Mining Act, R.S.O. 1970; c. 274; R.C.M.P. Pension Continuation Act, R.S.C. 1970, c. R-10.

38. See the Law Commission Report, *The Interpretation of Statutes* (1969), at 26-7: "a statute is directed not merely to the courts but also to the community at large, who will tend to read the statute without giving any very refined attention to the exact legal status of its different parts".

39. Marginal notes now are not considered by some courts as part of the Act: see Driedger, *The Construction of Statutes* (1974), at 109; *Wright, McDermott and Feeley* v. *The Queen* [1964] S.C.R. 192, at 193; *Govedarov, Popovic and Askov* (1974) 3 O.R. (2d) 23, at 48. On the other hand, headings may be looked at as affording some indication of the legislative purpose: see *Brodie, Dansky and Rubin* v. *The Queen* [1962] S.C.R. 681, at 708; *Govedarov, Popovic and Askov* (1974) 3 O.R. (2d) 23, at 48. See generally the Law Commission Report, *The Interpretation of Statutes* (1969), at 26.

40. See the letter to the editor by Jacob S. Ziegel in the *Globe and Mail*, February 23, 1974. Note the use of a table of contents in the Revised Statutes of New Brunswick.

41. See P. A. Kolers, "Introduction", in Huey, *The Psychology and Pedagogy of Reading* (1968 ed.), at xxix.

42. See, e.g., the preamble to the Act to Amend the Canada Labour Code, 1972, c. 18, and the statement of purpose set out in s. 2 of the Foreign Investment Review Act, 1972.

43. See Driedger, supra note 9, at 93-4; Drafting rules prepared by the Committee on Legislative Drafting of the Conference of Commissioners on Uniform State Laws, 1953, reproduced in Read, MacDonald and Fordham, *Legislation* (1959), 309 at 313; *cf.* Thorson, supra note 5, at 17-18: "we should be willing to explore whether such statements of purpose could usefully be made part of our law."

44. Law Commission Report, *The Interpretation of Statutes* (1969), at 38 *et seq.* A similar proposal was recommended by Harold Laski in his dissent to the *Report of the Committee on Ministers' Powers* (1932), Cmd. 4060, at 136. It is presently the practice in Denmark: see Law Commission Report, at 39; and Ghana: see Namasivayam, *The Drafting of Legislation* (1967), at 1. The Law Commission proposal was accepted in the Ninth Report of the Law Reform Committee of South Australia, *Law Relating to Construction of Statutes* (1970). See also Conard, "New

Ways to Write Laws" (1947), 56 *Yale L.J.* 458, at 460-1; Lord Simon in *Borough of Ealing* v. *Race Relations Board* [1972] 1 All E.R. 105 (H.L.), at 114: "All this is not, of course, to say that an explanatory memorandum accompanying a complicated measure, such as accompanies almost every statutory instrument, might not often be useful both in apprising legislators of the details for which they are assuming responsibility and in assisting the courts in their task of interpretation."

45. A number of such possibilities are explored in the Law Commission Report, *The Interpretation of Statutes* (1969), at 40-1; see also pp. xxxi — xxxii of the Second Report from the Select Committee on Procedure, *The Process of Legislation* (1971).

46. See Driedger, *The Construction of Statutes* (1974), at 130.

47. A further concern is that the record of Hansard could be developed with an eye to later interpretation by the courts. This is now the situation in the United States.

48. See generally, Hewitt, "Legal Indexing", in Knight, *Training in Indexing* (1969), at 152 *et seq.*

49. See Skelly, "Computers and Statute Law" (1970), 3 *Law and Computer Technology* 30, at 37.

50. Moreover, we are fortunate that we use the textual rather than the referential form of amendment. This means that the amendments will fit into and maintain the integrity of the existing statutory structure. In contrast, the English practice is sometimes to amend the law without necessarily fitting it into an existing statute.

51. On November 29, 1974 the Bill was given second reading by the House of Commons and referred to the Standing Committee on Justice and Legal Affairs.

52. See the Memorandum prepared by the Society of Public Teachers of Law, *Preparation of Legislation* (1974), 13 *J.S.P.T.L.* 96 at 103, which points out that "the statute will only be reprinted, as a whole, from time to time when the encrustations have reached substantial proportions". Moreover, the set is being proceeded with very slowly and so a user will have to use two sets of statutes for a considerable period of time: see Hutton in (1973), 89 *L.Q.R.* 21.

53. See Appendix 9. See generally the *Report of the Special Committee on Statutory Instruments* (Mark MacGuigan, Chairman) (1969) at 1477-8.

Chapter 5
PROVIDING BETTER ACCESS TO THE LAW

No single source of law or system of delivering legal information will provide the public with sufficient access to the law. People ask questions involving law for a wide variety of purposes. They ask about every area of law and direct their questions to a multitude of appropriate — and inappropriate — sources. Some want quick verbal answers to simple information questions; others wish to discuss problems with persons they regard as experts; and a few want to investigate an area of law in a more academic way.

We found that in many cases the information about law provided to the public by various information sources is inaccurate or incomplete. People answering legal inquiries find them more difficult to handle than many other kinds of questions. In addition, many members of the public do not recognize the legal dimension in many everyday situations; some people do not try to obtain information about their rights or obligations because it never occurs to them that they have any.

We believe that public access to the law can be improved in four ways: improvement of existing legal materials, basic education of the public about law, improvement of the quality of legal information dispensed by intermediary organizations, and development of a new source of law for non-lawyers. The form of existing legal materials was examined in the previous chapter. Our recommendations in the other three areas are set out below.

I. PUBLIC EDUCATION

An important component in improving access to the law is the education of the general public about law and the legal system. Non-lawyers should be familiar enough with the law and the legal system to recognize areas of activity covered by law. People should also be taught how to find the law in those areas where questions and problems most often arise — that is, how to use sources of law.

Since the law is always changing, it is important to distinguish between the ability to recognize situations covered by law and knowing the law itself. Even lawyers do not know the law except in the few areas they encounter continuously. They know how to look up the law. Similarly, law courses aimed at non-lawyers should stress the recognition of situations involving law and how to find the law, rather than what the law is at a particular moment in various areas. Care must be taken to avoid misleading people into thinking that they "know the law."

Fundamentals of law should be taught both in school and to those who have finished their formal education. In particular, courses about law and the legal system should be available in high schools and perhaps even in senior elementary schools. There are two major difficulties in undertaking such courses at present: finding suitable teachers and a lack of texts. Lawyers and law students are sometimes engaged to teach such courses in schools, but they often lack preparation time, familiarity with the students, and teacher training. The establishment of an undergraduate course concentration in law as part of a Bachelor of Arts program at university seems worth considering. Graduates of such a program, like those with degrees in history or physics, could become teachers of their special subject after completing teacher training. Such a program would also appeal to students wishing to study the law but having no real interest in specializing in law to the extent of entering law school.

The other problem encountered in connection with high school law courses is the lack of suitable texts and other supporting materials. Although several Canadian law texts for high schools are now in existence or in preparation, there are no suitable reference tools to back them up. An up-to-date reference work covering Canadian law suitable for high school libraries would also be used by university undergraduate students to research the law in connection with their courses.

Education about law is equally important for those outside the school system, and should be undertaken with the same objectives in mind: recognition of everyday situations involving law, and knowledge of resources available to supply specific legal information. In recent years the People's Law School in Vancouver has been running highly successful, free, one-week law courses aimed at non-lawyers. These courses combine lectures or videotapes featuring lawyers and specially prepared supporting materials that outline the basic law in various areas.[1] The People's Law School provides an example of legal education for non-lawyers which could be adapted for use in other communities.[2] It should be noted that the People's Law School has found it necessary to produce its own printed materials to supplement its courses. The availability of such materials would enable law courses for the public to be set up much more easily.

Another method of educating the public about law is through mass media advertising. Governments frequently use this method to inform members of the public of obligations placed upon them and of the law relevant to those obligations. For example, every spring the federal government sponsors television, radio and newspaper advertisements about filing income tax returns and about various aspects of income tax law. Such mass media campaigns have also been used at other times to inform the public of various legal rights. For example, in the past few years Manitoba's new landlord and tenant legislation and the Rentalsman office have been advertised successfully. Manitoba residents are increasingly recognizing a legal component in relationships between landlords and tenants and are using the Rentalsman for information as well as for service. Many people we spoke to, however, felt that such mass media campaigns are of limited usefulness because the audience is not faced with an immediate problem and is thus not motivated to listen to or remember the information being presented. Moreover, there are definite limits to the amount and complexity of the information that can be disseminated in this way.[3]

II.   IMPROVING DELIVERY SYSTEMS

The existing delivery of legal information should be improved by reducing the problems facing intermediary individuals and organizations in handling legal questions and by improving the quality of the information dispensed. In every case this involves training, as well as the provision of a well indexed source of Canadian and provincial law containing comprehensive, detailed, and up-to-date information. It also requires some recognition of the important role played by the telephone in transmitting information about law. Information is disseminated over the telephone more frequently than through face-to-face contact. It should not be treated as a second-class device interrupting the normal delivery system.

Many of the information sources we contacted believe that they handle legal inquiries successfully. However, the results of our tests described in chapter 2 indicate that all sources often make unsatisfactory referrals or provide incorrect or incomplete information. Those sources that said that they are not satisfied with the way they handle legal inquiries expressed concern about their own lack of knowledge about law. They often do not fully understand the questions or how to handle them, but are unhappy about referring them on because they are never sure that the inquirer will follow up the referral, or if he does, that he will in fact be assisted by the source referred to.

Because people have different types of legal problems and are seeking different types of responses to those problems, no one system of delivering legal information or services will suffice. As described in chapter 3, for example, there appears to be a strong need for a special delivery system for the Canadian Native People. What is needed is a variety of means of delivering legal information accurately and in a form useful to the people faced with the legal problems.

(A) Lawyers in Private Practice

One possibility would be to channel all legal inquiries to lawyers in private practice who have expert knowledge about law. However, such a solution is neither feasible nor satisfactory. Justifiably, lawyers charge for their time. If it is a citizen's right to find out about the laws affecting him, he should not be required to pay to exercise this right. Moreover, an individual should have the opportunity of determining whether or not a legal problem exists before making the decision to hire a lawyer. People will continue to rely on other organizations to answer their everyday legal questions no matter what attempts may be made to channel such inquiries to the private bar, both for monetary reasons and because many find lawyers and law offices intimidating. Moreover, Canada has comparatively few lawyers to serve the population, especially that part of it located outside major urban areas. Even if there were enough lawyers available, many of them would not want to handle the millions of simple inquiries that government departments, the police, and other organizations currently deal with each year. Most lawyers would find such questions a tiresome distraction from their work.

In addition, lawyers are not really trained to handle requests for information. Our experiments, described in chapter 2, revealed that lawyers in private practice sometimes made mistakes in answering relatively simple legal questions. Their mistakes usually arose from a failure to check the answers in readily available reference sources. It is not enough for a person handling information inquiries to have some expert knowledge about the subject matter of the inquiries; he must also be trained to handle information inquiries as such and to check answers in up-to-date sources of information rather than relying on his initial reactions.

(B) Legal Aid Clinics

There are strong arguments to be made for funnelling legal inquiries to legal aid offices and clinics if these organizations will accept answering them as part of their function. The staff of legal aid centres includes lawyers who already are trained to recognize complications in legal questions and problems and are familiar with existing legal materials. However, if all such inquiries were funnelled to lawyers in legal aid clinics, the number of such lawyers would have to be greatly increased.

One aspect of using legal aid offices as sources of legal information and summary advice that has not yet received as much attention as it deserves is the use of paralegals to handle the less complicated questions and problems. Normally, when a legal assistance clinic first opens, all the short-answer inquiries are passed on to the clinic's staff lawyers. However, as such a clinic becomes better known in the community, it attracts large numbers of such inquiries, and the staff lawyers become overburdened. Many existing clinics have found it necessary to establish a screening process to filter out questions and problems that can be satisfactorily handled by someone other than a lawyer.[4]

The use of paralegal personnel in this manner has many advantages. Our tests described in chapter 2 showed that non-lawyers often handle legal information questions and problems satisfactorily. Many of these questions simply do not require the use of expert legal knowledge, and directing them to lawyers is unnecessarily costly. A person with sufficient legal training to be able to categorize legal questions and to recognize problems that do require expert knowledge could handle such questions just as well.

One specific problem with the way legal inquiries are handled in some legal aid offices deserves special attention. In many offices, especially administration offices, office staff handle many of the questions without the supervision or knowledge of lawyers. As a result, mistakes and bad referrals are frequently made. Area Directors should make an effort to supervise this activity. At the very least, they should set some policy for dealing with such inquiries and should assist their staff in collecting referral information or act as a back-up for legal information.

Although legal aid clinics would be appropriate for many legal questions, some questions are more relevant to other organizations. Government offices, community information centres, the police, and libraries will continue to have a role in providing access to the law.

(C) Government Offices

At the present time government departments and information offices receive great numbers of legal inquiries each year. Many of these inquiries should continue to be directed to the government as they concern legislation and government services. It seems reasonable that specific departments should answer the legal questions they receive that relate to their own activities and responsibilities. But our tests indicated that at present the staff of individual government departments often give inaccurate or incomplete information, perhaps because of the difficulties of keeping up informally with the range of legislation and the many programs and services their department administers as well as relevant legislation and programs in other departments and other levels of government. In departments in which this information function remains unrecognized and is still handled informally, these problems are even more apparent. A comment by the supervisor of the public information section at the Toronto City Hall is apt in this regard. She said:[5] "In each department, it is often the lowest-paid person who gets all the inquiries, and that person often has no training at all to deal with them." These difficulties could be minimized if each department maintained an information bureau whose staff was responsible for receiving inquiries and trained to locate and co-ordinate appropriate answers.

As well as an information bureau in each department, it seems necessary for each government to have a general information branch, similar to Information Canada, to deal with inquiries not specific enough to direct to a particular department or involving matters that do not clearly fall within the jurisdiction of one department. The keys to the success of such a general information branch are a well qualified staff of information officers trained to check their information carefully and an up-to-date source of law in which answers can be verified.

Information Canada is an example of a centralized information office for an entire level of government. Several provincial governments also have established some form of central information service, although none is on the scale of Information Canada. As described in chapter 3, an important aspect of Information Canada's operations is the answering of questions from the public about the government's programs and policies. The Enquiry Centres seem to be the natural source for citizens and their advisors to use for information about federal statutory law such as old age pensions, unemployment insurance, immigration, and so forth. While specific federal departments have established information offices to give detailed information about programs like unemployment insurance and to assist applicants with special problems, the federal government has recognized and responded to the need for a general government information source.

The Standing Senate Committee on National Finance recommended that the number of Enquiry Centres be limited to the eleven existing ones.[6] However, rather than limiting the number of Centres, we think they should be opened in all the major cities in Canada. Victoria, Calgary, Regina, Thunder Bay, Windsor, Hamilton, Quebec City, Fredericton, and Saint John seem to be obvious future locations. These Enquiry Centres should be connected to the rest of their areas by toll-free lines, so that anyone would be able to contact the closest Centre with relative ease.

An effort should be made to establish an intensive training program for Enquiry Officers to ensure their ability to give accurate, detailed information about federal programs, policies, and laws. Inexperience and lack of training on the part of Enquiry Officers is currently a major reason for bad referrals and incorrect answers. Unfortunately, many of the Officers seem to lack experience in problem-solving and research methods, while the present training program places more emphasis on office skills than on information-handling and problem-solving techniques.

If more Enquiry Centres were established and the quality of their services upgraded, they could be utilized to a greater extent by local information sources as a back-up service. In this light, we endorse the following statement of the Senate Committee:[7]

> "... the Committee is of the opinion that Information Canada
> should encourage the use of local groups and facilities as much as
> is consistent with the aims of an information agency. Community
> information centres, libraries, church groups, etc., should be re-
> positories of government pamphlets and should be a source to
> which people can turn for initial information on government
> policies, programs and services. ... These local organizations
> should, in turn, be encouraged to make maximum use of the En-
> quiry Centre in their area."

The establishment of similar information branches at a provincial
level would be useful to complement the activities of the Information
Canada Enquiry Centres. In fact, the best solution might be to have
combined inquiry centres that could handle questions about both
levels of government.

(D)   Community Information Centres

As well as performing other useful functions, community information
centres act as an interface between the inexperienced citizen and the
multitude of government departments and regulations. They provide
the citizen with information in a form that he can understand and in an
atmosphere that he does not find intimidating or oppressive. For this
reason their establishment and growth should be encouraged by permanent or long-term funding derived from both public and private
sources.

The information centres throughout Canada are not linked together in any formal way. By contrast, in England the Citizens' Advice
Bureaus play a dominant and co-ordinated role in providing information to citizens. There are more than 600 such Bureaus, with over 80 in
Greater London alone.[8] An officer of one of them describes as follows
the background to their development and the special information materials that are made available to each Bureau:[9]

> The C.A.B. service was the outcome of inspired forward planning
> by a group of voluntary organizations which came together a year
> before the outbreak of war, at the time of the Munich crisis in 1938.
> Since war seemed imminent it was felt that a new service would be
> required which would be ready to answer the flood of queries
> which would inevitably arise about rationing, evacuation, con-
> scription, etc. Plans were laid for what was to become the Citizens'
> Advice Bureau service, and the day after war was declared a net-
> work of Bureaux opened up throughout the country. It is frustrating
> not to be able to quote statistics for this impressive organizational
> feat, but those who launched the C.A.B. service regarded it solely as
> a war-time emergency project. They did not at that stage expect the
> war to last more than months, or the C.A.B. service to survive it, so

none but a very few research-conscious staff kept records at the very beginning. However, the number of Bureaux rapidly reached a thousand and these were the responsibility of a varied assortment of already established voluntary organizations. Central government had been persuaded of the value of such a service, and a grant towards its organization was made available by the then Ministry of Health. For administrative tidiness, the grant was paid to the National Council of Social Service (N.C.S.S.) in its capacity as co-ordinating body for voluntary social work agencies throughout the country. The N.C.S.S. shared out the grant to those agencies which were already active in social work and had an administrative framework onto which C.A.B. could logically be grafted.

At the head of the C.A.B. service is the National Citizens' Advice Bureaux Council (N.C.A.B.C.) — still under the aegis of the National Council of Social Service. The N.C.A.B.C. provides the information service which is central to the efficient running of any individual Bureau. Of first importance is CANS — *Citizens' Advice Notes* — a loose-leaf volume which contains, summarized with great accuracy, a digest of all current legislation, official regulations, etc. CANS is under constant revision, and three times a year a supplement is issued to bring the reference material up to date. CANS is available on subscription outside the C.A.B. service, and can be found in libraries, solicitors' offices, and welfare rights organizations. To make a bridge between CANS supplements and to pass on to Bureaux information which is inappropriate for inclusion in CANS, a monthly circular is issued. C.A.B. may also call upon the services of the Information Department of the N.C.A.B.C., which can provide specialized information — for instance, finding out the liquidators of a firm which has ceased to trade — or can advise a Bureau on handling a particularly complex problem. General guidelines on C.A.B. policy and practice is given. If an individual Bureau fails to comply with the basic requirements laid down by the N.C.A.B.C. for the efficient operation of a C.A.B. and persists in its error despite prolonged persuasion and encouragement, the only course open to the N.C.A.B.C. is to withdraw the information service from it.

In Canada, the staffs of most community information centres are not trained to use reference materials to find specific information. As a result, most of the legal questions they receive are referred to specific government departments, legal aid clinics, or lawyers in private practice. The most effective way to improve this process is to provide an expanded system of legal aid clinics and a reliable source of information at each level of government.

The legal questions that information centres now try to answer themselves are generally handled less adequately than those they refer. Centres wishing to provide legal information and assistance directly should have staff members with paralegal training who can recognize complications requiring a lawyer's assistance. Although it is important that information centres remain approachable and unbureaucratic, it is vital that they ensure completeness and accuracy in the information they dispense.

There are a number of organizations that act as information centres for particular groups — for example, the Native Friendship Centres. They are able to tailor their operations to the needs of a specific clientele and to provide a contact point from which a successful referral to another service can be made. In most cases these organizations already have the skills necessary to reach their special audience; however, they sometimes are unable to provide adequate information or referrals in response to questions or problems involving law. In Native Friendship Centres, for example, although criminal law problems are usually recognized by the staff at the Centre and referred to their courtworkers or to lawyers in private practice, the legal aspects of housing and financial problems may go unidentified. The staff members need training to recognize the legal component in non-criminal problems and to know when these problems should be referred to an organization such as a legal aid clinic which can provide legal information and assistance.

For all information centres, therefore, the two most obvious needs are staff training to recognize the legal aspect of certain inquiries, and the availability of a centre specializing in law to which individuals can be referred.

(E) Police

As described in chapter 3, the police in Canada at present receive millions of telephone calls involving legal knowledge. Many of these calls are complaint-type calls dealing with matters commonly associated with the police, and it seems inevitable that the police will receive and respond to such calls. Indeed, for questions about laws in "police" areas, a police officer in many cases may be in as good a position as anyone else to provide an answer. In "non-police" areas, however, the police may not be an appropriate information source. Time pressures on police personnel and a tendency for them to give quick concrete answers sometimes affect the quality of the information given. In addition, the interest of the police in maintaining a quiet and orderly atmosphere may lead them to interpret a person's rights more narrowly than necessary. In appropriate cases, therefore, they should advise inquirers to consult other sources of information as well.

It seems likely that large numbers of people will continue to call the police with questions about law. Thus, the problem is not whether police departments should deal with such questions but rather to find the best method for them to do so.

Lack of training is a major problem at present in the way in which such questions are handled by the police, whether they attempt to give information themselves or refer the questions to other information sources. While officers receive training in various areas of law at police college, and thus have some of the knowledge necessary to deal with questions in "police related" subjects, they should also receive training in handling questions and properly researching answers to prevent reliance on out-of-date or partially forgotten information.[10] Such training should also attempt to inform officers when a question ought to be referred elsewhere and where to refer it.

The volume of inquiries received by the police justifies the establishment within each communications section of an information centre. Inquiries are now handled in a somewhat unorganized fashion by officers who are really supposed to be doing something else — receiving complaints and dispatching police personnel. If an information centre were established, questions of all kinds could then be switched to the centre where they would be handled by specially-trained officers assigned to this duty. The experience of the Calgary Police Department, described in chapter 3, is instructive in this regard. The establishment of such information centres in other police departments would ensure that the many information questions received by the police would be handled in an organized manner by trained personnel accustomed to dealing with information.

(F) Libraries

Many of the problems faced by public library staff in answering legal questions stem from the libraries' lack of suitable Canadian legal materials. Their availability would allow citizens to exercise their right to legal information while minimizing the possibility of misleading people with out-of-date information. It would also allow students, who make up a large proportion of public library users, easily and quickly to find the law related to their course of study.

However, whether or not new materials are produced, librarians need more training to facilitate the provision of legal information to the public.[11] Some background training in law would enable the librarian to categorize legal questions more accurately and thus to find relevant information more easily. Many librarians have already recognized the value of subject knowledge for staff in fields like science and fine arts; it is just as important in law.

Training of librarians in the use of legal materials is even more important. It is up to the librarian to help the user locate needed information as efficiently as possible; but many public librarians are not familiar enough with legal materials to perform this service adequately. Familiarity with existing legal materials will also allow the librarian with only a basic collection to be aware of resources available elsewhere.

Organized programs to learn about other community resources that provide legal information and assistance to the public should also be included in the training of library staff. A knowledge of such organizations would allow librarians to refer to them patrons who require more or different assistance than a library can provide. Moreover, an awareness of other community resources allows librarians to focus on their own distinctive skills and the resources of their libraries.

Paralegal training for librarians is another alternative we have considered. Paralegal personnel are able to perform such services as giving basic explanations of legal topics, assisting in the completion of legal forms, and advising individuals with relatively straightforward problems, while referring more complicated questions to lawyers. A few libraries have already begun to offer this kind of service, particularly to people in low-income areas. However, many librarians would be reluctant to become involved in paralegal activities, even if they were given special training. In addition, many of the legal inquiries now received by public libraries are from people who want to use printed materials to find information rather than to discuss a particular legal problem. At the present time most public libraries seem neither to want nor to need paralegal staff members. On the other hand, public libraries may be an ideal location for non-librarians to establish paralegal services. Legal aid clinics that have commenced operation in library buildings have had notable success. Similarly, some successful information centres in England have operated out of public libraries. [12]

University librarians and law librarians experience many of the same problems as public librarians in handling legal questions from the public. University libraries in general have collections of legal materials which contain more statutes and law-related textbooks than most urban public libraries but fewer popular legal handbooks. In addition, the bulk of the users of university libraries are students doing academic research, whose inquiries are general enough or vague enough that the librarians need some legal knowledge to categorize them properly. Like public librarians, they also need to learn about existing reference materials so that they can assess and plan their legal collections.

Law libraries, of course, have most of the existing materials. However, they also tend to receive more complicated inquiries about law, often referred to them by other libraries. Law librarians require considerable knowledge of existing materials and should be trained in their use. In addition, just as librarians in other special libraries are assisted by subject training, law librarians would benefit from some training in law.

III. AN ENCYCLOPEDIA OF LAW FOR NON-LAWYERS

As indicated throughout this study, one of the major difficulties in handling legal inquiries is trying to find specific information in existing legal reference materials. The changes in the form of law proposed in the previous chapter will assist the non-lawyer in looking up law, but they will not provide the needed solution to the problem. Although the law may become more readable, it will still be virtually inaccessible. For one thing, merely changing the form of legislation will not achieve the objective of integrating federal and provincial legislation and regulations, which is necessary to enable the non-lawyer (or even the lawyer) to look at both systems together. Moreover, case law and discretionary administrative practices would not be brought into the exposition of the law. In any event, it will probably be a long time before statutes are written in a form in which they can be easily understood. What is needed is a new printed source of law. What we propose is a multivolume legal encyclopedia, regularly updated, which could be directly available to those providing legal information and to citizens in public libraries and in such locations as government offices and school libraries.

Many of the persons to whom we talked suggested that they would find a readable, easy-to-use, up-to-date, quick reference source very useful. The police, for example, suggested that such a source would be used not only to answer questions from the public but also to assist in police training and in a department's daily operations. All intermediaries would benefit from such materials.

Legal aid and assistance centres, for example, require an easy-to-use printed source of legal information. There is little doubt that government-financed legal aid schemes will move towards clinics located in the parts of the community where the services are needed. Non-lawyers will more and more be used in these clinics to handle matters that do not initially require a lawyer's expertise. But even when a lawyer is involved, a better source of law would be useful. For reasons of cost and space legal aid clinics cannot have a proper lawyers' library. A substitute source would help with the summary advice often given by lawyers in these centres. And in fact, many of the areas of law most frequently dealt with in legal aid clinics are not covered by existing legal materials at all. A source of law dealing with these areas would be extremely useful to them.

Libraries do not now provide as much legal information and assistance as they could. Libraries constitute a largely untapped and — except to librarians — a relatively unknown source of legal services. They are usually centrally located within the community and fairly accessible to most people. In Metropolitan Toronto, for example, there are about 75 public libraries. The placing of understandable legal materials in public libraries is important in making it possible for everyone who wishes to do so to look up the law himself.

The materials could also be used in schools in conjunction with courses in law and the legal system. Students could be trained to look up points of law. As previously mentioned, courses in law at all levels of education — in the primary and secondary schools, in universities and community colleges, and in continuing education courses — would serve an important function in giving the citizen a grasp of our legal system; but they cannot teach him *the law*. The law is changing too quickly for that, and in any event no one can remember details of law learned in formal courses of instruction. By giving students training in the use of legal materials they would be able in the future to make effective use of the proposed encyclopedia.

The non-lawyers using our proposed reference collection to answer questions from the public would require some training in order to understand the materials with which they would be dealing. Perhaps a four- or five-week course would be all that would be necessary in order to enable them to know how to keep the material up to date and how to identify a problem sufficiently to locate the required volume.

(A)   Format

We envisage a set of binders occupying perhaps five or six feet of shelf space. The binders would have the general appearance of the CCH binders.

The encyclopedia would be comprehensive both in the areas of law covered and in the detail in which each area is covered. Many information sources complained about the interdependency of existing legal reference materials. For example, textbooks refer to statutes and cases and all three are needed to fully understand the text. Even if a community information centre, for example, manages to scrape together enough resources to purchase a few reference tools, it certainly cannot afford a small law library.

A related problem, frequently mentioned, is that many areas of law are not at present dealt with in existing materials. Many of the areas of law most frequently encountered by legal aid offices, such as workmen's compensation, welfare law, and unemployment insurance are not covered by traditional legal reference tools. Many legal aid programs have had to produce their own handbooks for their staff lawyers and students to use for quick reference in these areas.

The encyclopedia would therefore be intended to constitute the basic legal collection for those providing legal information and for most libraries: separate collections of statutes, regulations, and case reports would not be necessary, and essentially all areas of law would be covered. If persons wanted further information they could either go to a library with a specialized legal collection or consult a lawyer in private practice.

A separate set of materials would be required for each province because provincial legislation varies from province to province. There would therefore be 10 different encyclopedias, or 12 if they were also prepared for the Territories. However, the federal and, with minor changes, much of the provincial materials could be used in more than one jurisdiction. Therefore, once a set of materials had been produced for one province it could be easily altered for other provinces.

The encyclopedia would include references to a limited number of cases and other materials, which might be included in supplementary volumes to the encyclopedia. The authors, in appropriate cases, would attempt to give an accurate picture of how the law is actually administered. This would require dealing with such matters as policy statements, directives and other descriptions of how discretionary power is exercised.

One problem is the inclusion of by-laws, which vary from municipality to municipality and are often extremely bulky and contain much technical matter. The solution may be to have an additional supplementary volume in which the municipality sets out and keeps up-to-date the more commonly used by-laws and tells the citizen where he can locate the full text of all the municipal by-laws. It should be noted, of course, that some municipalities do not now have their by-laws in a readily retrievable form. One possible way of overcoming this difficulty is to establish a central registry in each province in which all municipal by-laws would be filed. Perhaps a computer terminal could be used to give the citizen access to the exact wording of the by-laws in the registry. However, this is a matter that requires more study than we have been able to give it.

(B) Classification

The materials would be classified according to headings most useful to the non-lawyer. Some would be quite broad, such as labour law and family law; others might be relatively narrow, such as workmen's compensation and immigration. The classifications set out in the present encyclopedias (such as *Halsbury's Laws of England*, the *Canadian Encyclopedic Digest*, and the American *Corpus Juris Secundum*) are designed for lawyers who have an understanding of the legal system. A non-lawyer would have difficulty in using and understanding these publications because of a lack of familiarity with the structure of the law. The idea therefore would be to divide the law into subject areas that would be recognizable to the ordinary citizen. For example, there would be no heading "torts." Instead, a section on motor vehicles would cover the negligence aspects of motor vehicle accidents and matters such as trespass and assault would be dealt with in a section on injuries to persons and property. In addition, there would be an introductory volume on the legal system itself covering many areas of constitutional law, various aspects of government, and the operation of the courts.

Our own attempts at classification indicate that the law can be classified into about 50 subject categories. Not all of the law would be contained in these classifications; some matters of a very technical nature that are not often used would be omitted, but a reference would be made to the relevant statutes and regulations and where they can be found.

We do not envisage a separate binder for each subject category. There might be only 15 binders in all, each containing a number of subjects, grouped according to the unity of the material. For example, there might be one binder relating to family law and social welfare and another relating to criminal law and procedure. With a good table of contents and index the set should be relatively easy to use.

(C) Severability

Although there might be 50 or more subject categories in 15 binders, the material would all be severable, that is, each subject would be divided into sections, each contained in a separate pamphlet. In the standard set of binders, all the pamphlets making up one subject would be put together. However, pamphlets from various subjects could be selected and combined in special binders to construct sets of materials for people with special interests. For example, persons interested in real property and real estate transactions might wish to have the pamphlet in the income tax section dealing with buying and selling a house, but not the whole of the material in the tax law binder.

(D) Models

There are very few existing models of the format we have in mind for the material in the encyclopedia. We collected several examples of existing publications that attempt to set out law for non-lawyers and have reproduced excerpts from some of them in Appendix 10 at page 151. These publications were produced by various governments, by private social service organizations, and by commercial publishers. Note, in particular, the excerpt from the *Citizens' Advice Notes* (CANS) at page 162, which is widely used in England by over 600 Citizens' Advice Bureaus.

Many of the pamphlets we examined (especially those published by governments) tended to contain too little detail to assist a person to ascertain his rights, and the popular legal handbooks produced by commercial publishers typically do not contain the relevant statutory material and are not designed for quick retrieval of specific information. Moreover, unlike the *Citizens' Advice Notes* the government pamphlets and the popular handbooks are quickly out of date.

To give better examples of the format that might be used in the materials and to get a better idea of some of the problems involved in writing about law for non-lawyers, we asked a number of lawyers and journalists to try their hand at preparing models. Excerpts from these models are contained in Appendix 11 at page 170. The excerpts on the Organizational Drive, The Tax Consequences of Selling Real Estate, Eavesdropping, and the Ontario Land Speculation Tax were all prepared by lawyers. The one on the Ontario Workmen's Compensation Act was prepared by a law student; the excerpt on the British Columbia Criminal Injuries Compensation Act was prepared by a journalist; and the article on the Ontario Mechanics' Lien Act was written by a journalist with legal training.

All of these models set out the law in a much clearer, more readable fashion than traditional legal sources. It is interesting to see that even technical concepts in the Income Tax Act can be handled so that any reasonably intelligent layman could understand them.

There was very little agreement amongst those who we asked to comment on these models. Almost all the models were selected by some as being close to what should be adopted. We have not selected one model as the ideal. No doubt the style will vary from subject to subject, depending to some extent on the likely users. Before a decision on style can be made some controlled tests asking subjects to look up the law should be undertaken using the same subject matter, but set out in different ways. Our impression is, however, that the best result will be achieved by combining the lawyer's precision with the skills of the professional writer.

Perhaps a team approach should be used, with a lawyer and a professional writer working together to produce and update a subject or a section of it. The lawyer would be responsible for the legal content and there might be an advisory committee (which could include persons from the appropriate government department) to assist him to ensure the accuracy of the contents. An attempt should be made to present the law in a way that would be useful both to a lawyer operating out of a legal aid clinic and to a reasonably intelligent citizen faced with, or assisting someone else with, a simple problem involving law. The combination of the lawyer and the professional writer would help ensure that both groups could understand and use the materials. An editorial committee would of course have overall responsibility for the content and style of all the materials.

As to the content of the materials, our conclusion is that the best approach for each section of a subject category is to set out the federal and provincial statutes and regulations and to write an explanatory accompaniment to them that would normally be as long or longer than the statutory and regulatory materials themselves. This accompanying explanation would explain the structure of the legislation and the regulations, highlighting the important parts, and would refer the reader to any important relevant case law as well as discretionary practices. The exact format would no doubt change with the subject matter of the category. In some instances the sections of a statute might be integrated with the explanatory material; in others they might be left to the end. In still others, as pointed out above, very technical and little used parts of the legislation and regulations might be referred to but not actually included. Names and addresses of organizations and government offices able to give further assistance would also be given.

Areas consisting mainly of case law, such as the law of contracts, present special problems. Rather than having statutory material with an introductory article, such sections of the encyclopedia would contain a summary of the case law. While this may be a more difficult task since cases are less definite than statutes, there seems to be no reason why it cannot be done.

Should the encyclopedia include how-to-do-it instructions? In general, it should not. Our view is that the encyclopedia should set out the law clearly; it should not be a step-by-step, do-it-yourself manual. There would, no doubt, be exceptions, however; for example the encyclopedia might usefully set out in detail how a citizen can change his or her name, file a mechanic's lien, or appear in a small claims' court. But the purpose of the encyclopedia would not be to encourage the citizen to act as his own lawyer in court or to draft his own contract (although it would obviously assist him in doing these things), but rather to allow him to understand the nature of his problem and the possible steps that might be taken. Throughout the encyclopedia the reader would be warned when a particular matter was complex or required an analysis of a body of case law, and wherever appropriate the suggestion would be made that legal advice be obtained.

(E) Updating

One constant problem information sources have with existing legal materials is keeping them up-to-date.[13] Legislative bodies are continually passing new Acts and amending old ones, and courts frequently alter areas of law in their judgments. It is vital, therefore, for any useful printed source of law to be updated frequently.

The people responsible for preparing a section of the encyclopedia would also be responsible for updating it. A dated supplement to each section could be sent out, possibly every two months, and complete replacement pamphlets whenever necessary. The legal publishers have had considerable experience with the problems of updating and seem to have solved it successfully for looseleaf services intended for use by lawyers and tax experts. One problem with current looseleaf services, however, is the difficult and tedious task of replacing individual pages. As mentioned above, we envisage that the material in the encyclopedia would be in the form of pamphlets that could be replaced easily. This would also enable the user to check quickly and easily that his binders contained all the current pamphlets. Several commercial publishers have recently been experimenting with such pamphlet updating systems.

(F) Indexing
The index to the materials would of course be one of the most important parts of the set. As the discussion in the previous chapter emphasized, the key to good indexing is to index according to topics, not just according to words. Each subject category would have its own index, and in addition there would be an index for the complete encyclopedia. The index itself would be kept current, possibly by a supplementary index or by a computer-produced consolidation.

(G) Production and Costs
Subsidization would undoubtedly be needed for the initial cost of writing the material but the total cost would not be as high as one might expect. We estimate that about $300,000 would cover the initial cost of writing the materials for the first province. Once the material is written the production and upkeep costs would be considerable, but, if demand proved adequate, would not be excessive. Obviously, the more that the production and upkeep costs are subsidized, the lower the price could be to the users. Some potential users, such as community information centres, probably could only afford to purchase the materials if the price were lowered by subsidization. Perhaps the best approach would be to subsidize both the production itself and some of the potential purchasers.

We saw in chapter 1 that the Standing Senate Committee on National Finance estimated that in the fiscal year ending March 31, 1974 the total cost of information within the departments and agencies of the federal government was as high as $200 million.[14] Even if $500,000 were set aside to subsidize the writing and production of the encyclopedia for the first province, that would still be only ¼ of 1 percent of the federal government's annual information cost.

One could begin with the most commonly used areas, producing perhaps ten subject categories a year, so that the entire encyclopedia could be produced for one province in about five years. The subsidization cost could therefore be spread over a similar time span.

(H)   Implementation

The implementation of this concept would require a continuing co-operative effort between the federal government and the provinces. The body entrusted with the job of implementing the scheme would have to be established on a secure basis, so that it would not collapse after a few years. One of the best bodies to engage in the task might be the Canadian Law Information Council (CLIC), which was set up by the federal and provincial governments in 1973 and has the support of the Canadian Bar Association and other interested groups. It could work closely with one or more publishers to produce the volumes. It may be that one of the Foundations would be interested in being a partner in producing the materials. A diversity of funding would help ensure the objectivity of the materials.

If an encyclopedia as envisaged in this chapter were to be attempted, many of the details touched on here, and others which have not been mentioned, would have to be worked out in the course of actually producing the materials. However, it is our belief that if a serious attempt were made to produce a legal encyclopedia for the non-lawyer, it could be done successfully.

IV.   CONCLUSION

Improving access to the law will not be an easy task. Attention must be given to all four approaches suggested in this study: improving existing legal materials, providing courses on law for non-lawyers, ensuring an adequate information delivery system, and producing a new source of law for non-lawyers. As we said in the introductory chapter, surely it is time for the law to be available to those it is meant to govern.

NOTES

1. Over the first three years of operation, the People's Law School lectures were attended by more than 16,000 people.

2. The Community Law School, similar in nature to the People's Law School, began presenting lectures in Toronto during the summer of 1974 with notable success.

3. Some campaigns have concentrated on just bringing legal problems to the public's attention rather than giving details about the problems. For example, the Quebec Legal Services Commission launched a campaign against pyramid selling. The Commission used posters which said nothing more than "Pyramid Sales Are Dangerous."

4. Several legal aid plans, most notably Manitoba Legal Aid, are now training paralegal personnel to receive and initially deal with questions and problems directed to the clinics.

5. Sue Kelly, quoted in *The Toronto Star*, July 17, 1974.

6. *Report of the Standing Senate Committee on National Finance on Information Canada*, Ottawa, Queen's Printer (1974) at 25.

7. *Report of the Standing Senate Committee on National Finance on Information Canada*, supra note 6, at 21-2.

8. In 1968: see Abel-Smith, Zander and Brooke, *Legal Problems and the Citizen: A Study in Three London Boroughs* (1973), at 39.

9. Rowland, "Citizens' Advice Bureaux: a Personal View" (1973), 4 *Community Health* 173, at 174-5. See also Abel-Smith, Zander and Brooke, supra note 8, at 39 *et seq.*; Brooke, *Information and Advice Services*, Occasional Papers on Social Administration, No 46, (1972).

10. In our testing of sources described in chapter 2, one of the incorrect answers given by the police was to the question "What does section 195.1 of the Criminal Code say?" The subsection that was read to the caller was taken from a two-year-old copy of the Code which was printed before section 195.1 was passed. The subsection actually read to the caller was 195(1).

11. Librarians themselves pointed out lack of training as a major problem in this area.

12. See Brooke, supra note 9, at 94-6 and 104.

13. We were amazed to find across the country that there is no organized attempt made to give police departments immediate notice of changes in statutory and regulatory laws, even in cases in which the police will immediately be called upon to enforce new or different laws. For example, we were told by the Calgary Police Department that when the Alberta Government decided to extend the deadline for new motor vehicle licence plates, the Department found out about the change through the newspapers.

14. *Report of the Standing Senate Committee on National Finance on Information Canada*, supra note 6, at 17.

Appendix 1

ORGANIZATIONS VISITED AND CONTACTED BY MAIL

We would like to acknowledge the assistance of the following organizations in providing information to us for this report. In particular, we wish to thank the staffs of these organizations for taking the time to meet with us or to complete questionnaires for us.

We also thank the Deputy Attorneys-General and their staff in all ten provinces who took the time to discuss the study with us.

I. LEGAL AID OFFICES AND LEGAL ASSISTANCE CENTRES

(A) Centres Visited

1. Nova Scotia Legal Aid, Provincial Office (Halifax).
2. Legal Aid New Brunswick, Provincial Director's Office (Fredericton).
3. Legal Aid New Brunswick, Saint John Area Office (Saint John).
4. Saint John Legal Aid Inc. (Saint John).
5. Commission des Services Juridiques (Montréal).
6. Centre Communautaire Juridique de Québec (Québec).
7. Services Juridiques Communautaires Inc., Point St. Charles, (Montréal).
8. Ontario Legal Aid Plan, Carleton County Area Office (Ottawa).
9. Ontario Legal Aid Plan, Essex County Area Office (Windsor).
10. Ontario Legal Aid Plan, Middlesex County Area Office (London).
11. Ontario Legal Aid Plan, Thunder Bay District Area Office (Thunder Bay).
12. Ontario Legal Aid Plan, Waterloo County Area Office (Kitchener).
13. Ontario Legal Aid Plan, York County Area Office (Toronto).
14. Victoria Park Legal Aid Clinic (Hamilton).
15. Legal Aid Clinic, Rexdale Community Information Directory (Toronto).
16. Parkdale Community Legal Services (Toronto).
17. Student Legal Aid Society (University of Toronto).
18. Legal Aid Manitoba, Provincial Office (Winnipeg).
19. Isabel Street Neighbourhood Law Centre (Winnipeg).
20. Saskatoon Legal Assistance Clinic Society (Saskatoon).
21. Regina Community Legal Services Society (Regina).

22. Legal Aid Society of Alberta, Provincial Office (Edmonton).
23. Legal Aid Society of British Columbia, Provincial Office (Vancouver).
24. Legal Aid Society of British Columbia, Victoria Area Office (Victoria).
25. Vancouver Community Legal Assistance Society (Vancouver).

(B)   Centres From Which We Received Completed Questionnaires
1. Nova Scotia Legal Aid, Cape Breton Metro Office (Sydney).
2. Nova Scotia Legal Aid, Annapolis Valley Office (Kentville).
3. Nova Scotia Legal Aid, Pictou County Office (New Glasgow).
4. Office of the Public Defender, Prince Edward Island (Charlottetown).
5. Legal Aid New Brunswick, Bathurst Area Office (Bathurst).
6. Legal Aid New Brunswick, Woodstock Area Office (Woodstock).
7. Community Legal Aid Services (Fredericton).
8. Centre Communautaire Juridique du Bas St. Laurent–Gaspésie (New Richmond, Québec).
9. Centre Communautaire Juridique de l'Estrie (Sherbrooke, Québec).
10. Centre Communautaire Juridique des Laurentides (St. Antoinedes Laurentides, Québec).
11. Centre Communautaire Juridique de Montréal (Montréal).
12. Clinique Juridique Populaire de Hull Inc. (Hull, Québec).
13. Services Juridiques Populaires de Sherbrooke (Sherbrooke, Québec).
14. Ontario Legal Aid Plan, Algoma District Area Office (Sault Ste. Marie).
15. Ontario Legal Aid Plan, Brant County Area Office (Brantford).
16. Ontario Legal Aid Plan, Frontenac County Area Office (Kingston).
17. Ontario Legal Aid Plan, Halton County Area Office (Oakville).
18. Ontario Legal Aid Plan, Kent County Area Office (Chatham).
19. Ontario Legal Aid Plan, Lambton County Area Office (Sarnia).
20. Ontario Legal Aid Plan, Leeds and Grenville Counties Area Office (Brockville).
21. Ontario Legal Aid Plan, Lincoln County Area Office (St. Catharines).
22. Ontario Legal Aid Plan, Norfolk County Area Office (Simcoe).
23. Ontario Legal Aid Plan, Peel County Area Office (Brampton).
24. Ontario Legal Aid Plan, Perth County Area Office (Stratford).
25. Ontario Legal Aid Plan, Wentworth County Area Office (Hamilton).

26. Legal Assistance of Windsor (University of Windsor).
27. Student Legal Aid Society (University of Ottawa).
28. Legal Aid Manitoba, Selkirk–Interlake Judicial District Area Office (Selkirk).
29. Legal Aid Manitoba, Northern Judicial District (Thompson) Area Office (Thompson).
30. Legal Aid Manitoba, Northern Judicial District (Flin Flon) Area Office (Flin Flon).
31. Main Street Neighbourhood Law Clinic (Winnipeg).
32. University of Manitoba Law Centre (University of Manitoba, Winnipeg).
33. Calgary Legal Guidance Services (Calgary).

II. GOVERNMENT OFFICES

(A) Information Canada

Enquiry Centres Visited

1. Halifax Enquiry Centre.
2. Charlottetown Enquiry Centre.
3. Montréal Enquiry Centre.
4. Toronto Enquiry Centre.
5. Winnipeg Enquiry Centre.
6. Saskatoon Enquiry Centre.
7. Edmonton Enquiry Centre.
8. Vancouver Enquiry Centre.

Enquiry Centres From Which We Received Completed Questionnaires

1. St. John's Enquiry Centre.

(B) Provincial Government Information Branches

Branches Visited

1. Nova Scotian Communications and Information Centre (Halifax).
2. Communication–Québec, Québec City Office.
3. Communication–Québec, Montréal Office.
4. Citizens' Inquiry Branch (Toronto).
5. Provincial Inquiry Office (Regina).
6. Alberta Information Service (Edmonton).

(C) Specific Government Departments

Departments Visited

1. Consumer Protection Bureau (Québec).

2. Ontario Ministry of Labour, Employment Services Division (Toronto).

3. Ontario Ministry of Labour, Women's Bureau (Toronto).

4. Ontario Ministry of Natural Resources, Northern Affairs Branch, Thunder Bay Regional Office (Thunder Bay).

5. Consumers' Bureau and Office of the Rentalsman (Winnipeg).

Departments From Which We Received
Completed Questionnaires

1. Ontario Ministry of Social Services, Regional Municipality of Durham Office (Oshawa).

2. Edmonton Department of Social Services (Edmonton).

(D)   Provincial Ombudsmen

Ombudsman's Offices From Whom We Received
Completed Questionnaires

1. Office of the Ombudsman, Nova Scotia (Halifax).

2. Office of the Ombudsman, New Brunswick (Fredericton).

3. Office of the Ombudsman, Saskatchewan (Regina).

4. Office of the Ombudsman, Alberta (Edmonton).

III.   COMMUNITY INFORMATION CENTRES

(A)   Centres Visited

1. Consumer and Social Action Centre (St. John's).

2. Halifax Neighbourhood Centre.

3. Volunteer Bureau/Help Line (Halifax).

4. Charlottetown Youth Services.

5. Chimo Help and Assistance Centre (Fredericton).

6. Social Services Council (Saint John).

7. Greater Montreal Anti-Poverty Coordinating Committee.

8. Information and Referral Centre of Greater Montreal.

9. Information Montreal.

10. Community Information Services of Ottawa–Carleton.

11. Information Gloucester (Ottawa).

12. New Canadian Services (Ottawa).

13. Ottawa Women's Centre.

14. Action Service Contact Centre (Toronto).

15. Bloor–Bathurst Information Centre (Toronto).

16. Community Information Centre of Metropolitan Toronto.

17. Don Mills Information and Assistance (Toronto).
18. Etobicoke Central Information and Referral (Toronto).
19. Information Fairview (Toronto).
20. Neighbourhood Information Centre (Toronto).
21. Neighbourhood Information Post (Toronto).
22. New Welfare Action Centre (Toronto).
23. People and Law Research Foundation Incorporated (Toronto).
24. Rexdale Community Information Directory (Toronto).
25. Services for Working People (Toronto).
26. Weston Information and Referral Centre (Toronto).
27. York Information Centre (Toronto).
28. Central Information Services of Hamilton and District.
29. North End Information Service (Hamilton).
30. Victoria Park and Northwest Community Organization (Hamilton).
31. Community Information Centre (Kitchener).
32. Information London.
33. Community Information Service (Windsor).
34. Council of Self-Help Groups (Winnipeg).
35. Fort Rouge Information and Resource Centre (Winnipeg).
36. Community Switchboard (Regina).
37. Community Aid Resource Centre (Saskatoon).
38. AID Service of Edmonton.
39. Advice, Information and Direction Centre (Calgary).
40. Cool-Aid Crisis/Counselling Centre (Victoria).
41. NEED Victoria Crisis Line (Victoria).
42. Community Information Centre (Vancouver).
43. Frog Hollow Information Centre (Vancouver).
44. Grandview–Woodland Information Centre (Vancouver).
45. Kitsilano Information Centre (Vancouver).
46. Red Door Information Centre (Vancouver).
47. West End Information Centre (Vancouver).
48. "Action Line", *The Province* (Vancouver).

(B)   Centres From Which We Received Completed Questionnaires

1. FISH (Bedford, Nova Scotia).
2. Centre de Référence et d'Information de la Région de Sherbrooke.
3. Consumers Association of Canada (Montréal).
4. Services de Renseignements (Plessisville, Québec).

5. Consumer Help (Cornwall, Ontario).

6. United Community Services (Peterborough, Ontario).

7. Information Oshawa (Oshawa, Ontario).

8. Information Burlington (Burlington, Ontario).

9. Community Torchlight Crisis and Information Centre (Guelph, Ontario).

10. H.O.P.E. — Social Service Bureau (Sarnia, Ontario).

11. Information Orillia (Orillia, Ontario).

12. Sudbury Regional Information Centre (Sudbury, Ontario).

13. Windsor Park Information and Resource Centre (Winnipeg).

14. Alberta Committee of Actions Groups for the Disabled (Edmonton).

15. Edmonton Social Planning Council.

16. Edmonton Social Services for the Disabled.

17. Open Door (Edmonton).

18. West 10 Information Centre (Edmonton).

19. Community Information Service Bureau (New Westminster, B.C.).

20. Dunbar–West Point Grey Information Centre (Vancouver).

21. Fairview Information Centre (Vancouver).

22. Fraserview–Killarney Action Centre (Vancouver).

23. The HUB (Vancouver).

24. Lower Lonsdale Information Centre (Vancouver).

25. Marpole–Oakridge Information Centre (Vancouver).

26. Young Women's Christian Association (Vancouver).

(C)   Native Friendship Centres

Centres Visited

1. Canadian Native Friendship Centre of Toronto.

2. Winnipeg Indian & Métis Friendship Centre.

3. Edmonton Native Friendship Centre.

4. Native Counselling Services of Alberta (Edmonton).

5. Calgary Indian Friendship Society, Inc.

6. Vancouver Indian Centre Society.

7. Victoria Native Friendship Centre.

Centres From Which We Received
Completed Questionnaires

1. Half & Half Indian Friendship Centre (Armstrong, Ontario).

2. Kenora Fellowship Centre.

3. Brandon Indian & Métis Friendship Centre.

4. Regina Friendship Centre.
5. Grande Prairie Indian Friendship Centre.
6. Central Okanagan Indian Friendship Society (Kelowna, British Columbia).
7. Sinu'Lulusta Indian Friendship Centre (Pentiction, British Columbia).
8. Quesnel Tillicum Society (Quesnel, British Columbia).
9. Skookum Jim Memorial Hall Friendship Centre (Whitehorse, Yukon).

IV. POLICE

(A) Departments Visited

1. St. John's Constabulary.
2. Halifax Police Department.
3. Charlottetown Police Department.
4. Fredericton Police Department.
5. Saint John Police Department.
6. Québec City Police Department.
7. Montréal Police Department.
8. Metropolitan Toronto Police Department.
9. Hamilton-Wentworth Regional Police Department (Hamilton).
10. Waterloo Regional Police Department (Kitchener).
11. London Police Department.
12. Windsor Police Department.
13. Thunder Bay Police Department.
14. Winnipeg Police Department.
15. Regina Police Department.
16. Saskatoon Police Department.
17. Edmonton Police Department.
18. Calgary Police Department.
19. Vancouver Police Department.
20. Victoria Police Department.

V. LIBRARIES

(A) Public Libraries

Libraries Visited

1. Provincial Reference Library (St. John's).
2. Halifax City Regional Library.
3. Dartmouth Regional Library.

4. Confederation Centre Library (Charlottetown).
5. Fredericton Public Library.
6. Saint John Public Library.
7. Bibliothèque Nationale du Québec (Montréal).
8. Bibliothèque Municipale de Montréal.
9. Fraser-Hickson Institute (Montréal).
10. Ottawa Public Library.
11. Carlingwood Branch, Ottawa Public Library.
12. Rideau Branch, Ottawa Public Library.
13. Metropolitan Toronto Central Library.
14. Richview Library, Etobicoke Public Library (Toronto).
15. Main Branch, East York Public Library (Toronto).
16. Willowdale Branch, North York Public Library (Toronto).
17. Don Mills Branch, North York Public Library (Toronto).
18. Bloor and Gladstone Branch, Toronto Public Libraries.
19. Parliament Branch, Toronto Public Libraries.
20. Parkdale Branch, Toronto Public Libraries.
21. Cedarbrae Branch, Scarborough Public Library (Toronto).
22. Main Branch, York Public Library (Toronto).
23. Hamilton Public Library.
24. Kitchener Public Library.
25. London Public Library and Art Museum.
26. Windsor Public Library.
27. Thunder Bay Public Library.
28. Winnipeg Public Library.
29. Saskatchewan Provincial Library (Regina).
30. Regina Public Library.
31. Saskatoon Public Library.
32. Edmonton Public Library.
33. Calgary Public Library.
34. Greater Victoria Public Library.
35. Vancouver Public Library.
36. Kitsilano Branch, Vancouver Public Library.
37. Yukon Regional Library (Whitehorse).

Libraries From Which We Received
Completed Questionnaires

NOVA SCOTIA
1. Halifax County Regional Library (Halifax).

NEW BRUNSWICK

2. Chaleur Regional Library (Campbellton).

3. Grand Falls Public Library.

4. Oromocto Public Library.

5. St. Croix Public Library (St. Stephen).

6. Fisher Library (Woodstock).

ONTARIO

7. Brantford Public Library.

8. Burlington Public Library.

9. Essex County Public Library (Essex).

10. Kingston Public Library.

11. Kirkland Lake Public Library.

12. Markham Public Library.

13. Mississauga Public Library.

14. Nepean Public Library (Nepean Township).

15. North Bay Public Library.

16. Orillia Public Library.

17. Oshawa Public Library.

18. Parry Sound Public Library.

19. Pembroke Public Library.

20. Peterborough Public Library.

21. Richmond Hill Public Library.

22. St. Catharines Public Library.

23. Stratford Public Library.

24. Sudbury Public Library.

25. Brookbanks Branch, North York Public Library (Toronto).

26. Fairview Branch, North York Public Library (Toronto).

27. Deer Park Branch, Toronto Public Libraries.

28. Forest Hill Branch, Toronto Public Libraries.

29. George Locke Branch, Toronto Public Libraries.

30. Riverdale Branch, Toronto Public Libraries.

31. Yorkville Branch, Toronto Public Libraries.

ALBERTA

32. Beaverlodge Public Library.

33. Canmore Public Library.

34. Cessford Public Library.

35. Devon Public Library.

36. Capilano Branch, Edmonton Public Library.
37. Tidsbury Public Library.
38. Edson Public Library.
39. Fairview Municipal Library.
40. Forestburg Public Library.
41. Hanna Public Library.
42. High Prairie Public Library.
43. Innisfail Public Library.
44. Jasper Municipal Library.
45. Nanton Public Library.
46. Plamondon Public Library.
47. Redcliff Centennial Library.
48. Rimbey Public Library.
49. St. Albert Public Library.
50. St. Paul Public Library.
51. Tofield Public Library.
52. Vegreville Public Library.
53. Viking Public Library.
54. Vulcan Public Library.
55. Wetaskiwin Public Library.
56. Unidentified library serving a Municipality of 5,000.

(B)   University Libraries

Libraries Visited

1. The Library, Memorial University (St. John's).
2. The Library, University of Prince Edward Island (Charlottetown).
3. Ward Chipman Library, University of New Brunswick (Saint John).
4. Social Sciences and Humanities Library, McGill University (Montréal).
5. The Library, Lakehead University (Thunder Bay).
6. Dana Porter Arts Library, University of Waterloo.
7. Elizabeth Dafoe Library, University of Manitoba (Winnipeg).
8. Regina Campus Library, University of Saskatchewan.
9. The Library, University of Calgary.
10. D. E. Cameron Library, University of Alberta (Edmonton).
11. McPherson Library, University of Victoria.

Libraries From Which We Received Completed Questionnaires

1. The Library, Laurentian University (Sudbury).

(C) University Law Libraries

Libraries Visited

1. The Library, Faculty of Law, Dalhousie University (Halifax).
2. The Law Library, University of New Brunswick (Fredericton).
3. Bibliothèque de droit, Université de Montréal.
4. The Law Library, McGill University (Montréal).
5. Bibliothèque, Université Laval (Québec).
6. The Law Library, University of Western Ontario (London).
7. Common Law Section, Law Library, University of Ottawa.
8. Law Library, University of Toronto.
9. Law Library, York University (Toronto).
10. Law Library, University of Windsor.
11. Law Library, University of Manitoba (Winnipeg).
12. The Library, College of Law, University of Saskatchewan (Saskatoon).
13. The J. A. Weir Memorial Library, University of Alberta (Edmonton).
14. The Law Library, University of British Columbia (Vancouver).

Libraries From Which We Received
Completed Questionnaires

1. Bibliothèque de droit, Université de Sherbrooke.

(D) Legislative Libraries

Libraries Visited

1. Bibliothèque de la législature, Québec.
2. Legislative Library, Winnipeg.
3. Legislative Library, Regina.

Appendix 2

WORKSHOP PARTICIPANTS

The following people attended a Workshop on Access to the Law on
March 15, 1974 at the University of Toronto.

J. B. Allen	Assistant Provincial Director, Ontario Legal Aid Plan.
Juanita Bay	Field Representative, Canadian Civil Liberties Association.
Ethel Bradley	Librarian, Mississauga Public Library.
Barbara Casson-Robin	Parkdale Community Legal Services.
Mollie E. Christie	Executive Director, Community Information Centre of Metropolitan Toronto.
Ken Danson	Cameron, Brewin & Scott.
W. R. Donkin	Area Director, York, Ontario Legal Aid Plan.
Gail Dykstra	Librarian.
Lyle S. Fairbairn	Counsel, Ontario Law Reform Commission.
Marion Falconbridge	Advocate, People and Law.
Kate Fitzgerald	Librarian, Metropolitan Toronto Central Library.
Clive Foster	Regional Manager, Employment Standards Branch, Ontario Ministry of Labour.
James D. Gallagher	Social Worker, Catholic Family Services.
Dick Gathercole	Ontario Ministry of the Attorney-General.
Rod Goodman	Editor, Star Probe.
Donald V. Goudy	Registrar, Consumer Protection Bureau, Ontario Ministry of Consumer and Commercial Relations.

111

J. S. Grant	Co-ordinator, Northern Affairs Branch, Ontario Ministry of Natural Resources.
Balfour J. Halévy	Law Librarian, York University Law Library.
Francess Halpenny	Dean, Faculty of Library Science, University of Toronto.
Roz Harley	Advocate, People and Law.
Elizabeth Harrison	Librarian, Etobicoke Public Library.
Margot Hewings	Librarian, Metropolitan Toronto Business Library.
Brig. George Hickman	Court Chaplain, Salvation Army.
Diana Hunt	Librarian, McCarthy & McCarthy.
D. E. Hushion	Executive Director, Employment Services Division, Ontario Ministry of Labour.
B. Kershner	Ontario Institute for Studies in Education.
John B. Laskin	Director, Campus Legal Assistance Centre.
Lucia Maguire	Librarian, Toronto Public Libraries.
Sarah Maley	Librarian, Barrie Public Library.
Rosemary McCormick	Chief Librarian, Law Society of Upper Canada.
Tom McDonnell	Osler, Hoskin & Harcourt.
Stanley McDougall	Librarian, Etobicoke Public Library.
Isabel K. McLean	Faculty of Library Science, University of Toronto.
Judy Miyauchi	Social Worker, Family Service Association of Metropolitan Toronto.
J. W. Mohr	Commissioner, Law Reform Commission of Canada.

Margaret Murray	Law Librarian, Faculty of Law, University of Toronto.
Cpl. Herman Myer	Safety and Information Branch, Ontario Provincial Police.
Richard Nellis	Advocate, People and Law.
Elizabeth Neville	Director, Women's Bureau, Ontario Ministry of Labour.
Maryka Omatsu	Parkdale Community Legal Services.
Jean Orpwood	Librarian, North York Public Library.
Helen Peterson	Director, Scarborough Public Library.
T. L. Pickard	Regional Supervisor, Northern Affairs Branch, Ontario Ministry of Natural Resources.
J. Robert S. Prichard	Co-Chairperson, Students' Legal Aid Society, University of Toronto.
Melvyn P. Robbins	Ontario Institute for Studies in Education.
Marianne Rogers	Librarian, York University Law Library.
Sherrill M. Rogers	Bloor–Bathurst Information Centre.
Alexander Ross	Ontario Task Force on Legal Aid.
William F. Ryan	Commissioner, Law Reform Commission of Canada.
Dorothy J. Service	Reference Librarian, Faculty of Law, University of Toronto.
Jerry Shultack	Bloor–Bathurst Information Centre.
Bill Somerville	Media Centre, University of Toronto.
Albert Spratt	Librarian, Mississauga Public Library.
Mel Springman	Ontario Law Reform Commission.
Sgt. Donald W. Stanley	Co-ordinator, Community Service Officers, Metropolitan Toronto Police Department.

John Swan   Faculty of Law,
                         University of Toronto.

Charles E. Taylor   Administrator and Secretary-Treasurer,
                         Committee of Adjustment,
                         City of Toronto.

Elizabeth Tyrwhitt   Bloor–Bathurst Information Centre.

Penny Watson   Librarian,
                         Richmond Hill Public Library.

A. R. Woadden   Archivist,
                         City of Toronto.

Wendy Wright   Co-ordinator of Community Development,
                         Scarborough Public Library.

Leslie Yager   Co-Chairperson,
                         Students' Legal Aid Society,
                         University of Toronto.

Appendix 3

SUPPLEMENTARY TABLES, CHAPTER 2, SECTION I

Appendix 3 Table 1

Old Age Benefits Question

	Sample (Number of Responses)		
	Toronto (72)	Kitchener (25)	Lindsay (21)
A. *Percentage who would seek information or help:* TOTAL	90.3	76.0	66.7
From:			
1. Federal Government General Inquiry	18.0	20.0	38.1
2. Provincial Government General Inquiry	22.2	20.0	9.5
3. Health & Welfare/Old Age Security	18.0	—	4.8
4. Friend/Family	8.3	—	4.8
5. Municipal Government General Inquiry	1.4	16.0	—
6. Canada Pension Plan	4.2	8.0	—
7. Unemployment Insurance Office	4.2	—	4.8
8. Canada Manpower Office	—	4.0	4.8
9. Welfare Office	1.4	4.0	—
10. Employer	2.8	—	—
11. MPP	1.4	—	—
12. Alderwoman/Alderman	1.4	—	—
13. Vital Statistics Office	1.4	—	—
14. Neighbourhood Information Centre	—	4.0	—
15. Star Probe/Action Line	1.4	—	—
16. Doctor	1.4	—	—
17. Church	1.4	—	—
18. Telephone Operator	1.4	—	—
B. *Percentage who would contact a lawyer*	1.4	0.0	0.0
C. *Percentage who would act without first seeking information or help:* TOTAL	1.4	20.0	14.3
By:			
1. Going to Post Office for application	1.4	20.0	14.3
D. *Percentage who did not know what they would do*	6.9	4.0	19.0
TOTAL	100.0	100.0	100.0

115

Appendix 3 Table 2

Leaking Roof Problem

	Sample (Number of Responses)		
	Toronto (72)	Kitchener (26)	Lindsay (22)
A. *Percentage who would seek* information or help: TOTAL	41.7	30.8	22.7
From:			
1. City Government General Inquiry	6.9	11.5	9.1
2. Landlord-Tenant Bureau	2.8	7.7	—
3. Mayor's Office	—	7.7	9.1
4. City Building Department	5.5	—	—
5. Alderman/Alderwoman	4.2	—	—
6. Consumer Protection Bureau	4.2	—	—
7. Legal Aid	4.2	—	—
8. Star Probe/Action Line	4.2	—	—
9. Tenant's Association	4.2	—	—
10. Federal Government General Inquiry	1.4	—	—
11. Provincial Government General Inquiry	1.4	—	—
12. City Health Department	1.4	—	—
13. Member of Parliament	1.4	—	—
14. Student Legal Aid Clinic	—	3.8	—
15. Better Business Bureau	—	—	4.5
B. *Percentage who would contact a lawyer*	8.3	3.8	0.0
C. *Percentage who would act without first seeking information or help:* TOTAL	47.2	57.7	68.2
By:			
1. Moving	8.3	38.5	13.6
2. Fixing roof at own expense	12.5	11,5	9.1
3. Fixing roof and deducting cost from rent	8.3	3.8	22.7
4. Not paying rent	11.1	3.8	13.6
5. Pestering Landlord	5.5	—	—
6. Doing nothing	1.4	—	9.1
D. *Percentage who did not know what they would do*	2.8	7.7	9.1
TOTAL	100.0	100.0	100.0

Appendix 3 Table 3
Pregnancy Leave Question

	Sample (Number of Responses)		
	Toronto (73)	Kitchener (30)	Lindsay (30)
A. *Percentage who would seek* *information or help: TOTAL*	95.9	83.3	93.3
From:			
1. Unemployment Insurance Commission	35.6	30.0	26.7
2. Employer	20.5	23.3	30.0
3. Canada Manpower Office	4.1	6.7	20.0
4. Welfare Office	9.6	3.3	—
5. Labour Relations Board	4.1	6.7	6.7
6. Trade Union	—	6.7	6.7
7. Federal Government General Inquiry	2.7	—	3.3
8. Children's Aid	2.7	3.3	—
9. Human Rights Commission	2.7	—	—
10. City Government General Inquiry	2.7	—	—
11. Workmen's Compensation Board	1.4	3.3	—
12. Provincial Government General Inquiry	1.4	—	—
13. Ontario Hospital Insurance Plan	1.4	—	—
14. Better Business Bureau	1.4	—	—
15. Women's Place (Information Centre)	1.4	—	—
16. Family Services-United Appeal	1.4	—	—
17. Women's College Hospital	1.4	—	—
18. Doctor	1.4	—	—
B. *Percentage who would contact a lawyer*	0.0	0.0	0.0
C. *Percentage who would act without first* *seeking information or help: TOTAL*	0.0	6.7	0.0
By:			
1. Doing nothing because there are no benefits	—	6.7	—
D. *Percentage who did not know what* *they would do*	4.1	10.0	6.7
TOTAL	100.0	100.0	100.0

Appendix 3 Table 4
Door-To-Door Salesman Question

	Sample (Number of Responses)		
	Toronto (101)	Kitchener (35)	Lindsay (26)
A. *Percentage who would seek information or help:* TOTAL	22.8	17.1	11.5
From:			
1. Better Business Bureau	5.9	11.4	3.8
2. Consumer Protection	5.9	—	—
3. Star Probe/Action Line	3.0	—	7.7
4. Federal Government General Inquiry	2.0	—	—
5. Friend/Family	2.0	—	—
6. Legal Aid	2.0	—	—
7. Provincial Government General Inquiry	1.0	—	—
8. City Hall	—	2.9	—
9. Chamber of Commerce	—	2.9	—
10. Police	1.0	—	—
B. *Percentage who would contact a lawyer*	6.9	5.7	3.8
C. *Percentage who would act without first seeking information or help:* TOTAL	67.3	77.2	80.9
By:			
1. Calling company to cancel	25.7	25.7	26.9
2. Notifying company in writing	7.9	8.6	34.6
3. Notifying company by registered letter	5.9	14.3	7.7
4. Refusing to pay	14.8	14.3	3.8
5. Paying and accepting encyclopedia	12.9	14.3	7.7
D. *Percentage who did not know what they would do*	3.0	0.0	3.8
TOTAL	100.0	100.0	100.0

Appendix 3 Table 5
Car Repair Question

	Sample (Number of Responses)		
	Toronto (102)	Kitchener (38)	Lindsay (32)
A. Percentage who would seek information or help: TOTAL	40.2	34.2	21.9
From:			
1. Better Business Bureau	8.8	15.8	9.4
2. Legal Aid	11.8	7.9	—
3. Star Probe/Action Line	6.9	—	6.2
4. Consumer Protection Bureau	4.9	—	—
5. Police	3.9	2.6	—
6. Provincial Government General Inquiry	1.0	—	3.1
7. Student Legal Aid Clinic	1.0	2.6	—
8. Insurance Company	1.0	—	3.1
9. City Government General Inquiry	1.0	—	—
10. Credit Bureau	—	2.6	—
11. Ontario Motor League	—	2.6	—
B. Percentage who would contact a lawyer	21.6	18.4	3.1
C. Percentage who would act without first seeking information or help: TOTAL	33.3	39.5	68.8
By:			
1. Complaining to garage	20.6	31.6	46.9
2. Doing nothing	9.8	7.9	21.9
3. Going to Small Claims Court	2.0	—	—
4. Going to Court	1.0	—	—
D. Percentage who did not know what they would do	4.9	7.9	6.2
TOTAL	100.0	100.0	100.0

Appendix 3 Table 6
Deserted Wife Question

	Sample (Number of Responses)		
	Toronto (90)	Kitchener (29)	Lindsay (28)
A. *Percentage who would seek information or help: TOTAL*	58.9	69.9	53.6
From:			
1. City Welfare Office	4.4	37.9	35.7
2. Welfare Office	18.9	—	—
3. Legal Aid	11.1	6.9	14.3
4. Provincial Welfare Office	6.7	—	—
5. Police	3.3	6.9	—
6. Provincial Government General Inquiry	4.4	—	—
7. Court Office	2.2	6.9	—
8. City Government General Inquiry	1.1	6.9	—
9. Children's Aid	1.1	3.4	3.6
10. Federal Government General Inquiry	2.2	—	—
11. Federal Welfare Office	1.1	—	—
12. Women's Place (Information Centre)	1.1	—	—
13. Student Legal Aid Clinic	1.1	—	—
B. *Percentage who would contact a lawyer*	26.7	17.2	25.0
C. *Percentage who would act without first seeking information or help: TOTAL*	13.3	6.9	17.8
By:			
1. Going to Family Court	6.7	6.9	10.7
2. Getting a job	6.7	—	3.6
3. Complaining to husband's employer	—	—	3.6
D. *Percentage who did not know what they would do*	1.1	6.9	3.6
TOTAL	100.0	100.0	100.0

Appendix 3 Table 7

Popular Song Question

	Sample (Number of Responses)		
	Toronto (74)	Kitchener (22)	Lindsay (22)
A. *Percentage who would seek information or help:* TOTAL	28.4	9.1	9.1
From:			
1. An entertainment expert re: copyright	20.3	9.1	9.1
2. Federal Government General Inquiry	4.1	—	—
3. City Government General Inquiry	2.7	—	—
4. Provincial Government General Inquiry	1.4	—	—
B. *Percentage who would contact a lawyer*	8.1	4.5	0.0
C. *Percentage who would act without first seeking information or help:* TOTAL	55.4	63.6	81.8
By:			
1. Contacting an entertainment expert to publish song	55.4	59.1	72.7
2. Contacting a patent officer	—	4.5	4.5
3. Duplicating copy of song	—	—	4.5
D. *Percentage who did not know what they would do*	8.1	22.8	9.1
TOTAL	100.0	100.0	100.0

Appendix 3 Table 8

Speeding Ticket Question

	Sample (Number of Responses)		
	Toronto (68)	Kitchener (25)	Lindsay (22)
A. *Percentage who would seek information or help:* TOTAL	20.6	8.0	4.5
From:			
1. Court Office	11.8	—	—
2. Police	5.9	4.0	4.5
3. City Government General Inquiry	—	4.0	—
4. Department of Transport	1.5	—	—
5. Ontario Motor League	1.5	—	—
B. *Percentage who would contact a lawyer*	0.0	0.0	4.5
C. *Percentage who would act without first seeking information or help:* TOTAL	79.4	92.0	91.0
By:			
1. Going to court to fight ticket	41.2	12.0	27.3
2. Paying fine	16.2	32.0	22.7
3. Not paying and ignoring ticket	19.1	24.0	22.7
4. Calling Police to cancel ticket	2.9	24.0	18.2
D. *Percentage who did not know what they would do*	0.0	0.0	0.0
TOTAL	100.0	100.0	100.0

Appendix 3 Table 9
Swimming Pool Fence Question

	Sample (Number of Responses)		
	Toronto (98)	Kitchener (29)	Lindsay (21)
A. *Percentage who would seek information or help:* TOTAL	48.0	58.6	66.6
From:			
1. City Government General Inquiry	21.4	37.9	47.6
2. City Building Department	8.2	6.9	—
3. Police	4.1	3.5	14.3
4. Alderwoman/Alderman	4.1	—	—
5. Provincial Government General Inquiry	3.1	—	—
6. MPP	3.1	—	—
7. Swimming Pool Company	2.0	3.5	—
8. Federal Government General Inquiry	1.0	—	—
9. Health Department	—	—	4.8
10. Mayor's Office	—	3.5	—
11. Court Office	1.0	—	—
12. Star Probe/Action Line	—	3.5	—
B. *Percentage who would contact a lawyer*	2.0	0.0	4.8
C. *Percentage who would act without first seeking information or help:* TOTAL	45.9	37.9	28.6
By:			
1. Negotiating with Neighbour	45.9	37.9	28.6
D. *Percentage who did not know what they would do*	4.1	3.5	0.0
TOTAL	100.0	100.0	100.0

Appendix 3 Table 10

Criminal Code Question

	Sample (Number of Responses)		
	Toronto (84)	Kitchener (29)	Lindsay (23)
A. *Percentage who would seek information or help: TOTAL*	77.3	100.0	91.3
From:			
1. Library	25.0	34.5	13.0
2. Police	11.9	20.7	34.8
3. Court Office	6.0	13.8	26.1
4. Family/Friend	3.6	17.2	8.7
5. Legal Aid	7.1	—	4.3
6. City Government General Inquiry	4.8	6.9	—
7. Law School Library	4.8	—	—
8. Law School	3.6	—	—
9. Law Society	3.6	—	—
10. Federal Government General Inquiry	2.4	—	—
11. Department of Highways	2.4	—	—
12. Student Legal Aid Clinic	1.2	—	—
13. University	—	3.4	—
14. Registry Office	—	—	4.3
15. Mayor's Office	—	3.4	—
16. LINK-Community Information Service	1.2	—	—
B. *Percentage who would contact a lawyer*	16.7	0.0	8.7
C. *Percentage who would act without first seeking information or help: TOTAL*	0.0	0.0	0.0
D. *Percentage who did not know what they would do*	6.0	0.0	0.0
TOTAL	100.0	100.0	100.0

Appendix 3 Table 11

Percentage Who Would Seek Information or Help

Question	Sample		
	Toronto	Kitchener	Lindsay
1. Old Age Benefits	90.3	76.0	66.7
2. Leaking Roof	41.7	30.8	22.7
3. Pregnancy Leave	95.9	83.3	93.3
4. Door-to-Door Salesman	22.8	17.1	11.5
5. Car Repair	40.2	34.2	21.9
6. Deserted Wife	58.9	69.0	53.6
7. Popular Song	28.4	9.1	9.1
8. Speeding Ticket	20.6	8.0	4.5
9. Swimming Pool Fence	48.0	58.6	66.6
10. Criminal Code	77.3	100.0	91.3
AVERAGE	52.4	48.6	44.1

Appendix 3 Table 12

Percentage Who Would Contact a Lawyer

Question	Sample		
	Toronto	Kitchener	Lindsay
1. Old Age Benefits	1.4	0.0	0.0
2. Leaking Roof	8.3	3.8	0.0
3. Pregnancy Leave	0.0	0.0	0.0
4. Door-to-Door Salesman	6.9	5.7	3.8
5. Car Repair	21.6	18.4	3.1
6. Deserted Wife	26.7	17.2	25.0
7. Popular Song	8.1	4.5	0.0
8. Speeding Ticket	0.0	0.0	4.5
9. Swimming Pool Fence	2.0	0.0	4.8
10. Criminal Code	16.7	0.0	8.7
AVERAGE	9.2	5.0	5.0

Appendix 3 Table 13

**Percentage Who Would Act Without First
Seeking Information or Help**

Question	Sample		
	Toronto	Kitchener	Lindsay
1. Old Age Benefits	1.4	20.0	14.3
2. Leaking Roof	47.2	57.7	68.2
3. Pregnancy Leave	0.0	6.7	0.0
4. Door-to-Door Salesman	67.3	77.2	80.9
5. Car Repair	33.3	39.5	68.8
6. Deserted Wife	13.3	6.9	17.8
7. Popular Song	55.4	63.6	81.8
8. Speeding Ticket	79.4	92.0	91.0
9. Swimming Pool Fence	45.9	37.9	28.6
10. Criminal Code	0.0	0.0	0.0
AVERAGE	34.3	40.1	45.1

Appendix 3 Table 14

**Percentage Who Did Not Know
What They Would Do**

Question	Sample		
	Toronto	Kitchener	Lindsay
1. Old Age Benefits	6.9	4.0	19.0
2. Leaking Roof	2.8	7.7	9.1
3. Pregnancy Leave	4.1	10.0	6.7
4. Door-to-Door Salesman	3.0	0.0	3.8
5. Car Repair	4.9	7.9	6.2
6. Deserted Wife	1.1	6.9	3.6
7. Popular Song	8.1	22.8	9.1
8. Speeding Ticket	0.0	0.0	0.0
9. Swimming Pool Fence	4.1	3.5	0.0
10. Criminal Code	6.0	0.0	0.0
AVERAGE	4.1	6.3	5.8

Appendix 4

SUPPLEMENTARY TABLES, CHAPTER 2, SECTION II

TABLE 1

Solutions To Test Questions

1. *Old Age Benefits*: To get old age benefits a person must apply to the Old Age Security Branch of the Canadian Department of Health and Welfare. Application forms may be picked up at a post office or at the local Health and Welfare Office.

2. *Leaking Roof*: By Section 96(1) of the Landlord and Tenant Act, R.S.O. 1970, c. 236, a landlord "is responsible for providing and maintaining the rented premises in a good state of repair and fit for habitation." Under Section 96(3) a tenant may enforce the landlord's obligation by making a summary application to a county court judge. Thus an answer to this question is to make an application under Section 96(3) although in practical terms the most sensible first step would be to point out the landlord's obligation to him and show him that it can be enforced.

3. *Pregnancy Leave*: Section 13a of the Employment Standards Act, R.S.O. 1970, c. 147, as amended, protects the woman's job for 12 weeks while she takes pregnancy leave. At the end of the leave period she can resume work "with no loss of seniority or benefits accrued to the commencement of the maternity leave." By Section 30 of the Unemployment Insurance Act, S.C. 1971, c. 48, she can collect benefits under the Act for up to 15 weeks.

4. *Door-to-Door Salesman*: Under Section 33 of the Consumer Protection Act, R.S.O. 1970, c. 82, the purchaser may rescind such a contract by delivering a notice of rescission in writing to the seller within two days after a duplicate original copy of the sales contract comes into the purchaser's possession. The notice may be delivered personally or mailed by registered mail within the two days.

5. *Car Repair*: If negotiations to recover the money from the first garage fail even after a threat of legal proceedings is made, the car owner would have to sue the garage. By Section 54 of the Small Claims Courts Act, R.S.O. 1970, c. 439, a claim for $250.00 falls within the jurisdiction of the Small Claims Court. If the car owner does not hire a lawyer to carry out the lawsuit for him, he should go

to the Small Claims Court in the area and ask the Clerk what he must do to bring an action.

6. *Deserted Wife*: The wife may obtain an order for the maintenance of herself and her children under Section 2 of the Deserted Wives' and Children's Maintenance Act, R.S.O. 1970, c. 128, or an order for the maintenance of her children under Section 3 if the judge will not make an order for her support as well. The procedure for the wife to follow is to lay an information before a justice of the peace who may then issue a summons against the husband. The husband will be brought before a judge in the provincial court (family division) and the judge may make a support order.

7. *Popular Song*: The writer of the song should be sure that his authorship is protected. Any method of establishing a date of ownership will suffice since copyright arises automatically as the song is written. The writer's problem is one of proving that he wrote the song before some one else who claims to have written it. The best way to ensure such proof is to register the copyright under the Copyright Act, R.S.C. 1970, c. C-30. This may be done by completing Form K under the Act and mailing it to the Commissioner of Patents at the Copyright Office in Hull.

8. *Speeding Ticket*: Section 148 of the Highway Traffic Act, R.S.O. 1970, c. 202, states that penalties imposed by the Act are recoverable under the Summary Convictions Act, R.S.O. 1970, c. 450. Section 3 of the Summary Convictions Act states that Part XXIV of the Criminal Code, R.S.C. 1970, c. C-34 applies to every case to which the Summary Convictions Act applies. Section 729 (in Part XXIV) of the Criminal Code states that sections 510 and 512 of the Code apply to informations under Part XXIV of the Code. Section 510 states that an information is sufficient if it contains in substance a statement that the accused committed the offence specified. In this case, the accused might go to traffic court and argue that the ticket was defective since it did not identify him with certainty; however, the court might well decide that in substance the statement of the offence and of the identity of the accused was clear and that is all that is required.

9. *Swimming Pool Fence*: For the City of Toronto, by-law no. 72-74 states that "every fence erected around a privately-owned outdoor swimming pool . . . 'shall extend from the ground to a height of not less than 4 feet'." A person should be able to obtain this information by calling City Hall. If the neighbour's fence was under 4 feet and

he refused to change it, one could have the by-law enforced by informing the city building inspector.

10. *Criminal Code:* Section 195.1 of the Criminal Code (added to the Code by the Criminal Law Amendment Act, S.C. 1972, c. 13, s. 15) states that:

"Every person who solicits any person in a public place for the purpose of prostitution is guilty of an offence punishable on summary conviction."

Appendix 4 Table 2

Percentage of Subjects Who Recommended Sources Which Gave Various Responses When Called

RESEARCHER X

Result of Inquiry	Old Age Benefits	Leaking Roof	Pregnancy Leave	Door-to-Door Salesman	Car Repair	Deserted Wife	Popular Song	Speeding Ticket	Swimming Pool Fence	Criminal Code	Average
A. Correct answer given:											
1. By source called	31.0	—	5.5	71.4	32.5	7.5	71.4	85.7	74.5	53.2	43.3
2. After 1 referral	32.9	—	—	4.8	25.0	15.1	14.3	7.1	8.5	17.8	12.5
3. After 2 referrals	31.0	—	—	—	—	—	14.3	—	8.5	—	5.8
4. After 3 or more referrals	3.4	—	—	—	2.5	3.8	—	—	—	3.2	.9
B. Incomplete answer given:											
1. By source called	—	—	5.5	—	17.5	45.3	—	—	—	—	6.8
2. After 1 referral	—	—	1.8	—	—	3.8	—	—	—	—	.6
3. After 2 referrals	—	—	1.8	—	—	—	—	—	—	—	.2
4. After 3 or more referrals	—	—	—	—	—	—	—	—	—	—	—
C. Incorrect answer given:											
1. By source called	1.7	14.8	67.3	14.3	22.5	—	—	7.1	—	16.1	14.4
2. After 1 referral	—	11.1	9.1	—	—	—	—	—	8.5	—	2.9
3. After 2 referrals	—	74.1	5.5	—	—	—	—	—	—	—	8.0
4. After 3 or more referrals	—	—	—	—	—	—	—	—	—	—	—
D. No answer given:	—	—	3.6	9.5	—	24.5	—	—	—	9.7	4.7
TOTAL	100.0	100.0	100.0	100.0	100.0	100.0	100.0	100.0	100.0	100.0	100.0

Appendix 4 Table 3

Percentage of Subjects Who Recommended Sources Which Gave Various Responses When Called

RESEARCHER Y

Result of Inquiry	Question										
	Old Age Benefits	Leaking Roof	Pregnancy Leave	Door-To-Door Salesman	Car Repair	Deserted Wife	Popular Song	Speeding Ticket	Swimming Pool Fence	Criminal Code	Average
A. *Correct answer given:*											
1. By source called	29.3	—	5.5	81.0	2.5	1.9	—	35.7	80.8	8.1	24.5
2. After 1 referral	31.0	—	9.1	—	10.0	5.7	14.3	57.1	4.3	4.8	13.6
3. After 2 referrals	37.9	—	3.6	—	—	—	4.8	—	—	—	4.6
4. After 3 or more referrals	1.7	—	3.6	—	2.5	—	9.5	—	—	—	1.7
B. *Incomplete answer given:*											
1. By source called	—	11.1	1.8	—	17.5	20.8	71.4	—	—	—	12.3
2. After 1 referral	—	66.7	—	—	—	9.4	—	—	—	—	7.6
3. After 2 referrals	—	18.5	—	—	—	45.3	—	—	—	—	6.4
4. After 3 or more referrals	—	—	—	—	—	—	—	—	—	—	—
C. *Incorrect answer given:*											
1. By source called	—	—	52.7	19.0	35.0	11.3	—	7.1	8.5	37.1	17.1
2. After 1 referral	—	—	21.8	—	30.0	5.7	—	—	6.4	29.0	9.3
3. After 2 referrals	—	—	—	—	2.5	—	—	—	—	3.2	.6
4. After 3 or more referrals	—	—	—	—	—	—	—	—	—	6.5	.6
D. *No answer given:*	—	3.7	1.8	—	—	—	—	—	—	11.4	1.7
TOTAL	100.0	100.0	100.0	100.0	100.0	100.0	100.0	100.0	100.0	100.0	100.0

Appendix 4 Table 4

Summary of Results Received from the Government Sources — line 1 of Table E

Researcher X

Source	Number of Times Called	Referral		No Answer or Referral	Result of Inquiry		
		Satisfactory	Unsatisfactory		Correct	Incomplete	Incorrect
						Information	
A. *Federal Government* TOTAL	16	7	3	—	3	—	3
1. General Inquiry	8	4	2	—	1	—	1
2. Specific Departments	7	3	—	—	2	—	2
3. Member of Parliament	1	—	1	—	—	—	—
B. *Provincial Government* TOTAL	25	9	8	—	6	2	—
1. General Inquiry	8	3	5	—	—	—	—
2. Specific Departments	15	5	3	—	5	2	—
3. Member of Legislature	2	1	—	—	1	—	—
C. *City Government* TOTAL	20	5	7	—	5	1	2
1. General Inquiry	8	2	5	—	1	—	—
2. Specific Department	9	2	1	—	3	1	2
3. Alderman/Alderwoman	3	1	1	—	1	—	—
TOTAL	61	21	18	—	14	3	5

Appendix 4 Table 5

Summary of Results Received from the Government Sources — line 1 of Table F

Researcher Y

Source	Number of Times Called	Referral Satisfactory	Referral Unsatisfactory	Result of Inquiry No Answer or Referral	Correct	Information Incomplete	Incorrect
A. *Federal Government TOTAL*	16	7	4	—	2	—	3
1. General Inquiry	8	4	2	—	—	—	2
2. Specific Departments	7	3	1	—	2	—	1
3. Member of Parliament	1	—	1	—	—	—	—
B. *Provincial Government TOTAL*	25	9	6	—	6	—	4
1. General Inquiry	8	2	5	—	—	—	1
2. Specific Departments	15	7	1	—	4	—	3
3. Member of Legislature	2	—	—	—	2	—	—
C. *City Government TOTAL*	20	6	8	—	3	2	1
1. General Inquiry	8	2	5	—	1	—	—
2. Specific Departments	9	4	1	—	2	2	—
3. Alderman	3	—	2	—	—	—	1
TOTAL	61	22	18	—	11	2	8

131

Appendix 5

RESPONSES TO TEST QUESTIONS

I. The responses received to the landlord and tenant question in the testing described in Section III of chapter 2 were as follows:

(a) **LAWYERS**: Out of the 10 lawyers or law firms called:
   7 — gave the correct answer immediately over the telephone;
   1 — referred the caller to the York County Area Legal Aid Office, which gave the correct answer over the telephone when it was called;
   1 — told the caller to come in to the office for an appointment; and,
   1 — gave no answer at all. (The law firm that gave no answer at all was a large firm located in the centre of Toronto. When our researcher telephoned the firm the call was answered by a switchboard operator who tried to transfer the call to one of the lawyers. The lawyer chosen was not in the office at the time so our researcher explained the problem briefly to the lawyer's secretary who took a message and said the lawyer would call back. The call was never returned.)

(b) **PUBLIC LIBRARIES**: Out of the 10 public libraries called:
   4 — referred the caller to the Landlord and Tenant Bureau, which gave the correct answer over the telephone when it was called;
   2 — told the caller to contact a lawyer;
   2 — told the caller to come in to the library and they would assist in looking up the answer;
   1 — gave the correct answer immediately over the telephone; and
   1 — referred the caller to the York County Area Legal Aid Office, which gave the correct answer over the telephone when it was called.

(c) **INFORMATION CENTRES**: Out of the 10 information centres called:
   6 — referred the caller to the Landlord and Tenant Bureau, which gave the correct answer over the telephone when it was called; and
   4 — gave the correct answer immediately over the telephone.

(d) **OTHER SOURCES**: Out of the 10 other sources called:
   5 — gave the correct answer immediately over the telephone; and
   5 — referred the caller to the Landlord and Tenant Bureau, which gave the correct answer over the telephone when it was called.

II. The responses received to the criminal records question in the testing described in section III of chapter 2 were as follows:

(a) **LAWYERS**: Out of the 10 lawyers or law firms called:

3 — told the caller that they did not practice that type of law. Only one out of the three suggested another lawyer who might help the caller, and none suggested any other sources of information.

2 — told the caller that in the circumstances he should not worry about a record and that it would be a waste of time and money to do anything about it;

2 — told the caller that since he had been given an absolute discharge he had no record to be expunged;

1 — referred the caller to the National Parole Board, which, when it was called, told the caller when and how to apply to have his record expunged and pointed out that there was no need for him to retain a lawyer;

1 — referred the caller to the Provincial Court, which, when it was called, referred the caller to the National Parole Board; and

1 — referred the caller to the Police Department, which, when it was called, explained the relevant law to the caller and told him that application forms could be obtained from the National Parole Board.

(b) **PUBLIC LIBRARIES**: Out of the 10 public libraries called:

2 — told the caller to come in to the library and they would assist in looking up the answer;

2 — referred the caller to the Neighbourhood Information Post (a local information centre), which explained the law to the caller correctly when it was called;

1 — told the caller to contact a lawyer;

1 — referred the caller to the Police Department, which explained the law to the caller correctly when it was called;

1 — told the caller to contact the local legal aid clinic run by the York County Area Legal Aid Office;

1 — referred the caller to the Student Defenders at the City Hall who, when called, told the caller that since he had been given an absolute discharge he had no record to be expunged;

1 — told the caller that there was nothing he could do to expunge his record; and

1 — told the caller that since he had been given an absolute discharge he had no record to be expunged.

(c) **INFORMATION CENTRES**: Out of the 10 information centres called:

3 — referred the caller to the Campus Legal Assistance Centre,

which, when called, told the caller that since he had been given an absolute discharge he had no record to be expunged;

1 — explained the law correctly to the caller;

1 — told the caller to contact a lawyer;

1 — referred the caller to the National Parole Board, which, when called, explained the law correctly to the caller;

1 — referred the caller to the Police Department, which, when called, explained the law correctly to the caller;

1 — referred the caller to the York County Area Legal Aid Office, which, when called, referred the caller to the National Parole Board;

1 — told the caller that he must wait seven years before he could apply to have his record expunged and that at that time he should apply to the Solicitor-General of Canada; and

1 — told the caller that since he had been given an absolute discharge he had no record to be expunged.

(d) **OTHER SOURCES**: Out of the 10 other sources called:

7 — referred the caller to the National Parole Board, which, when called, explained the law correctly to the caller; and

3 — told the caller that since he had been given an absolute discharge he had no record to be expunged. (These three sources were all legal aid sources — Parkdale Community Legal Services, the Campus Legal Assistance Centre, and the Community and Legal Aid Services Programme.)

Appendix 6

LIST OF TEST QUESTIONS

Questions used in the test described in section IV of chapter 2 of how successfully members of the public can look up law on their own.
1. Can anyone under 18 obtain a marriage licence? (Answer is in The Marriage Act, R.S.O. 1970, c. 261, ss. 7(4), 8.)

2. (a) Is a person entitled to vacation pay after working for one year? (Answer is in The Employment Standards Act, R.S.O. 1970, c. 147, s. 27.)
(b) What is the rate of vacation pay? (Answer is in The Employment Standards Amendment Act, 1973, S.O., c. 172, s. 5.)

3. Are you required to either pay for or return a book received through the mail that you did not order? (Answer is in The Consumer Protection Act, R.S.O. 1970, c. 82, s. 46(3).)

4. Is a taxi driver entitled to overtime pay? (Answer is in the Regulations to The Employment Standards Act, R.R.O. 1970, Reg. 250.)

5. Can a landlord give a tenant notice in the winter months? (Answer is in The Landlord and Tenant Act, R.S.O. 1970, c. 236, ss. 98-103.)

6. What is the penalty for leaving the scene of a traffic accident? (The answer is in The Highway Traffic Act, R.S.O. 1970, c. 202, s. 140(2), and the Criminal Code, R.S.C. 1970, c. C-34, s. 233(2).)

7. Can a police officer without a warrant search a person and/or a house for marijuana? (The answer is in the Narcotic Control Act, R.S.C. 1970, c. N-1, s. 10(1).)

8. How long must a person live in Canada before he/she can apply for a divorce? (The answer is in the Divorce Act, R.S.C. 1970, c. D-8, s. 5(1).)

9. If an employee drives to work and spends $1.00 a day to park, can this person deduct this money in 'his' or 'her' income tax return? (The answer is in the Income Tax Act, S.C., 1970-71-72, Volume 2, c. 63, s. 8(1)(a).)

10. For how many years must a person reside in Canada before he/she can apply for Canadian citizenship? (The answer is in the Canadian Citizenship Act, R.S.C. 1970, c. C-19, s. 10(1).)

Appendix 7

READABILITY: by P. A. Kolers

The following excerpt is from a letter, dated September 6, 1974, written by Professor Paul A. Kolers of the Department of Psychology at the University of Toronto in response to our request that he examine some Canadian statutes and comment on the language used:

"Complying with your request, I read some law and made notes on the reading. . . .

I approached the task from the dual views of the educated layman who might at some time want to learn the details of a law, and of a student of the psychological aspects of literacy. The query underlying my reading was: Is the law readily comprehended, both as to fact and intention; and if it is not, why is it not?

Some of the difficulties of comprehension . . . are related to the special requirements of written law, but others seem to be created by a perverse use of English. Consider the two points separately.

Every formal discipline develops its own symbolism — words, phrases, and constructions special to the discipline. The usual reason is that natural language is stretched beyond its capability when it is required to handle exceedingly specific details and relations between them. Natural language seems to have emerged as a parallel structure for gesture and is well suited to expressing affect; precision in and specification of abstraction do not come so readily. In some fields of science this restrictive property of natural language is circumvented by the use of artificial languages, in which arbitrary symbols are assigned precise meanings, as exigency requires. In the arts, dance notation and staff notation provide fairly clear instructions to dancers and musicians. The social and political sciences have not attained equivalent degrees of precision of statement; indeed, even a suitable system of notation is missing in the social sciences and mere words still must make do. Hence the linguistically dreadful usages of social science, and the misshapen forms which, in the United States, are called "Federalese." In these fields we see, aside from the jargon and faddism, excessive reliance upon qualification, restrictive relative clauses, and clauses embedded within them by whose means the writer tries with words to identify exactly and precisely who he has in mind and the conditions under which a statement will hold.

This effort toward precision of definition is handled in law, apparently, not only by qualification in the statements, but also by use of formulas, some quite aged. The most striking to the layman is the parallel linguistic structure whose parts are separated by the semicolon rather than the full stop. It is possible that this is little more than custom, derived from medieval Latin and French (English was not used in English courts, following the Norman invasion, until ordered by the *Statute of Pleading* of 1362). Once one penetrates the structure — that the qualifications and restrictions come first, the action last — it is not too difficult to reconstruct a sentence in mind. . . . The main question is whether one should have to learn so much in order to penetrate the structure, whether the phrasing should not be more transparent. This brings us to the second point, the particular use of language in written law.

Most languages of the world state the main point first, and then the restrictions and qualifications. They are called "right-branching" (because the graph that describes their parsing branches to the right). Japanese and Turkish, in contrast, are left-branching; they state their qualifications first. . . . This structural device of listing qualifications and restrictions first seems to be especially favored in English legal prose. . . .

The main consequences of this inverted style is that a complex law may cite a very large number of exceptions, qualifications, reservations, and the like, all of which must be borne in mind when one subsequently reads the main facts of the law (the main noun and verb), and the need of remembering all this can exceed the limits of normal attention or apprehension. Here the problem is more in the domain of psychology than of linguistics, and has to do with the much-measured and so-called span of apprehension, the number of distinct items that one can hold simultaneously in mind. Under proper test conditions, that is, conditions fairly free of memorized background information, the size of that span is quite small for distinct items (about half a dozen) and even smaller for complex relationships expressed in embedded relative clauses (about three). Hence, writing sentences in the "backward" fashion described not only violates a customary structure of English, which creates one difficulty for comprehension; it also creates a difficulty for intelligence by requiring much supportive detail to be remembered while one seeks the point of the sentence. In English we first express our feelings and then mention the locale; in Japanese the qualifying context dominates. Neither of these is necessarily better as a structure than the other; but certainly having grown accustomed to processing language in a right-branching fashion, the typical reader of English finds his comprehension retarded by left-branching constructions. . . .

The problem of comprehension of legal prose is not a matter of "readability" in the usual sense of that term. Indeed I understand that you have attempted to apply some "readability" measures to legal prose, such as are used for some textbooks, and I am not surprised at the lack of useful results. Readability measures are usually directed at fairly straightforward accounts of fairly simple events; they are not well suited, as I perceive them, to coping with material that is intrinsically abstract and necessarily qualified. . . ."

Appendix 8

INDEXING: by K. H. Packer and A. H. Schabas

The following are excerpts taken from an article entitled "Indexing of Official Legal Publications for the Layman: Present Practices and Possible Alternatives" written for the study by Professors K. H. Packer and A. H. Schabas of the Faculty of Library Science at the University of Toronto.

"The general premises on which an index is designed should be clearly stated at the beginning of an index. Exactly what is indexed, for whom, its currency, format, and other such explanatory details should be included for the guidance of the users. It is generally assumed that, within the limits set down in such a statement of scope and intent, the indexing will be consistent and complete in all respects and for all parts. . . .

The level of indexing should be geared to the level of information needed by the user of the index. Indexing can be at a high level of generality or very specific or both. Exhaustive indexing must be highly selective so as not to lead the user to trivia, or to increase the bulk of the index unnecessarily. Guidelines governing the levels of indexing should be applied consistently. The way of referring to the section indexed should be specific without being unnecessarily so. The user should not have to scan the text extensively to find the passage referred to by the index entry. On the other hand, references which are overly specific tend to require a complex notation which clutters the index and opens the way for misinterpretation and transcription errors.

The vocabulary from which index terms are drawn should be the vocabulary of the intended users: popular terms for the layman, technical terms for the specialist. If both approaches are desirable, both can be provided, either by duplicate entries or by cross-references. Basic decisions on syntax should be made and applied consistently (e.g. use of singular versus plural). . . .

There is nothing more frustrating to the user than giving careful thought to choosing a likely term to look up in an index only to find, on looking it up, that it is not present at all or, more frustrating yet, to find that it is present with obviously unsuitable references. The cause may be that the material indexed does not contain what the user is looking for, or it may be insufficient cross-referencing. The index design should anticipate this need and provide a useful cross-reference structure to lead the user from sought terms to index terms actually used, and from index terms to other subject-related index terms. These references can link synonyms, alternate spellings, generically related terms and more loosely related terms. . . .

Both the English and the French versions of the RSI [Index to the Revised Statutes of Canada, 1970] were published in one volume; the English version (on which the present study is based) is 448 pages long. No directions on the use of the index, the users for whom it was intended, or any explanation of the abbreviations employed in the citations are included in the index volume, with the exception of a cryptic comment appearing under the heading on *all* pages "(References are to sections)". . . .

The RSI is printed three columns to a page, and a variety of type faces have been used to distinguish the various types of entries included in the RSI. The entries can be divided into two main categories which are distinguished typographically. The first category includes terms or other headings from which reference is made to individual statutes or to other terms. The second category includes only the short titles of individual Acts followed by entries that relate only to the Act itself. This second category of entry accounts for a very considerable portion of the RSI. The names of the Acts appear in their alphabetical position in the RSI followed by what amounts to a mini-index of all the key terms contained in a particular Act. These terms and phrases are printed in bold-face type and indented below the name of the Act. They in turn are followed by subheadings which identify more precisely the context in which the term occurs. These subheadings are indented below the terms they amplify and include references to specific sections of the Act being indexed. The length of these mini-indexes varies from fewer than 10 entries to over 30 pages. Relationships to other Acts are made explicit in a "see also" paragraph at the head of each mini-index. . . .

The mini-indexes provided for individual Acts are of value to anyone who enters the index knowing the correct short title of the Act he wishes to consult, or to anyone interested in locating information in a specific Act who succeeds in locating the title in the RSI regardless of how he does so. The presence of the mini-indexes, mingled as they are with the terms designed to provide subject access to the Statutes, however, interferes with efficient use of the subject portions of the RSI. In spite of the fact that they have been distinguished typographically from the subject terms, when they extend for several pages it is not easy to skip past the mini-indexes and pick up the main alphabet. There is danger of terms being overlooked when . . . only one or two subject terms occur between two mini-indexes. It is extremely difficult to follow one alphabetic sequence when other alphabetic sequences intervene and extend beyond the confines of one page. . . .

In order to reveal the general characteristics of the RSI all the entries that did not form part of the mini-indexes were stored in machine-readable form. All the codes used to identify the Acts to which each entry referred were also stored with the entry. Once the data was available in this form it was possible to tally the frequencies of references to individual Acts and to resequence the file by the individual Acts to identify all the terms that had been used as index entries for each Act. . . .

The total number of different index terms used is approximately 1550. While one term refers to 124 Acts, 66 percent of the terms refer to only one, and only .5 percent refer to more than ten. Of this .5 percent, two-thirds are proper names. The other third are very general topical terms such as Agriculture (41 references), Trade (34 references) and Fish (21 references). These findings reveal more about the material being indexed (Acts that deal with a wide variety of subjects) than about the quality of the indexing.

Viewed from the standpoint of the number of access points provided for the Acts, the total is 4500 approximately. This figure averages out to about 12 terms per indexed chapter. The range is from 124 subject entries for the Canada Shipping Act to no entries for ten Acts including the Income Tax Act. Fifteen percent of the Acts are indexed by 18 or more terms and another 15 percent by fewer than four terms.

It was not thought useful to test the complete file for a possible relationship between the length of an Act (number of pages) and the number of terms used to index it. In the process of studying the data in order to select Acts that would be of particular interest to the layman and that would also present a variety of indexing problems, some information on this point did emerge. For example, two Acts, one of 384 pages and one of 64 pages were both indexed with 51 terms. A comparison of the actual terms revealed another significant feature of the RSI index. Of the 51 terms used for the 384-page Act, the Criminal Code, all but four fell into the category of proper names; names of places (e.g. England, Quebec, Strait of Juan de Fuca) names of federal agencies, names of government departments or ministers, and other similar types of proper names. The four terms were: Aircraft, Alcohol, Explosives and Quartz. There appears to be no obvious explanation why a reference from Quartz should have been included when none was made from Gold or Silver (terms that occur in the same section and appear to be at least as likely if not more likely to be sought as access points). The same pattern of entries obtained for the 64-page Act, the Prisons and Reformatories Act. Of the 51 entries only four could by any stretch of the imagination be considered topics. They were: Justice, Prisons, Reformatory and Religion. While appropriate access points, they are grossly inadequate as the only access points to this Act for the layman. Three of them, the first three, are so general that no section references were provided. The fourth covers only one very specific and rather minor aspect of the Act. Entries under Imprisonment, Discipline (of prisoners), Escape (from prison) suggest themselves immediately, on examining the Act, as essential access points.

A rough calculation of the proportion of true subject entries provided in the RSI as opposed to entries for proper names (Acts or other Codes, geographic areas and governmental jurisdictions, government departments, boards, officers and ministers, and also non-governmental agencies and bodies, treaties, funds and courts) revealed that only approximately 40 percent of the 1550 entries are true subject entries. In other words, there are roughly 600 topical subject entries. It is the subject terms that are likely to be of use to the layman. The name approaches may be exceedingly valuable for experts who want to find out what Acts mention a specific country or government agency, but such approaches are less likely to be of use to the general public. A layman is more likely to be problem-oriented. He will want to know about Acts as they affect his personal and business life and he will have to identify them through the terms he himself employs to describe the matter in question.

This leads to a consideration of the terms selected as subject entries in the RSI. . . . It would appear that the terminology of the index was closely related to the terminology of the Acts themselves rather than to that of any potential user group. By implication, this identifies its intended users as legal experts.

A practice in the RSI that is of questionable usefulness is that of making an index entry that files directly ahead of the name of the Act to which it refers; for example: Agricultural Products Board see Agricultural Products Board Act, or Arctic Waters see Arctic Waters Pollution Prevention Act, or Carriage by Air see Carriage by Air Act. There are approximately 100 entries of this type. . . .

Other irregularities and errors that were identified include the following. A number of entries begin with "Her Majesty"; other entries begin with Queen, Queen's or Crown, and one entry appears under Elizabeth II. No links have been provided from Majesty to Her Majesty (for those who would not expect to find an entry under a personal pronoun) or between the four entries that have been used, all of which are very closely related. Some errors in filing were identified and the entry for "An Act respecting the Incorporation of Livestock Record Associations, 1900" was filed under "An." It is always easier to criticize errors than it is to eliminate them, especially from an index as involved and complicated as RSI, but the fact remains that errors do seriously interfere with the use of the index, and cannot be disregarded in an evaluation. . . .

To sum up, the present index does not satisfy the criteria that have been generally accepted as the hallmarks of sound indexing practice regardless of its intended users, and it is woefully inadequate to meet the needs of the layman. . . .

Recognizing that the RSI was not prepared with the layman in mind, it was decided to experiment with various methods of selecting index terms appropriate for the layman. With this in mind, it was decided to select three Acts for in-depth study. Criteria for this selection were: that the Acts deal with matters of likely interest to the layman; that they represent three different interest areas; that they be of different lengths; and that they vary with regard to the number of index terms provided for them in the RSI. . . .

The three Acts chosen were: the Canadian Citizenship Act, 26 pages long with 20 index terms in the RSI, the Family Allowances Act, six pages long with ten index terms in the RSI, the Trade Unions Act, 11 pages long with three index terms in the RSI. (The fact that the Family Allowances Act has recently been revised does not affect its use for this study.)

It was thought desirable to draw on the special knowledge, experience and skills of others to identify as completely as possible the layman's requirements in the way of an index. Two people were approached and each was asked to index the three Acts. They were given free rein to index in any way they considered appropriate for the layman. The main objective was to identify the topics that would be most useful as index entry points and the vocabulary that would be most suitable. Each indexer was provided with standard tools (subject heading lists, thesauri, classification schedules) for indexing legal materials, although these were to be used or not as the indexer saw fit. It should be noted that a literature search was conducted to identify any such tools for indexing legal material *for the layman* and none was found. . . .

Five times more terms were assigned to the three Acts by the two indexers than had been used in RSI. The RSI terms were all included by Indexer-1 or Indexer-2 or both. . . .

. . . the major improvement needed in the RSI to make it useful to the layman is to provide more subject access, phrased in user (layman) vocabulary. Because different users approach information with different terms in mind the index must provide for all reasonable alternatives: variant spellings, multiword phrases and inversions, synonyms and different levels of generality. Because of the bulk that would result if a direct lead were provided from every variant to information in the Statutes it is recommended that two kinds of cross-references be used: general references . . . and specific references from terms not used to the preferred term. Finally, the importance of providing context with the index entry as a selection aid to the user has to be stressed, and further it is recommended that a systematic approach to this be adopted. . . .

One of the limitations in present indexing is the fact that it is first necessary to identify the appropriate index to consult. Without any change in present methods of publication of legal documents it would be possible to provide improved access by incorporating in one index access points to a number of related publications. For example, as a first step, indexing to the Regulations could be incorporated into the RSI. To test this idea, as part of this study, the Regulations to the Family Allowances Act were converted to machine-readable form and its terminology analysed and compared with the lists from the Family Allowances Act itself. A few additional useful terms emerged, but in the main it was found that the majority of the terms selected for the Family Allowances Act would also lead to useful information contained in the Regulations.

As a second stage it would be possible to merge the Federal and the Provincial indexing. Such a recommendation assumes that indexing to the Provincial materials be based on the same principles as that of the Federal materials. Since it would be inappropriate to combine indexing for the publications of all provinces with the Federal publications, this recommendation presupposes machine-readable data bases from which a number of indexes could be generated such as Federal and Ontario, Federal and Alberta, Federal and Quebec. Indexes limited in scope to certain subject areas could also be generated from the same data basis.

This approach also offers a solution to the problem of currency. The machine-readable indexes can be as up to date as the publication they index. Access to revisions and amendments can be provided. The hard copy indexes could be kept up to date with frequent supplements and new editions. . . ."

Appendix 9

INDEXING: by A. H. Janisch

The following are excerpts taken from an article entitled "A Critical Evaluation of Canadian Statute and Regulations Indexes" written for the study by A. H. Janisch, a librarian from Halifax. The article is a further development of ideas expressed originally as part of a panel on indexing of Canadian legal materials at the 1974 Annual Meeting of the Canadian Association of Law Libraries.

". . . Whether accompanying an encyclopedia, a history, a text-book, or a set of statutes, an index is constructed the same way and serves the same purpose: to locate specific parts of the work without having to read the entire contents. . . .

While little has been written concerning the problems of law index-ing and even less about the indexing of statutes or regulations, the *Chicago Manual of Style* maxim that "Every serious book of non-fiction should have an index if it is to achieve its maximum usefulness" can certainly be applied to statutes and regulations, as what more serious non-fiction can be found than the law? Yet in Canada, the statute index-es are inadequate (little more than expanded tables of contents) and regulations indexes are non-existent!

For the purposes of this paper the term "index" means a topical (i.e. subject) list arranged in alphabetical order. The term "table" means a list of items arranged or grouped in some order other than by topic, for example, all the regulations made under an Act listed under that Act regardless of the subject of each regulation. A table of contents is a different table, being a list of the chapters of a volume, in the order that they are found in the volume.

According to these definitions the Index to the *Revised Statutes of Canada, 1970* is a partial table of contents and partial index. The so-called "Index" to the *Canada Gazette, Pt. II*, is a set of three tables, none of which is an index. . . .

Canadian statute indexes at the present time range from four to 23 years in age, not counting those which do not exist. . . . The *Index to the Statutes* in Gt. Britain is cumulated annually, and the *United States Code* Index is cumulated annually in its pocket part supplements. Au-stralia, like Canada and its provinces, has not only a small index, but a hopelessly out-of-date one.

No dates can be given for Canadian regulations indexes because there are none. The British *Index to Government Orders* has been

145

cumulated periodically since its first publication in 1891. Though not an annual publication, it is a much more comprehensive index than the Index to the U.S. *Code of Federal Regulations*, which is cumulated annually. . . .

There is no statute index at all for Newfoundland. The 1952 Index in the old Newfoundland consolidation can hardly be used with the 1970 consolidation.

The federal government and all provinces except Newfoundland and P.E.I. publish tables of regulations arranged by empowering Act, but these tables bear no resemblance to indexes.

The federal and provincial statute indexes in Canada are all, upon close examination, found to be lists of acts, with each Act indexed to some extent, and with some cross-references for topics. If all of these "Act analyses" were removed from the statutes indexes (and perhaps placed at the top of chapters in the statutes) there would be very little left of the indexes.

The Canadian indexes are very different from the American topical statute indexes, and from ordinary topical indexes that one encounters frequently — encyclopedia, textbook, or yellow pages for example. They appear to be modelled on the British *Index to the Statutes*, but with one major and fatal divergence in style: where the British Index is organized in broad topics with many subheadings arranged under the topics referring to many different acts, the Canadian indexes are organized by Act, with the many subheadings all referring to the Act under which they are found. There are topical cross-references, but these are simply not adequate in number or in conception. Thus the British Index, for all its different appearance, is a topical index, while the Canadian ones are, at best, Act indexes. If a person knows the Act he needs he is unlikely to go to the index for the particular section number (unless it is a very large Act); the index should serve the purpose of locating a topic in one or several Acts, when the Acts are not already known. The Canadian indexes do this only to the extent that the cross-references help to locate the Acts in which some topics are found. . . .

The type of index produced in Canada (for both provincial and federal statutes) is not a topical index, but merely a modified, expanded table of contents, with some subject analysis and some cross-referencing. Thus, in the 1970 R.S.C. Index, The Canada Evidence Act is listed in the "C" section, with a see-reference from Evidence, but no see-references to all the other Acts in which the topic "evidence" is found.

To illustrate the difference between a list or table of Acts and a true topical index a comparison is made between the treatment of the topic "fire" in the 1970 R.S.C. Index and the treatment it should receive. The example is taken entirely from the existing Index, which is to say there may be mention of fire or a related term such as flammable in the text of the *Revised Statutes* which was not picked up as a subheading for any of the Acts. In other words, this is simply a topical re-arrangement of the Index. The entries under "fire" in the R.S.C. 1970 Index are:

Fire, *See* Fire Losses Replacement Account Act,
R.S., c. F-11
FIRE LOSSES REPLACEMENT ACCOUNT ACT,
   R.S., c. F-11
   * * * [analysis omitted]
Fireworks, *See* Explosives Act, R.S., c. E-15, s. 2.

A section of a topical index for "fire" should resemble the left-hand column below:

index	(where found)
Fire, *See* Arson c.C.-34, s. 17, 331, 385, 389-392, 405	Criminal Code
Fire, false alarm of, c. C-34, s. 393	Criminal Code
Fire, prevention & extinguishing in national parks, reg- ulations re. c.N-13, s. 7(1)(d)(e)	National Parks Act
Fire Drill entry in ship's log-book c. S-9, s.263(b) reg's re, ship. c.S-9, s. 400(1)(r) reg's re, steamship. c. S-9, s.441(1)	Canada Shipping Act
Fire fighters, Pensions to Corps of (Civilian) Canadian Fire Fighters. c.C-20, s.22, 23 75(1)(c); c.P-36, s.5(2).	Civilian War Pensions and Allowances Act; Public Service Superannuation Act.
Fire from locomotive, liability for damages. c.G-11, s.64, 65; c.R-2, s.338	Government Railways Act; Railway Act.
Fire guards on railway, reg. re. c.R-2, s.221(1)(a)	Railway Act
Fire insurance, classes avail- able without deposit. C. I-15, s. 107	Canadian and British Insurance Companies Act

FIRE LOSSES REPLACEMENT ACCOUNT
ACT, c. F-11
*** [analysis omitted]

Fire protection for railway, regs. re. c.R-2, s.221(1) (4), 227(1)(f)	Railway Act
Fire protection for ships, regs. re. c.S-9, s.460(1) (2)	Canada Shipping Act
Fire-rangers powers re railway. c. R-2, s. 221(3) reg's. re railway. c. R-2 s. 221(1)(b)	Railway Act
Fires, causing-service offence. c. N-4, s.? [no s. no. in index]	National Defence Act

It is not expected that anyone (lawyer or layman) would be interested in all these diverse references to "fire." However, the lawyer needs to find the particular statutory reference he requires as quickly as possible, and the layman is handicapped by lack of expertise. The average person, without intimate knowledge of the law, doesn't say to himself, "I wonder what the requirements of the X Act are concerning Y?" He is much more likely to say "I need to know something about the law concerning Y." The topical approach is an indexing technique to enable both to locate rapidly (or at all) the one reference each requires. Bringing together all references relative to one topic could be useful (as, for example, all of the duties of the master of a ship). Nevertheless, quick location, not commonality, is the justification for the topical approach.

That the Canadian index represents a different type of index is not, in itself, adequate reason for condemning it. It could be made to perform the function for which it is intended through use of copious, accurate, complete and specific cross-references. However, none of the Canadian indexes does this.

A close examination of the 1970 R.S.C. Index reveals gross inconsistencies in terminology, and generally haphazard, incomplete and inaccurate cross-references. . . .

. . . [For example], some topics are not used at all in the Index. The only entry under "Children" is an Act: "Children of War Dead (Education Assistance) Act," although children (infants, etc.) are treated in at least 22 other acts, including the Canada Shipping Act, the Judges Act, the Juvenile Delinquents Act, the Land Titles Act, the Proprietary or Patent Medicines Act and the Yukon Act. There are entries with cross-references under other classes of persons, e.g. "Veterans," "Indian," but not under some classes of persons, e.g. children, widows. Why? . . .

While the lawyer may, in time, learn his way around the statutes and the regulations, the layman, on the few occasions that he tries, is faced with a maze difficult, if not impossible, to navigate.

If, for example, a conscientious Canadian consumer should want to find out what his government has done about the problem of flammable fabrics (a not unreasonable pursuit for a conscientious consumer) he would find the way blocked, not by want of government action, but by near impossibility of locating the action taken in the form of law.

In the United States the consumer could look in the Index to the *United States Code* under "Flammable Fabrics" and find more than 75 specific references. He could then look in the Index to the *Code of Federal Regulations* and find a cross-reference, "Flammable Substances, See Fire Prevention and Control," under which he would find two subheadings "Fabrics" and "Flammable Fabrics Act" with three references to the regulations made under this act.

In Great Britain the consumer would find nothing under flammable as the *Index to the Statutes* uses the traditional term. "Inflammable Textile Fabrics" is a topic with four general see-also references and eight specific references to sections under it. In the *Index to Government Orders*, under the same topic, he would find a cross-reference to "Consumer Protection, 2", which is "2. Inflammable goods" and lists, with general description of the subject matter, three regulations.

In Canada, the consumer would not have such an easy time. If he looked first in the 1970 Index he would find nothing under Flammable, nothing under Fabric, and nothing under Inflammable. He would look in all subsequent (yellow) statute indexes and find nothing. He would try looking in the "Index" to the *Canada Gazette, Part II*, and would discover that it is not an index. Should he assume that the government has done nothing? In this instance, no.

This intrepid consumer could choose between reading the 1970 *Revised Statutes*, and all subsequent statute volumes from cover to cover, plus the entire *Canada Gazette Part II* working back from the latest issue, and consulting a lawyer or government department specializing in consumer affairs. Should he pursue the quest doggedly in one way or another he would find that flammable fabrics are dealt with in Part I of the Schedule to the Hazardous Products Act, as amended by S.O.R./70-73. As this was added to the Act after publication of the *Revised Statutes*, flammable fabrics appears nowhere in the 1970 Index. As the *Canada Gazette, Pt. II* is not indexed, flammable fabrics cannot be found there. The only possible way for the consumer to find this section would be for him to sense somehow that this problem must be dealt with in the Hazardous Products Act (knowing first, of course, of the existence of this act), to read the Act, and amendments (and find nothing), to look in Table II of the *Canada Gazette, Pt. II*, for regulations made under the Act, to find regulations concerning charcoal, car seats and other products referred to, but none concerning flammable fabrics, to decide that perhaps the undifferentiated list of 21 S.O.R.'s under "Schedule to the Act" was worth investigation, and to locate and read through all or some of them until he finds the one dealing with flammable fabrics. That's a lot to expect of a layman, no matter how deep his interest in a problem — especially when none of it would be necessary if the statutes and regulations were provided with timely topical indexes. . . .

A new approach needs to be made to federal and provincial statute and regulation indexes. An attempt is being made in Quebec where all "legislative instruments" (i.e. statutes and regulations) are being published in Pt. II of the *Gazette Officielle du Québec/ Quebec Official Gazette* with an annual combined index. This index is interesting in that it includes both statutes and regulations in one list, but falls short of the ideal in that it is not cumulative (as yet) so that the last cumulative Quebec statute index dates from 1964, and it is not a true topical index so that unless the first word of a regulation is its subject, the regulation is difficult to find.

The Quebec Index presents an example of a combined index; another format could be a companion set of two volumes. If the federal and provincial statutes and regulations are to be provided with adequate indexes, a standard should be set within the framework of which the indexes could vary in format and design:

1. The indexes should be issued annually.
2. The indexes should cumulate all new material, together with all material since the last consolidation, in each issue.
3. The indexes should be topical, arranged alphabetically, with either duplication of references for alternative terminology or adequate cross-reference.
4. The indexes should include, separately, the tables now issued.
5. Whether issued as one combined index or as separate indexes, statute and regulations indexes should be treated equally."

Appendix 10

GOVERNMENT PUBLICATIONS AND POPULAR LEGAL HANDBOOKS

The excerpts on the following pages are reprinted from existing publications that explain law or an area of law for non-lawyers. They are published by commercial publishers, government, and a variety of other organizations, including legal aid, law societies, consumers' organizations, community groups, and educational institutions.

COMMERCIAL PUBLISHERS

You and the Law, Reader's Digest.
Layman's Guide to Ontario Traffic Court, Gilchrist.
Mental Patients and the Law, Page.
The Guide to Family Law, Kronby.

GOVERNMENT

Labour Standards in Canada, Department of Labour.
Moving Back to Canada, Department of Revenue.
Social Assistance Handbook, B.C. Department of Human Resources.
The Consumer Protection Act and How It Helps You, Ontario Department of Consumer and Commercial Relations.
The Driver's Handbook, Ontario Department of Transport.
Guide Pratique de La Loi des Petites Créances, Québec Ministère de la Justice.

VARIOUS ORGANIZATIONS

CANS: Citizens' Advice Notes, U.K.
Landlord Tenant Act Problems, Vancouver Community Legal Assistance Society.
The Landlord and Tenant Act, Law Society of Manitoba.
How to Adopt, U.K. Consumers' Assoc.
What to Do When Someone Dies, U.K. Consumers' Assoc.
A Handbook on Youth and the Law, B.C. Civil Liberties Assoc.
A Hard Act to Follow: Notes on Ontario School Law, U. of T. Fac. of Ed.
Many Laws, Métis Assoc. of Alberta.

YOU AND THE LAW*

It is generally agreed that however good and dedicated a children's institution might be, it is still inferior to all but the worst family environment. The *foster home* provides a popular substitute for the real thing.

A Children's Aid society may decide in the interests of the child to place its ward in a foster home. Foster parents should be friendly, sympathetic persons who take wards of the society into their homes and care for them on a temporary basis. They are paid for the maintenance of the child.

Foster parents should not be confused with adopting (or adoptive) parents. The child placed in a foster home is usually still in the custody of a Children's Aid society, and the society can demand that the child be returned at any time. The foster home can supply a child with the affection and family life that is exceedingly difficult to provide in an institution. Not infrequently, foster parents end up adopting a child put into their care, having grown to love it genuinely.

Adoption procedure

All of our provinces and territories have legislation setting out the requirements for adoption. These laws are generally similar, with only minor variations from one province to the next. However, since the laws concerning the young are changing rapidly, those who would like to adopt should check the current position at their provincial welfare ministry, or with any branch of the local Children's Aid society.

Most provinces permit you to adopt only persons younger than 21 who have never been married. Others will allow you to adopt someone older than 21, providing you had earlier brought the person up.

To qualify as an adopting parent, unmarried applicant must be older than 21. A husband and a wife may adopt a child provided that one of them is older than 21. This age requirement does not apply, however, if one of the spouses is a parent of the child.

The requirements are somewhat different in Ontario. An Ontario court may refuse an adoption application where either of the applicants is younger than 25

or where the applicant is 21 years older than the person to be adopted. The court may also refuse an adoption where the applicant is a widow, a widower, divorced or unmarried. The religion of a child available for adoption is an important factor everywhere.

Each province insists that the consent of the child's parent or guardian be obtained. Here again, there are local variations. Some provinces (Alberta and New Brunswick, for example) require only the consent of the child's guardian, whether he is a parent or not. If the child is a permanent ward of the Crown, the consent of the parent is not required; the society makes the decision. Ontario insists that the parent's consent be obtained, regardless of who has custody of the child.

An illegitimate child can be put up for adoption only with the written consent of the mother—which must be given seven days or more after the child is born. If the child resides with and is maintained by the father, the father's consent is also necessary. Either parent may withdraw consent within 21 days after it is given. And the court reserves the right to permit a parent to withdraw consent even after the 21 days have passed.

Most jurisdictions also require consent to an adoption by the director of a Children's Aid society; this is issued only after a set period during which the child has resided with the prospective parents under the scrutiny of the society. This waiting period is usually a year; in a few provinces, it is six months.

In most provinces, if a child is older than 15, you must also get his consent before you can legally adopt him. (In Alberta, the age is 14.)

The courts reserve the right to dispense with the consent of a parent or guardian. Perhaps the parent has abandoned, neglected, or has persistently ill-treated the child or otherwise failed to discharge his obligations as a parent. It might be that he cannot be found or is incapable of giving his consent. The parent might be withholding consent unreasonably, perhaps to spite the persons wishing to adopt the child. The court will overrule the parent's objections if it feels . . . .

---

*YOU AND THE LAW, Montreal, Reader's Digest Association (Canada) Ltd., 1973, p. 200.

LAYMAN'S GUIDE TO ONTARIO TRAFFIC COURT*

The essential elements are:

(1) That the accused was the driver;

(2) Of a motor vehicle;

(3) Upon a highway;

(4) Within a city, town, etc.;

(5) At a greater rate of speed than thirty miles per hour.

If any of these elements are not proven, then when the Crown closes its case you may move for a dismissal. For example you may say: "Reserving my right to call evidence, I make a motion that the charge be dismissed on the grounds that there is no evidence of one of the essential elements, namely, that I was the driver of the motor vehicle in question."

If the judge finds that there is <u>some</u> evidence that you were the driver of the motor vehicle in question, he will dismiss your motion. You will then have to decide whether or not to call your own evidence. Refer to page 46 for further notes on what to do at this point.

Here are some more cases of violations under the Highway Traffic Act where evidence of one or more of the essential elements was found lacking.

<u>Example 1:</u> Section 96(5) -- "red light--intersection--no stop for cross-walk."

The relevant section of the Highway Traffic Act, section 96(5) reads as follows:

"When a red signal light is shown at an intersection, every driver or operator of a vehicle or car of an electric railway that is ....

*GILCHRIST, PETER, LAYMAN'S GUIDE TO ONTARIO TRAFFIC COURT, Toronto, Self-Counsel Press, 1972, p. 19.

MENTAL PATIENTS AND THE LAW*

Strictly speaking, it is not up to the voluntary patient to "wait around" to see if he can leave, although in the past there sometimes were "waiting periods" and certain red-tape hassles to be undergone in order to determine if such a person could leave. At present, the onus is clearly on the physician in charge to take definite steps to prevent a person from leaving an institution — otherwise it appears that the voluntary patient may legally leave whenever he wishes. He is usually asked to "sign himself out", and sometimes these people are allowed to leave even "against medical advice". It is important to note that any change in a patient's status while he is in the institution whether from voluntary to involuntary or vice versa must be communicated to the patient.

For some persons — perhaps those who simply aren't sure whether they want to be institutionalized or not — there can develop a type of dead-end situation. For example, if you are considered "sane", you might be said to have the capacity to make some sort of reasoned decision regarding your confinement in a mental institution. Probably you'd choose, therefore, not to let it happen to you. But if you don't choose to be institutionalized, then you may be suspected of "avoiding" or denying the situation and of perhaps being afflicted, therefore, with mental illness.

The "true" voluntary mental patient thus appears to be one who is both: (a) not judged by a doctor to be dangerous to himself or to others and (b) one who enters the institution voluntarily.

C. Criminal Commitment

The laws dealing with mental health and criminal procedures are complex and ill-defined. We will outline briefly the three major areas in which mental health considerations enter into criminal procedures:

1. Deciding whether or not a person is mentally fit to stand trial;

2. What happens when a person is acquitted of a crime on the grounds that he is insane; ....

---

*PAGE, STEWART, *MENTAL PATIENTS AND THE LAW*, Toronto, Self-Counsel Press, 1973, p. 12.

THE GUIDE TO FAMILY LAW*

Each province has established "prohibited degrees of consanguinity", blood relationships which prevent valid marriage. You already know that brother and sister can't marry, but did you know, for example, that a man can't marry his ex-wife's aunt? Information about the prohibited degrees of consanguinity is available wherever marriage licences are issued.

Prior Marriages

You musn't already be married to someone else. Lots of people are already married in a strict legal sense. So if you were previously married and your spouse is still alive, that prior marriage must have been effectively dissolved by divorce or annulment (or death) before you can marry again.*

This is no problem if, say, the prior marriage was solemnized in Saskatchewan, the spouses always lived there together, and later got divorced there. But the situation can become greatly complicated where the prior marriage (or marriages) were solemnized in one place and dissolved in another. Suppose for instance that the wife was first married in California, moved with her husband to ...

*There is another way. If your spouse has disappeared and been absent for at least seven years without any information whatever about the spouse in that time, you can apply for a court order permitting remarriage. If the spouse turns up later, your first marriage is still valid and your second marriage is void, and children of it are illegitimate. However, you haven't committed bigamy. The Divorce Act now permits a divorce after three years' disappearance, so applications merely to allow remarriage ....

*KRONBY, MALCOLM C., THE GUIDE TO FAMILY LAW, Toronto, New Press, 1972, p. 5.

LABOUR STANDARDS IN CANADA*

EQUAL PAY

The Parliament of Canada and all provinces but Québec have enacted laws which require equal pay for equal work without discrimination on the grounds of sex.

The Québec fair employment practices law forbids discrimination in employment on the basis of sex, thus prohibiting, among other things, discrimination in rates of pay solely on the grounds of sex. Similar prohibitions against discrimination in employment are contained in Alberta, British Columbia, Manitoba, New Brunswick, Newfoundland and Ontario human rights legislation.

In four jurisdictions equal pay provisions are contained in the labour code — the Canada Labour Code, Part III, Division II.1; the Ontario Employment Standards Act, Part V; the Saskatchewan Labour Standards Act, Part V; and the Nova Scotia Labour Standards Code (sections 55-57)[1]. In four other provinces equal pay provisions form part of human rights legislation — the Alberta Individual's Rights Protection Act, the British Columbia Human Rights Act and the Newfoundland and Prince Edward Island Human Rights Codes. Manitoba and New Brunswick have separate equal pay Acts.

The Newfoundland and New Brunswick legislation forbids an employer to pay a female employee at a rate of pay less than the rate paid to a male employee for **the same work done in the same establishment.**

The Prince Edward Island Act states that an employer may not pay a female employee at a rate of pay less than the rate paid to a male employee for **substantially the same work done in the same establishment.** The British Columbia Act refers to the **same work or substantially the same work done in the same establishment.**

In Saskatchewan, an employer is forbidden to pay a female employee at a rate of pay less than the rate paid to a male employee for **work of comparable character done in the same establishment.**

The Alberta Act forbids an employer to employ a female employee for any work at a rate of pay that is less than the rate of pay at which a male employee is employed by that employer for **similar or substantially similar work.** The work is deemed to be similar or substantially similar if the job, duties or services the employees are called upon to perform are similar or substantially similar. Reduction of an employee's rate of pay in order to comply with the legislation is prohibited....

---

*CANADA, DEPT. OF LABOUR, LEGISLATIVE RESEARCH, *LABOUR STANDARDS IN CANADA*, Ottawa, Information Canada, 1974, p. 21.

MOVING BACK TO CANADA?/VOUS REVENEZ VIVRE AU CANADA?*

you should know

vous devriez savoir

If you are a former resident of Canada who has been abroad for at least 365 days, there are some things that you should know about Canada Customs.

First, the good news.

You may bring back duty-free all of your household or personal effects including your car, boat, or even private airplane, provided they have been acquired and used six months before your return to Canada. That means six months before the day of your arrival back into Canada.

And here's a break if you are a new bride. In this case, the six months business does not apply to your trousseau or wedding gifts. In other words, you can get married, leave for Canada the next day and still bring in your gifts without paying duty provided they are actually owned and possessed prior to your return to Canada.

If you are a former resident of Canada who has surrendered his Canadian citizenship and hold foreign citizenship or have resided abroad for at least five years, you also can bring back all your possessions without the time limitation of six months but all goods must have been actually owned in your possession and used prior to return to Canada.

Now the bad news.

Alcoholic beverages, cigars, cigarettes and manufactured tobacco products are not considered as household goods or effects and these may not be included on your formal entry declaration. However, Customs do allow returning former Canadian residents who meet the age requirements of their home province to each bring back, as personal baggage, 40 ounces of either wine or liquor or 24 pints of beer as well as 200 cigarettes, 50 cigars and . . . .

Si vous êtes un ancien résident du Canada ayant séjourné au moins 365 jours à l'étranger, voici quelques renseignements indispensables au sujet de Douanes Canada.

D'abord les bonnes nouvelles . . .

Vous pouvez rapporter en franchise des droits tous vos effets domestiques ou personnels y compris votre auto, votre bateau, ou même votre avion privé, pourvu qu'ils aient été acquis et utilisés au moins six mois avant le jour de votre arrivée au Canada.

Si vous êtes récemment mariée, voici une belle occasion . . . la période de six mois ne s'applique pas à votre trousseau et à vos cadeaux de noces. En d'autres mots, vous pouvez vous marier, partir pour le Canada le jour suivant et apporter vos cadeaux sans payer de droits pourvu que vous en ayez pris possession avant votre retour au Canada.

Si vous êtes un ancien résident du Canada ayant renoncé à sa citoyenneté canadienne pour devenir citoyen d'un autre pays, ou ayant résidé à l'étranger pendant au moins cinq années, vous pouvez aussi rapporter tous vos biens sans avoir à respecter le délai de six mois. Toutes les marchandises doivent cependant avoir été réellement possédées et utilisées avant votre retour au Canada.

Ensuite les moins bonnes nouvelles

Les boissons alcooliques, les cigares, les cigarettes et les produits du tabac fabriqué ne sont pas considérés comme des marchandises ou des effets domestiques et ils ne peuvent être visés par votre déclaration d'entrée officielle. Toutefois, tout ancien résident du Canada qui revient au pays et qui satisfait aux exigences relatives à l'âge, dans sa propre province, peut rapporter dans ses bagages personnels, 40 onces de vin ou de spiritueux ou 24 chopines de bière ainsi que 200 cigarettes, 50 cigares et . . . .

---

* CANADA, DEPT. OF REVENUE, CUSTOMS AND EXCISE, *MOVING BACK TO CANADA?/VOUS REVENEZ VIVRE AU CANADA?*n.d.

SOCIAL ASSISTANCE HANDBOOK*

Eligibility

3

Who May Apply:

Any Canadian citizen may apply for Social Assistance in British Columbia, no matter how long he or she has lived in the province. A landed immigrant may apply for Social Assistance under certain circumstances and will be advised that if such assistance is granted, the Immigration Department will be notified. Enquire for details at your local Human Resources office.

Assets Requirements:

You may own certain things and still receive assistance. You may:

1. Own or be purchasing a home providing you are living in it.
2. Own one motor vehicle providing the sale value is less than $1500.
3. Have cash, bonds, stock, securities or any other assets that can be converted into cash and will total not more than $500 if you are single, or $1000 of such assets singly or jointly owned if you are married or with children.
4. Have an insurance policy which can provide $1000 loan or cash surrender value.

Note: Mortgages and agreements for sale are considered personal assets at their resale rate.

Important Eligibility Notes

1. In all marriages, the head of the family must be eligible if the family is to receive a social allowance.
2. In common law situations, the common law husband is considered the head of the family. A social allowance can be paid to the family only if the total family assets and income are within eligibility guidelines.

3. Employable applicants for Social Assistance are expected to actively seek employment. If an applicant for Social Assistance refuses employment without good cause, his application for assistance can be refused.
4. An applicant for Social Assistance may not forego income from any other source and still receive a social allowance.
5. Children under age 19, if living in their parent's home, may usually only receive Social Assistance if the parents are eligible.
6. Under the Family Relations Act, children under nineteen are the responsibility of their parents. When children under 19 years of age, living away from their parent's home, apply for a social allowance, their parents will be interviewed or contacted as to their ability to provide for their child and the desireability of their child living away from home. . . .

---

*BRITISH COLUMBIA, MINISTRY OF HUMAN RESOURCES, *SOCIAL ASSISTANCE HANDBOOK*, 1973, p. 3.

THE CONSUMER PROTECTION ACT
AND HOW IT HELPS YOU, THE CONSUMER*

Cooling-off Period

Even with all the above details, the consumer still has the right to break such a contract if he does so by registered mail or by letter personally delivered within two working days after the contract has been signed. **A telephone call is no good. This "cooling off" period applies only when the contract involves more than $50 and has been negotiated and signed at a place other than the seller's regular place of business, for example in your home.**

If the consumer terminates the contract, he is responsible for returning the goods to the seller immediately at the seller's expense. The seller, in turn, must return all monies received or realized in the transaction and return any trade-in.

Repossession of Goods

When goods have been purchased, delivered and accepted and the buyer falls behind in payments, he cannot have the goods taken away from him except by a court order after he has paid two-thirds of the purchase price.

Buying on credit

Buying on credit is so widespread that it would be hard to imagine a world without it.

The Act protects the consumer in credit transactions. Credit rates vary according to the source and the type of transaction. Factors which influence the interest charged are: the degree of risk involved; the cost of money at a particular time, plus the expense of collection and record keeping. Anyone selling merchandise costing more than $50 on credit must provide the purchaser, before credit is given, with a clearly written statement, showing the total finance charges both in dollars and cents and the annual percentage rate being charged. The seller must also show, in writing, the additional charges he intends to make if the purchaser defaults on payments. This detailing of costs not only applies to contracts for goods purchased on credit, but also to monthly charge accounts and to all loans. (For further information on credit, write: Using Credit Wisely, Consumer Buy-Line, 555 Yonge Street, Toronto, Ontario.)

Unsolicited goods

The Act also limits the consumer's liability in the area of unsolicited goods, including credit cards. The consumer is not responsible for any unsolicited goods delivered to him and has no legal obligation in respect to their use or disposal, unless he knows they were intended for some other person.

If a consumer receives unordered merchandise through the mail, or placed on his doorstep, he can legally keep it or throw it out.

If you receive an unsolicited credit card you have no legal obligation as to its use or disposal unless you accept the card in writing or you purchase goods with it. In this case you are responsible for the goods purchased. But, if you don't want the card simply cut it up and throw it out.

Referral selling

The Act prohibits a seller from offering a consumer a special discount on goods if the consumer can get his friends to place a similar order. Any . . . .

---

*ONTARIO, MINISTRY OF CONSUMER AND COMMERCIAL RELATIONS, *THE CONSUMER PROTECTION ACT AND HOW IT HELPS YOU, THE CONSUMER*, n.d. (unpaged).

THE DRIVER'S HANDBOOK*

SIGNALLING

The law requires you to signal other drivers of your intention to stop or suddenly decrease the speed of your vehicle . . . to turn to the left or the right . . . to change from one lane for traffic to another lane for traffic . . . to leave the roadway . . . to set your vehicle in motion from a parked position. **Signals shall be given by turn signals, stop light or hand and arm.** [94.]

Turn signals must not be used for any purpose other than when turning, changing lanes, or pulling away from a parked position. [94 (6).] They must not be used to indicate a stationary vehicle.

SIGNAL IN TIME

Give correct signals well in advance and in such a way as to be plainly visible to other drivers. Check your signalling devices frequently to ensure they are working properly.

TO TURN LEFT

Always give the required signal.   [94 (4) (a).]

TO TURN RIGHT

Always give the required signal.   [94 (4) (b).]

TO STOP OR SLOW DOWN

Always give the required signal.   [94 (7).]

TO CHANGE LANES

Never move from one lane for traffic to another until you make certain that you can do so safely. This means you must have safe clearance to the side, ahead and behind your vehicle in addition to giving the proper signal.

TURNS AT INTERSECTIONS

RIGHT TURNS

Well back from the intersection, signal for turn and **move to right-hand lane when the way is clear.** Look ahead and to left and right before starting to make turn. Keep as close as possible to the right. Watch for pedestrians.

LEFT TURNS

Well back from intersection, slow down and signal intention to turn left. Look behind for traffic and **move as close to centre line as possible.** Look ahead and to left and right before starting to make turn. Enter the intersection to right of the centre point (as shown). Leave the intersection by passing to the right of and **as closely as practicable** to the centre line of the highway being entered. **Left turn must not be made in front of oncoming traffic unless such turn can be made safely.**

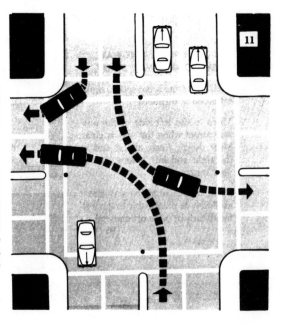

*ONTARIO, DEPT. OF TRANSPORTATION AND COMMUNICATIONS, *THE DRIVER'S HANDBOOK* 1971/72, p. 10.

GUIDE PRATIQUE DE LA LOI DES PETITES CREANCES *

D'autre part, le remboursement d'un dépôt de $300.00 ou moins ne peut être réclamé à la division des petites créances, s'il s'agit d'un bris de contrat dont le montant est supérieur à $300.00.

VI. LE RÉFÉRÉ

Une personne morale ne peut poursuivre un débiteur devant la Cour provinciale, division des petites créances. Elle doit plutôt s'adresser à la Cour provinciale. Mais le débiteur poursuivi devant cette dernière cour, peut, dans les dix (10) jours après avoir reçu le bref d'assignation, demander que la cause soit transférée à la division des petites créances s'il est poursuivi pour une somme de $300.00 et moins. C'est le débiteur qui doit faire cette demande au greffier de la Cour provinciale.

VII. LE MANDAT

S'il arrive que le créancier ou le débiteur soit dans l'incapacité de se présenter devant le juge pour cause de maladie, d'éloignement, d'âge avancé ou de tout autre motif jugé valable par le juge, il lui faudra mandater quelqu'un pour le représenter.Ce mandat se fait par écrit, signé par le mandant qui y mentionne la raison de son incapacité de se présenter. Le représentant ou mandataire doit être un parent ou un allié, au choix. Il n'y a pas d'ordre de priorité entre eux. Ce n'est que dans le cas où il n'y aurait ni parent ou allié que l'on peut avoir recours à un ami. Le mandataire doit tout de même être au courant des faits lorsqu'il se présente à la Cour d'accès à la justice

VIII. OÙ S'ADRESSER POUR PRÉSENTER SA REQUÊTE?

Tout citoyen (personne physique) qui veut réclamer un montant de $300.00 et moins doit adresser sa requête à la Cour provinciale, division des petites créances. Il existe, sur le territoire québécois, 84 tribunaux habilités à entendre les causes relevant de la loi des petites créances. On ne peut, toutefois, se présenter à n'importe lequel de ces tribunaux pour faire valoir sa requête; mais au choix ....

---

*QUEBEC, MINISTERE DE LA JUSTICE, SERVICE DE L'INFORMATION, *GUIDE PRATIQUE DE LA LOI DES PETITES CREANCES*, 1974, p. 6.

162 *Access to the Law*

CANS
(CITIZENS' ADVICE NOTES)*

payments to continue up to the age of 21, on the same terms as those for guardianship orders (see [14] 11), subject to modification to suit the special circumstances; but no order may be made requiring any person to pay any sum for the benefit of an illegitimate child of that person.

S.7 of the Act provides that, where exceptional circumstances make it impracticable or undesirable for a ward of court to be under the care of either of his parents or of any other individual, the Court may commit him to the care of a local authority. The Court is also empowered, in certain other circumstances, to place the ward under the supervision of a welfare officer or local authority.

The ward of court system does not apply in Scotland.

[14] 13   ADOPTION:
STATUTORY PROVISIONS

Reference has been made, inter alia, to—

Adoption Acts, 1958, 1960, 1964, and 1968

Family Law Reform Act, 1969

Age of Majority (Scotland) Act, 1969

Children and Young Persons Act, 1969

Guardianship of Minors Act, 1971

The Adoption Agencies Regulations, 1959, as amended (S.I. 1959 No. 639, 1961 No. 900, and 1965 No. 2054)

The Adoption Agencies (Scotland) Regulations, 1959, as amended (S.I. 1959 No. 773, 1961 No. 1270, and 1967 No. 34)

Home Office Circulars Nos. 61/1966 (April, 1966) and 276/1970 (December, 1970)

The statutory provisions relating to legal adoption are contained in the above Acts. The Act of 1958 consolidates the previous legislation, including those parts of the Children Act, 1958, which dealt with adoption.

Note.—The local authorities for the purpose of the Acts are, in England and Wales, the councils of counties, county boroughs, or London boroughs, or the Common Council of the City of London, and, in Scotland, the councils of counties and large burghs. Adoption matters are dealt with by the social services committees (in Scotland, social work committees) of these authorities.

Who may be an Adopter

The adopter must be domiciled in England and Wales, or in Scotland, and normally both the adopter and the infant must also reside in one of those countries (but see below as to applications for adoption orders by persons not resident in Great Britain). No adoption order may be made in respect of any child, unless the applicant for the order, or, in the case of a joint application, one of the applicants is—

(a) the father or mother of the child; or

(b) a relative of the child and over 21 years of age; or

(c) over 25 years of age.

Only where, in special circumstances, the court considers it justified, may a man be the sole adopter of a female child. The expression "relative" means a grandparent, brother, sister, uncle, or aunt, whether of the full blood, of the half blood, or by affinity; in the case of an illegitimate child, the expression includes the father, and persons who would be relatives if the child were legitimate; it should be noted that, for the purposes of determining relationship, an adopted person is treated as if he had been born to the adopter in lawful wedlock.

An adoption order may be made authorising the adoption of a child by its mother or father, either alone or jointly with her or his spouse. In certain circumstances, the adoption of a child by its own mother, usually with her husband, is very desirable.

Who may be Adopted

Only a child under the age of 18, who has never been married, may be adopted. It is not necessary for the child to be a British subject. The child must be resident in England or Wales or in Scotland.

Consent to Adoption

An order cannot usually be made on an application by one of two spouses without the consent of the other. The court has power, however, to dispense with such consent if the person concerned cannot be found, or is incapable of giving consent, or where the spouses have separated and are living apart and the separation is likely to be permanent.

The consent is ordinarily required of the parent or guardian of the infant; for the purpose of the Acts, a natural father is not a "parent" but such a father may, under the Guardianship of Minors Act, 1971 (applicable only to England and Wales— see Note [14] 11) apply to the court to obtain custody of the child. The court may, however, dispense with such consent if the parent or guardian has abandoned, neglected, or persistently ill-treated the child, or has persistently failed without reasonable cause to discharge the obligations of a parent or guardian, or if the . . . .

LANDLORD TENANT ACT PROBLEMS*

the rent cannot be increased until the **next March 1st**.

There is, however, one significant exception to eviction and rent provisions of the Act. **If, after proper notification of a rental increase, the tenant refuses to pay the increase on the day rent is due, the landlord is entitled to evict him within 10 days** rather than the usual required 30 days. However, as in the case of evictions for any other cause, the landlord must go through the courts to have the tenant evicted should the tenant refuse to leave.

OBLIGATIONS OF THE PARTIES

The B.C. Landlord - Tenant Act imposes obligations on both the landlord and tenant during the period of occupancy under a rental agreement.

A. **Tenant's Obligations — Under the Act, the tenant is responsible for ordinary cleanliness and he must maintain acceptable health and sanitary standards throughout the rented premises.** If damage is done deliberately or accidentally by the tenant or his visitors the tenant is responsible for the repairs. Most tenancy agreements provide that a tenant is required to keep the premises in a "tenant-like" manner. He is expected to do the **little things** like replacing burnt out light bulbs or unplugging sinks. On termination of the tenancy the tenant is expected to l e a v e the premises in good condition.

B. **Landlord's Obligations —** Prior to the Landlord - Tenant Act, the landlord was responsible for ensuring the premises were fit for human habitation only when it involved a furnished residence. Therefore it was up to the tenant to satisfy himself of the suitability of unfurnished premises before he entered into an agreement to rent. If the premises needed repair, the tenant had no recourse since he knew about it before he moved in.

Now, under the Act, the landlord m u s t m a i n t a i n both furnished and unfurnished premises in a good state of repair and fit for human habitation. This is true whether or not the tenant is aware of any defect at the time he agrees to rent. The obligation of the landlord to provide and maintain a good state of

repair is absolute. No exceptions are allowed. The landlord is further obligated to comply with all health, safety and housing standards as set down by existing municipal laws.

C. **Repair of Premises —** Either a landlord or a tenant may apply to provincial court to enforce the other's obligation to repair. The judge may authorize the repair to be made or may terminate the tenancy agreement. Although there is no legal obligation to do so, it would appear likely that before a tenant can get a tenancy agreement cancelled for non-repair, he should notify the landlord and give him a chance to make the needed repair.

Of course, the tenant can make the repair himself. But a tenant who rushes off to have something repaired may find himself out of pocket for the amount he spent. **The safe course of action is to apply and have the judge make the appropriate repair order.** The Landlord - Tenant Act does not make any specific provision for maintenance of appliances and fixtures included in a rental agreement nor for redecoration. However, municipal by-laws can fill this gap by outlining the landlord's obligation to carry out these functions.

D. **Entry by Landlord —** Under rental agreements made prior to the Act, the landlord often made agreements giving him unrestricted entry to the rented premises. The Act now makes such unrestricted entry illegal. Should a landlord wish to enter the rented premises, he must give 24 hours written notice of his intention to do so. He must say what time he will be coming and it cannot be before eight in the morning nor after nine at night. However, there are four exceptions w h e r e the landlord is not required to give this notice:

1. In case of emergency;
2. With the consent of the tenant given at time of entry;
3. Where the landlord has the right under the tenancy agreement to show the premises to prospective purchasers or tenants after notice of termination of the tenancy has been given.
4. Where the tenant abandons the premises. . . .

---

*VANCOUVER COMMUNITY LEGAL ASSISTANCE SOCIETY, *LANDLORD TENANT ACT PROBLEMS*, 1973.

THE LANDLORD AND TENANT ACT*

When a dispute arises between a landlord and a tenant about the return of the security deposit or any part of it and the landlord claims that:

(a) the tenant has caused damage to the premises; or

(b) the tenant is in arrears in payment of his rent;

The landlord must immediately:

(a) notify the Rentalsman and the tenant in writing of his reasons for objecting to the return of the security deposit and

(b) forward, at the same time, the amount of the security deposit, with interest, to the Rentalsman.

The Rentalsman will then try to mediate an agreement between the parties. If the landlord and tenant fail to reach an agreement, they may request the Rentalsman to act as an arbitrator.

DISTRESS

A landlord cannot seize personal property of a tenant for default in payment of rent.

RESPONSIBILITIES

A landlord is responsible for providing and maintaining the rented premises in good condition and fit for habitation during the tenancy.

The tenant shall:

(a) be responsible for ordinary cleanliness of the premises;

(b) take reasonable care of the premises and repair damage resulting from willful or negligent conduct by the tenant or his guests; and

(c) take reasonable action to avoid causing a nuisance or disturbance to other tenants in the building.

If a tenant or his guest is causing a disturbance or nuisance and doesn't stop when requested by the landlord or another tenant, the complaining person can make a complaint before a magistrate. If convicted, the offending party would be liable to a fine.

Failure by a landlord or tenant to fulfill any of the foregoing obligations or responsibilities shall be sufficient reason for the non-offending party to terminate a tenancy agreement.

When a tenant requests his landlord to make reasonable repairs and the landlord refuses or neglects to do so, the tenant may notify the Rentalsman....

*LAW SOCIETY OF MANITOBA, *THE LANDLORD AND TENANT ACT*, Winnipeg, n.d.

HOW TO ADOPT*

Others' consent

If the child has a guardian, the guardian's consent is required. A guardian is a person appointed by deed or by a will of a parent, or appointed by a court to be the guardian of the infant.

For the purpose of consent to a proposed adoption the natural father of an illegitimate child does not count as a parent. This applies whether or not he has contributed to the maintenance of the child. Some courts ask for a signed consent from the father if he is making payments, although this is not required in law. The fact that some courts ask for this and some do not, shows that the courts interpret their duties towards the natural father in different ways.

If the child being adopted is legitimate, the consent of both parents is required even if they are divorced and one of them has custody of the child. If the mother is married, her husband's consent to the proposed adoption is required, but the court may dispense with his consent if the mother swears an affidavit to the effect that he is not the child's father. If the court is willing to accept the mother's affidavit as proof of the child's illegitimacy, the consent of her husband will not be required, nor need he be notified of the adoption arrangements. However if the application to adopt is before a court which deems that the husband must be the father of the child, he will be informed of the adoption arrangements and his consent sought. It is difficult to know in advance what the requirements of a particular court ....

HOW TO ADOPT, London, Consumers' Association, 1973, p. 93.

WHAT TO DO WHEN SOMEONE DIES*

the death. If the death had been reported to the coroner direct, the registrar will not know who the next of kin are, so he has to wait until someone comes to him.

Post mortem
If the coroner orders a post mortem, no one can appeal against his decision. The coroner's officer becomes responsible for the body, and has it removed to the mortuary if it is not already there.

A post mortem is usually needed to establish with certainty the medical cause of death. It may be important to be able to state the medical cause of death accurately if there are any legal proceedings arising from the death.

If the post mortem should reveal that the death was due to a natural cause and no other circumstances warrant further investigation, the coroner notifies the registrar. The coroner has no duty to inform the next of kin of the result of the post mortem. In some districts, the coroner's officer or another policeman calls on the family to tell them; otherwise the next of kin have to enquire at the registrar's office every few days to find out whether the coroner's notification has arrived, or get the undertaker to find out.

After the post mortem the body becomes again the responsibility of the family, unless there is to be an inquest.

Inquest
The coroner can choose to hold an inquest on any death reported to him. But if he has reasonable grounds for suspecting that the death was violent or unnatural, he is legally obliged to hold an inquest. He is also obliged to hold one when a person has died in circumstances where the law requires an inquest to be held – for ....

WHAT TO DO WHEN SOMEONE DIES, London, Consumers' Association, 1973, p. 14.

A HANDBOOK ON YOUTH AND THE LAW*

11. WHAT CAN A PUPIL DO IF HE IS ABOUT TO BE SUSPENDED OR EXPELLED?

1. He can promise to make an effort to reform.
2. He can request a transfer to another school in the district.
3. He can ask the School Board to hold a hearing and allow him to present his case to the Board.

12. DOES THE PUPIL HAVE A RIGHT TO A HEARING IF THE BOARD IS CONSIDERING SUSPENDING OR EXPELLING HIM?

The pupil has the right to a hearing before the Board if he is about to be suspended or expelled. In making a decision to suspend or to expel a pupil, the Board is acting in a quasi-judicial capacity, and the student is entitled to be present with parents and counsel.

13. CAN A PUPIL BE READMITTED IF HE HAS BEEN SUSPENDED OR EXPELLED?

He and/or his parents may apply to the School Board for readmission. The School Board must be satisfied that he has sufficiently reformed. The Board will consult with the District Superintendent of Schools before making its decision. An optional procedure is to take the case before the B.C. Supreme Court within one year of the suspension or expulsion.

14. CAN A PUPIL BE FORCED TO TRANSFER FROM ONE SCHOOL TO ANOTHER?

Apparently the School Board cannot directly force a pupil to change schools. However, a student who has been dismissed from one school may have no option but to transfer to another school in the district if he wishes to continue his education.

15. IN WHAT CIRCUMSTANCES MAY A STUDENT BE REQUIRED TO TRANSFER FROM ONE SCHOOL TO ANOTHER?

Pursuant to the policy of the Vancouver School Board, a student may no longer attend his present school where:

1. He consumes liquor or takes drugs or narcotics on the school premises or at a school function.
2. He brings liquor or drugs or narcotics into school premises or to a school function....

---

*BRITISH COLUMBIA CIVIL LIBERTIES ASSOCIATION, *A HANDBOOK ON YOUTH AND THE LAW*, VANCOUVER, THE ASSOCIATION, 1971, p. 9.

A HARD ACT TO FOLLOW:
NOTES ON ONTARIO SCHOOL LAW*

II The Schools Administration Act

This act is one of the mainstays of the Ontario school system, since its contents give substance to most aspects of a local school system. A list of the parts of the act will indicate the wide application it has to the everyday operation of a school, a board, and, indeed, to many activities common to all systems in the Province of Ontario.

The Schools Administration Act contains eleven parts:
1 School Terms and Compulsory Attendance
2 Teachers
3 Schools Trustees' and Teachers' Boards of Reference
4 Boards and Trustees
5 School Sites
6 Supervisory Officers
7 Finance
8 Reduction of School Taxes on Residential and Farm Assessment
9 School Board Advisory Committees
10 Offences and Penalties
11 Miscellaneous

1 School terms and compulsory attendance
The school year is defined as comprising three terms; the dates are specified clearly. It should be noted that the provision for a holiday in March is a relatively recent (1970) amendment; previously the break had come at Easter which, being a movable feast, had caused variations in the lengths of terms. School holidays are defined; it is interesting to note that every Saturday and Sunday are included, thereby precluding any weekend classes. These terms apply to all schools in the province, with some minor exceptions in special cases.

Attendance is compulsory for all children between specified ages; there is, however, a long list of exemptions. One of these makes it possible for students to attend privately operated schools, since they are excused if they are "receiving satisfactory instruction at ....

*GILBERT, V.K., ET AL, *A HARD ACT TO FOLLOW: NOTES ON ONTARIO SCHOOL LAW*, Toronto, University of Toronto Faculty of Education, 1973, p. 6.

MANY LAWS*

is up to the magistrate anyways. What if the magistrate says that the person has to go back in jail until the next court date? Well, even in jail the person can get advice and help from the Native court worker and lawyer. He can even get witnesses to come to his next court time. Again it is up to the person. He must not be afraid to ask for help in how to do all this. People have a right to give their side of the story too.

"The person finally has his trial. What can happen?

"In court they have what is called a PROSECUTOR. He is the one who tries to prove you did wrong. Sometimes he will ask the magistrate to WITHDRAW THE CASE. Why? Because it turns out he cannot prove it. If they want, they can arrest you again if they find new evidence.

"Or another thing can happen. The PROSECUTOR will give his side of the story. He might ask the police officer who arrested you to speak too. After he speaks, then the accused person can speak and tell his side of the story.

"Again this is where it is good to have advice. So, after hearing both sides, the magistrate makes a decision. If he has doubt about the prosecutor's side of the story, he will decide that you are not guilty. If he believes the prosecutor, he will find you guilty.

"Remember the man who is caught stealing bread because he is hungry? This type of thing should be told. Maybe if the magistrate knows the man was hungry, he will not put him in jail. He might put him on PROBATION. This means he can go home but he has to report once a month, to a government man. This man is called a PROBATION OFFICER. If a person is found guilty and goes to jail he can get out under certain conditions.

"Now if you do not think you got a fair deal, you can make what is called an APPEAL. When you are brought back to the cell, you should ask for an APPEAL FORM from the police officer or you can ask the lawyer or the court worker for this form. This should be filled out right away. You should ask for help if you cannot write in English.

"This does not mean that you will get off. It means that you have a chance to bring it to court again.

"So you see . . . Eddy, it is important to know this. Our people must no longer fear these things. . . .

---

*METIS ASSOCIATION OF ALBERTA, *MANY LAWS*, Canindis Foundation, 1970, (unpaged).

Appendix 11

COMMISSIONED MODELS

The following excerpts are taken from models prepared especially for the Study.

MODEL I.
Jack Batten, A Guide to the Ontario Mechanics' Lien Act for Subcontractors, Suppliers and Renters of Equipment.

MODEL II.
David M. Beatty, Ontario Labour Relations Law: The Organizational Drive.

MODEL III.
Ray Chatelin, The British Columbia Criminal Injuries Compensation Act.

MODEL IV.
T. E. J. McDonnell, Tax Consequences of Selling Real Estate.

MODEL V.
A. W. Mewett, Eavesdropping.

MODEL VI.
E. P. Salsberg, Ontario Land Speculation Tax.

MODEL VII.
Leslie Yager, The Workmen's Compensation Act in Ontario.

MODEL I

A GUIDE TO THE ONTARIO MECHANICS' LIEN ACT
FOR SUBCONTRACTORS, SUPPLIERS AND RENTERS OF EQUIPMENT

prepared by Jack Batten

(Jack Batten is a freelance journalist who has practised law in Toronto.)

Let's suppose you're a carpenter or a mason or a pick-and-shovel man and you've finished your work on a small construction job, building a $9,000 addition to a house in the suburbs. Or let's suppose you run a company that has sold readi-mixed concrete to the job or that your outfit has supplied the nails or the lumber or the bricks. Or let's suppose that you've rented some equipment needed on the job, a small

170

steam shovel for excavation work or the scaffolding for the brick-laying.

Let's say you're one of these men — a worker or a supplier or a renter — and then let's say that you haven't been paid for your services. You haven't seen a penny of the $9,000. What do you do now? Answer: you turn to the Mechanics' Lien Act. That's the easy part — the Mechanics' Lien Act is intended to rescue people in just your position, and it's intended to do the job in a fast and cheap way, mainly by giving you the right to register your claim for payment against the property where the construction was going on and to leave it registered there until you're paid the money owing to you.

Now comes the hard part. Even though the elected members of the Ontario legislature who passed the Mechanics' Lien Act into law were no doubt filled with good intentions — to help you get your money as quickly and inexpensively as possible — the Act presents all kinds of built-in problems, particularly if you're going to interpret the Act on your own. And it's best to keep at least three of these built-in difficulties in the back of your mind at all times:

One: the Act sets out to protect other people besides you, you the worker or supplier or renter, and these people's interests usually fall on different sides of the fence than yours. The Act has something to say about the rights of the owner of the property where the work was being done, about the rights of the mortgagee of the property, about the rights of the fellow who got the job to work as general contractor on the construction, hiring the various workers and suppliers and renters of equipment. As you can see, the interests of these different people may easily come into conflict with yours, almost always over one subject — money — and it's the Mechanics' Lien Act's chore to sort out the conflict in a way that's fairest to all. (This article, as the title indicates, is going to be concerned almost entirely with the rights and remedies of the low men on the totem pole, the workers and suppliers and renters. The rights of the contractors will come into the article in those cases where the contractor has himself done some of the work on the job or supplied his own materials to the construction. That, however, isn't as often the case today as it once was; nowadays the general contractor's role is more specialized, and he usually performs no other job except supervision, direction and, hopefully, payment to the people he's hired. His interest in most cases, then, runs against the interests of the workers, suppliers and renters. In fact, it's to him that the others are almost always looking for payment.)

Two: the Mechanics' Lien Act is a complicated piece of legislation — complicated in its language and in its intentions — and some of the Act's sections can even be intimidating. These latter sections are the kind that you can figure out only with a lawyer looking over your shoulder and acting as a translator. That's how dense the wording of some parts of the Act is. The Act's trust section (about which more later) is an example of a tough-to-understand provision, and if your problem involves you in it, you shouldn't hesitate to call on a lawyer for help. Otherwise, awkwardly worded as much of the Act is, you should be able to make your way through it on your own.

Three: you must always take the Act as a whole, relating each section to all the others. If you go at it in separate chunks, then chances are that you'll short-change yourself by missing a crucial section that qualifies another section that you're relying on. You could, in other words, act on incomplete information, and in doing so, you could blow your rights to collect the money that's rightfully owing to you.

As an illustration of the last point, a natural place to start in at the Act isn't section 1, but section 21. Section 21 makes it clear that if you've done work on a construction job, such as the $9,000 house-addition project, or if you've supplied material to it or rented equipment to it, then you've got 37 days to register a claim for lien (in effect a claim for payment of the money owing to you) against the land on which the job was taking place. Remember the magic number — 37. Mark it down in your diary or on your calendar, and don't let it slip by unnoticed.

But before you mark it, you've first got to know the answer to this question: 37 days from *when*?

Well, in the case of the workman, the pick-and-shovel guy, the employee on the job, it's 37 days from the date when you did your last work on the job. In the case of the supplier, it's 37 days from the date when you supplied your last materials to the job. In the case of the renter of equipment, it's 37 days from the date when your piece of equipment was last used on the job. All of this is set out in section 21.

But that isn't all. Section 21 also gets into the more complicated area where you, as a contractor or a subcontractor, may be performing your work or service under a written contract. In that case, section 21 says your 37 days begin from the time of "the completion or abandonment of the contract or of the subcontract." To sort out exactly what "completion" means, you have to chase back to section 1 where you'll find a group of definitions of terms used in the Act including one for "completion of the contract" which goes this way: "'completion of the contract' means substantial performance, not necessarily total performance, of the contract."

What this bit of wording boils down to is that you don't have to have finished up all the work you promised to do under your contract before you can claim a lien. Which is good for you in some ways, bad in others. Never mind the good. It's the bad you have to worry about. The notion of substantial completion can possibly work against you because it means that if, say, you're an electrician and you've left a job and let the 37 days slide by, you can't return to the job, install a few cover plates that are necessary to wind up your contract, and then, thinking you've kept your 37 days alive, proceed to file your lien. No way. Your 37 days began when you were substantially finished, not when you returned to install the plates. You can't go back to a job weeks after you'd almost finished up, a common practice among many sub-trades in former times, and revive your lien rights.

Subsection 3 of section 1 helps out in this tricky area by explaining that a contract is "substantially performed" when two conditions are satisfied: when the work you've done under your contract is being used or is ready to be used for its intended purpose, and when the work still left to be done under the contract can be carried out at a cost of not more than three per cent of the first $250,000 of the contract price, two per cent of the next $250,000, and one per cent of the balance. Take an example: suppose a school board gives a general contractor a contract to put up a new school at a cost of one million dollars. Well, when the pupils are in that school, or it's at least ready to receive them, and when there's under $17,500 worth of work left to be done on the building, then the 37 days has started to run under the contract.

There's one more complication left to throw into this business of substantial performance. The very idea of substantial performance is a fairly new addition to the Mechanics' Lien Act — up until the time it came along, final and total completion was the only yardstick by which the 37-day period was measured — and the courts haven't yet made up their minds whether substantial performance applies to subcontractors. Certainly it applies to contractors, but different Ontario judges in some recent cases have waffled around on the real meaning of substantial performance as it may or may not relate to subcontractors. Does it or doesn't it? The truth, ridiculous as it seems, is that nobody knows for sure. So the best advice for any subcontractor operating under a written contract is to play it safe and to begin counting his 37 days from the earlier date, which is of course the date of substantial performance. If you miss that date, you can always register a lien within 37 days of final completion — that is, if you're an electrician, 37 days after you've fitted those cover plates — and hope a court will agree that substantial performance is strictly for contractors and not for the subs. That, however, may be taking a long chance. . . .

MODEL II

ONTARIO LABOUR RELATIONS LAW:
THE ORGANIZATIONAL DRIVE

prepared by David M. Beatty

(David Beatty is an Associate Professor in the Faculty of Law and Acting Director of the Centre for Industrial Relations, University of Toronto.)

Having identified which persons are entitled to the benefits under the Labour Relations Act in the first chapter, the immediate question that faces an employee or union organizer who desires to organize an employer's employees is — What rights and protections does the Act confer upon the organizers?

(a)   **Right to Solicit Employees**

(i)   *Union Organizers*

In the first place if the *union organizer* is not an employee of the employer, he is not entitled, with one exception, simply to enter the employer's premises and attempt to solicit his employees. The exception is found in s. 10 of the Act. It provides that a union official may enter an employer's property to persuade his employees to join a union where the employees live on that property or the employer controls access to that property. The most common cases where the exception would operate are company towns, logging camps, mines and the like. It is important to note that before entering such property, the union official must apply (Form 12a) to and receive permission from the Board before entering upon the property. If it has been established that the employees reside on the employer's property or that the employer controls access to the property where the employees live, the Board will grant permission for a named representative of the union to have access to that property at certain specified times for the purpose of persuading such employees to join the union. It is important to note that failure to obtain such permission from the Board could result in the organizer being charged with trespass.

(ii)   *Employees*

In so far as an *employee's* right to organize his fellow employees on company property and during working hours is concerned, the Act in Section 62 neither prohibits nor authorizes such activity. Rather, in a lengthy series of cases, the Board has decided that an employer may prohibit union activity on his premises and during working hours where he can show that such activity, whether by verbal persuasion or written circulars, disrupts his production, the order in the plant, or affects the cleanliness of his plant. So, for example, if an employee's soliciting results in fighting between himself and other employees it can be prohibited. Conversely, however, an employer could not ban only discussion about the union while permitting solicitation for the United Way, unless he can prove that union persuasion has disruptive affects that other appeals do not.

It should also be noted that an employee cannot be prohibited from engaging in "non-persuasive" activity during working hours such as wearing a union button. Further, the Act does not affect an employee's (nor a union organizer's) right to persuade employees off the company premises. Finally, unless the cleanliness of the plant were affected, it would appear an employer is not entitled to prohibit solicitation on his premises which occurs in non-working hours, for example during the luncheon break.

It should be apparent from what has been said that an employer is under no obligation to provide an employee or a union official with the names, addresses and phone numbers of his employees. Rather, the employee or union official must resort to his own methods to contact those employees he seeks to persuade to join the union. Usually this is achieved by contacting employees as they leave the plant, getting licence plate numbers and the like.

(iii) *Legitimate Organizing Activity by the Union and Employees*

Within the limits already described unions are essentially protected in their attempts to persuade employees to join the union. The only limitation imposed by the Act is that no one connected with the organizing drive may attempt to induce employees to join the union by means of "intimidation or coercion" (s. 61). What this prohibition has meant in practice is that any forms of physical assault or intimidation or certain kinds of economic threats (such as the assertion that if an employee failed to join the union, the union would see to it that such persons would lose their jobs) or appeals to employees based on racial or religious prejudices will result in either the Board refusing to certify the union by setting aside the vote or indeed finding the union guilty of an unfair labour practice with the possible consequence of serious fines being levied against it. Short of such coercion or intimidation, however, the Labour Board will not interfere with an aggressive and forceful campaign waged by the union in its attempt to persuade the employees to join the union. In that regard speeches or circulars outlining the potential benefits of membership in the union, deficiencies on the part of an employer toward his employees which the union promises to correct, even if exaggerated and put in the extreme, should not jeopardize the legality of the organizational drive.

(b)   Legitimate Employer Activity During Organizational Campaign

Assuming the union is able to commence an organizing drive either off the company premises, or on the employer's premises within the limits described above, the predominant legal issue that arises during an organizational campaign is what legal responses may an employer make to the union drive. Section 56 of the Act sets out the predominant theme of the legislation. It states that an employer can not . . . "participate in or interfere with the formation, selection or administration of a trade union . . .". However, it equally clearly preserves the employer's right "to express his views so long as he does not use coercion, intimidation, threats, promises or undue influence". In short, although the question of organization is primarily one between the trade union and the employees, the employer's right to state his position is protected. If the employer engages in certain kinds of conduct (which we shall describe below) which does interfere with the formation, selection or administration of a trade union, the Board has the power (to be described in detail in the last section of this Chapter) to permit the prosecution of the employer, to certify a union without a vote and to order the reinstatement of any employee found to have been discharged during the drive contrary to the provisions of the Act. That is not to say an employer is powerless to respond to an organizational drive, nor that he should remain completely passive. However, it is to say an employer must not engage in that kind of activity which interferes with or frustrates the organizational drive.

In each case the Board will examine whether the conduct complained of by the union was likely to coerce, intimidate or unduly influence the employees in their decision as to whether to join the union or not. As we shall see below there are certain kinds of conduct occasionally engaged in by an employer which clearly are coercive or plainly interfere with the union campaign. Other kinds of activity, however, such as the discharge of a union organizer, although obviously interfering with the drive and possibly coercive of the other employees not to join the union, may in fact have been done by the employer for perfectly legitimate reasons. For example, it would be quite proper for an employer to discharge an employee who attempts to organize during working hours and does not fulfil his assigned employment obligations. In these kinds of cases, in order to find the employer has committed an unfair labour practice, the complaining employee must prove that the real reason for the employer's action was to frustrate the organizational drive rather than to further some legitimate interest of his own. The key factor, in the Board's opinion, is to discover, not whether the employer had a legitimate reason for his action but rather what is the real or genuine reason for his action. If the Board finds that the employer was motivated by an anti-union intention, he will be found to have violated the Act. To illustrate the limits of legitimate employer response to an organizational drive, we can review certain kinds of conduct which employers have frequently used in the past and on which the Labour Board has stated its views. These would include:

1. interfering with or dominating the union
2. discussing the union's campaign with the employees
3. closing or relocating the plant on discovering the union's drive
4. discharging, suspending, etc. union organizers or sympathizers

MODEL III

THE BRITISH COLUMBIA CRIMINAL
INJURIES COMPENSATION ACT

prepared by Ray Chatelin

(Ray Chatelin is the Editor of the "Action Line" column in the Vancouver daily, The Province.)

Anyone in British Columbia injured as a result of a crime can collect benefits or receive other forms of compensation through the Criminal Injuries Compensation Act.

Until recently it has been the offender who has received the bulk of attention in any crime with the taxpayer paying the rehabilitation and medical expenses needed while the victim has gone unnoticed or has been ignored.

With the passing into law of this Act in 1972, crime victims and those injured during the commission of a crime can now claim the same benefits that had been previously reserved for the wrongdoer.

It brings to eight the total number of provinces in Canada that have such legislation. However, B.C. officials claim their Act is more far-reaching and will provide greater benefits than comparable legislation.

Administration

Claims under the legislation are processed through the Workers Compensation Board (WCB). The WCB was chosen because of its experience in handling compensation problems and because it already had the bureaucratic machinery to handle claims.

It also had the needed rehabilitation clinics plus experts in related fields.

Employers, who already pay for on-the-job injuries, do not pay a cent through direct assessment. Monies for either direct financial compensation or rehabilitation come from the provincial government's revenue fund.

Victims

Exactly who is a victim?

According to the legislation you are eligible for benefits if you've been hurt for the following reasons:

• Assisting a police officer in making an arrest.

• Making an arrest of a criminal suspect yourself.

• Preventing or attempting to prevent a crime from taking place.

• Being the direct victim of any one of 39 Criminal Code offences. The list of offences is quite comprehensive and includes most crimes of violence.

Crimes

[A list of crimes follows.]

It should be noted that the list of offences excludes any arising out of the operation of a motor vehicle. These offences are covered under the Motor Vehicle Act and regulations.

However, the list does include assault by means of a motor vehicle — running down someone deliberately.

In giving protection to persons aiding police, the Criminal Injuries Compensation Act replaced the Law Enforcement Officers Assistance Act made law in 1969. Features of that piece of legislation are incorporated into this one.

Application

While it might not be comforting to know, your immediate family is also covered should you be killed while attempting to stop a crime or if you are a direct victim.

In determining if you or your dependents should receive compensation, the WCB will examine several factors. The most important of these, of course, will be to determine if a crime indeed did occur.

For this, police co-operation is essential. Their reports will be examined and their opinion of whether or not a crime has occurred will be considered.

So it is up to the victim to report the crime to the police.

However, there needn't be a conviction of the wrongdoer for you to collect.

In evaluating evidence the WCB has powers similar to those of the Supreme Court of B.C. Officials can compel the attendance of witnesses and examine them under oath.

The WCB also has the power to examine books, papers and any other items that might be relevant to a claim.

In a case where a witness cannot appear, the board can demand a deposition. And once that is out of the way the board will base its decision on the following:

• The extent and degree of disability.

• The permanence of the disability

• The degree of lessening of earning power.

• Relationships of any family member to the victim (in case of death).

• The existence of dependency.

Any or all of these points will be applied to any case coming before the WCB depending upon the circumstances surrounding each case.

If you apply for compensation, expect to be examined by a doctor. If your own doctor doesn't look at the injury the WCB has its own team of medical experts and doctors.

Exclusions

There are, of course, some claims that obviously will not qualify. If, for example, you're a party to a crime and you're injured you won't be able to collect.

Also, if you've contributed to your injuries or even your own death through some "gross fault" the WCB will refuse either you or your dependents any compensation.

If you are collecting through some other provincial or federal Act, you'll be refused.

The Act applies only to crimes committed within B.C. and there must have been at least $100 damage . . .

MODEL IV

TAX CONSEQUENCES OF SELLING REAL ESTATE (HOUSE, COTTAGE, DUPLEX, CONDOMINIUM, ETC.)

prepared by T. E. J. McDonnell

(Tom McDonnell is an Associate Professor in the Faculty of Law, University of Toronto, who formerly practised in the tax law area.)

The first question to consider is whether the proceeds of sale of the real estate are taxable at all. For many persons, the proceeds of sale will be received on the sale of their family residence, and as such will be free from tax in whole or in part under the "principal residence" exemption.

The Principal Residence Exemption

If the property qualifies as a "principal residence", in many cases all of the gain will be totally exempt from tax. (The most important exception to this is a principal residence that includes more than one acre of surrounding land; in such a case, part of the proceeds may not qualify for exemption. For further discussion of this, see below).

There are two important sections of the Act to look at in connection with this exemption; paragraph 54(g) and paragraph 40(2)(b).

Paragraph 54(g) contains the basic definition of a principal residence. To qualify, all of the following conditions must be met:

(i) The property must be a housing unit or a leasehold interest therein, or a share of the capital stock of a co-operative housing corporation (including a condominium). There is no definition of "housing unit". Probably anything that is actually used as a place of residence qualifies, for example, a mobile home or trailer or perhaps even a houseboat, if occupied full time.

(ii) The property must be owned by the taxpayer in the year, whether jointly with another person or solely by the taxpayer ("jointly" includes ownership as joint tenants or tenants-in-common).

(iii) The property must have been "ordinarily inhabited" by the taxpayer in the year (more about this below), or,

(iv) if the property was being rented, the owner must have made a subsection 45(2) election (more about this below).

(v) The property must have been designated as the principal residence in prescribed manner and no other property may have been so designated. Basically, the exemption is claimed in the tax return which is filed for the year in which the property was sold. The actual mechanics for making the election are outlined in Interpretation Bulletin IT-120.

(vi) Only the house and as much of the surrounding lands that are necessary for the use and enjoyment of the house as a residence qualify for exemption. Normally, up to one acre of land will be presumed to be necessary for use and enjoyment without any evidence from the taxpayer. To get an exemption for more than one acre, the taxpayer will have to show that the excess was necessary for his use and enjoyment of the house as a residence. (See Interpretation Bulletin IT-120 for a discussion of the type of evidence the tax department will require to establish the exemption for land in excess of one acre.)

The Property Must Be "Ordinarily Inhabited"
As a Principal Residence

This means that the person claiming the exemption must have used the house as his usual place of residence. If a husband and wife own their home jointly and live together, both of them may claim the exemption when the home is sold. However, if they were living apart at the date of sale, only the spouse actually living in the house would qualify for the full exemption. The other spouse might qualify for a partial exemption, based on the number of years after 1971 that he or she did in fact live in the house. (More on the details of calculating the exemption below).

Spouses (or other persons) may own more than one property together; for example, a city house and a cottage property. If both properties are owned jointly, the full exemption can only be claimed on one of them, since the exemption can be claimed only in respect of one property in any year. However, if the city house was owned solely by one and the cottage solely by the other, it might be possible to get the full exemption for both. The question would then be whether each owner "ordinarily inhabited" each property as a residence, especially where the two owners were living together. It is not possible to make general comments that will cover all possible cases. However, it may be that if the owner of the cottage, to take just one example, regularly lives there during the summer, then that person can claim the exemption for the cottage notwithstanding that he or she spends the rest of the year residing in the city.

Rental Properties and "Ordinarily Inhabited"

In certain cases, a property may continue to qualify as a principal residence even though it is not actually inhabited by the owner for a period of time. If a person living in a house that otherwise qualifies decides to rent all or a part of it for a period of time, he may choose to file an election under subsection 45(2) of the Act. The effect of doing so is to treat the owner as if he continued to occupy the house, instead of renting it, for certain purposes. For principal residence purposes, the owner may continue to regard the house as a principal residence for up to four taxation years from the year in which he makes the election. Any rental income received during that period is taxable and no deduction may be made on account of capital cost allowance (depreciation). Other expenses such as mortgage interest, property taxes and maintenance charges may be deducted, however. Because there may be other tax consequences of making (or not making) the election at the time you decide to rent all, or part, of your house, it may be prudent to check with the information service of the tax department, or a lawyer or accountant, before doing so. For example, if you rent without making the election, you will be treated for tax purposes as if you had sold the property rented. This may require you to claim the principal residence exemption in your tax return for that year, even though there has been no actual sale.

Calculation of the Amount of the Exemption

If the property has been used as your principal residence continuously since you acquired it and you have been a resident of Canada throughout the same period, all of any gain on resale qualifies for exemption. However, if the property did not qualify as a principal residence for part of the time (say because the owner did not reside in it) or if the owner was a non-resident of Canada for part of the time, part only of the gain will be exempt. There is a formula in paragraph 40(2)(b) that is to be used in such cases. If you have a case in which the calculation must be made, it might be prudent to get professional help from a lawyer or accountant familiar with tax matters. (A sample calculation is attached as Appendix "A" for those interested in trying to work out their own situation.)

If the Real Property Does Not Qualify for the Principal Residence Exemption

If you cannot get the principal residence exemption, it will be necessary to decide whether the proceeds of sale of the real estate are taxable as income or as capital. . . .

MODEL V

EAVESDROPPING

prepared by A. W. Mewett

(Alan Mewett is a Professor in the Faculty of Law, University of Toronto and is the editor of the Criminal Law Quarterly. The excerpt is based upon materials for a book he is writing on Criminal Law and Procedure.)

Part IV.1 of the Criminal Code came into force in 1974 and is concerned with the offences that can conveniently be considered as dealing with the protection of privacy. Its provisions are somewhat complicated and the interpretation of some of the sections will be open to doubt until they have been fully considered by the courts. In general, the Part forbids the interception of private communications by various means, except in certain defined circumstances.

A private communication is defined to mean any oral communication or any telecommunication made under circumstances in which it is reasonable for the person making the communication to expect that it will not be intercepted by any person other than the person the communicator intended to receive it. "Intercept" includes listen to, record or acquire a communication or acquire the substance, meaning or purport of it.

Section 178.11(1) of the Criminal Code states:

Everyone who, by means of an electromagnetic, acoustic, mechanical or other device, wilfully intercepts a private communication is guilty of an indictable offence and liable to imprisonment for five years.

The phrase "electromagnetic, acoustic, mechanical or other device" means any device or apparatus that is used or is capable of being used to intercept a private communication, but does not include a hearing aid used to correct subnormal hearing of the user.

The offence set out in Section 178.11(1) is not committed where one of four different conditions apply. These are, first, where the accused has the consent to intercept, express or implied, of the person making the communication or of the person the communicator intended to receive it. Since a communication necessarily involves two persons, this condition refers to the consent of either of those two. This means, of course, that consent by the person, for example, making a telephone call will make any wire-tap legal even if the result of it is to intercept the statements made by the person at the other end of the telephone, even where he himself does not consent.

Second, an offence is not committed if the interception is by a person who is engaged in providing a telephone, telegraph or similar service and such interception is necessary for maintaining or protecting the person's rights or property related to the provision of such service.

Third, an employee of the federal government is permitted to intercept in the course of random monitoring that is necessarily incidental to radio frequency spectrum management.

Last, the interception may be authorized or it may be done by a person who in good faith aids a person whom he believes has such authorization.

The authorization referred to is provided in Sections 178.13 or 178.15(2). An application in writing is made under Section 178.12, to a judge of a superior court of criminal jurisdiction or a judge defined in Section 482 (a county court judge). The application is to be signed either by the provincial Attorney-General or the federal Solicitor-General or by a specifically designated agent, and it must be accompanied by an affidavit, sworn by a peace officer or public officer.

The affidavit must set out the following: (1) the facts justifying the belief that an authorization should be given, including the particulars of the offence under investigation; (2) the type of private communication to be intercepted; (3) the names and addresses, where known, of those persons whose private communications are to be intercepted, or, if not known, the general description of the place of the private communications; (4) the period for which the authorization is requested; (5) and whether other investigative procedures have been tried and have failed or why it appears they are unlikely to succeed or why there is some urgency in the matter.

The offence referred to in the application for authorization is not any offence but only those listed in Section 178.1 of the Criminal Code. These offences are the conspiracy to commit or attempt to commit or being accessory after the fact to such crimes as: (1) treason and sedition and related offences; (2) hijacking; (3) causing bodily injury; (4) bribery; (5) public fraud; (6) perjury; (7) invasion of privacy; (8) murder; (9) kidnapping; (10) hate-propaganda dissemination; (11) robbery and extortion; (12) breaking and entering; (13) possession of stolen property and related offences; (14) forgery; (15) threats; (16) fraudulent transactions; (17) counterfeiting and uttering; (18) some gambling offences; (19) theft over $200; (20) drug offences; (21) some excise offences relating to alcoholic spirits; or, generally, (22) any other indictable offence which forms part of a pattern of two or more persons acting together to commit similar offences which are part of the activities of organized crime.

Upon application, the judge may grant the authorization if he is satisfied that it is in the best interests of the administration of justice to do so and in addition to that, that other investigative procedures have been tried and have failed, or that other investigative procedures are unlikely to succeed or that the urgency of the matter is such that other investigative procedures only would be impractical.

If given, the authorization states the nature of the offence in question, the type of private communications to be intercepted, the identity of the persons involved if known, or the place involved if they are not known, the period of the authorization (up to a maximum of thirty days), and such terms and conditions as the judge considers advisable in the public interest. . . .

MODEL VI

ONTARIO LAND SPECULATION TAX

prepared by E. P. Salsberg

(Rick Salsberg is a solicitor with the Toronto firm of Tory, Tory DesLauriers & Binnington.)

Liability of an Individual to Pay Land Speculation Tax

In what situation does an individual become liable to pay land speculation tax?

Do not be misled into believing that you must be speculating in order for this tax to be payable. Unless you discover the opposite as you read further in this discussion, you are liable to pay this tax whenever you sell or otherwise give someone else any part of any interest which you have in any land or building located in Ontario.

The first example of such a situation which will spring to mind is selling a certain piece of land or a certain building which you own. In this case, you have the entire interest in the land or building, and you are selling that entire interest. However, it is easy to think of cases in which you have the entire interest in a piece of land or a building but you only give away part of it: for instance, if you sell someone a half-interest in your land, or you give someone an option to buy your land, or you rent someone part of your building. Similarly, you can imagine instances in which you only have a partial interest in a piece of land or a building and you give away all of that partial interest: for instance, if you only own a half-interest in a piece of land and you sell that half-interest, or if you are a tenant in a building and you sub-let to another person.

In all these cases, you are liable for land speculation tax unless there is a specific exemption mentioned below.

How much is the land speculation tax?

In order to calculate how much land speculation tax you must pay in any transaction, you must first determine two things: how much the interest in the land or building cost you to acquire and maintain, and how much you charged when you disposed of it. You will discover below that there are many specific rules telling you how to calculate both of these amounts. In general terms, though, your cost will be the amount you paid when you acquired the interest (or, if you acquired it on or before April 9, 1974, the market value of the interest on April 9, 1974) plus the amount which you have spent since April 9, 1974 on improvements and maintenance costs plus your costs involved in selling or otherwise giving the interest to someone else, and your Receipts will be the full price which you charged the person to whom you sold or gave the interest.

If your Receipts are less than or exactly equal to your Cost, you do not owe any land speculation tax. Otherwise, the land speculation tax which you must pay is one-half the difference between your Receipts and your Cost.

Which transactions never require the payment of land speculation tax?

It was mentioned above that there are certain situations in which you will never have to pay land speculation tax even though you are selling or giving someone else a part of an interest which you have in some land or building located in Ontario. These are listed below, and if your type of transaction appears in that list, you do not have to be concerned with paying land speculation tax.

(a) The most common situation is if you sell or give someone else the place where you ordinarily live. If you ordinarily live in more than one place, this must be your principal place. Furthermore, if that place contains more than 10 acres, or is partly used for purposes other than the residence of you and your family, this exception only relieves you of paying land speculation tax in respect of 10 acres of that place or the portion of that place which is used as the residence of you and your family. . . .

MODEL VII

THE WORKMEN'S COMPENSATION ACT IN ONTARIO

prepared by Leslie Yager

(Leslie Yager is a third-year student in the Faculty of Law, University of Toronto, who prepared the Workmen's Compensation Section of Law for Community Clinics, published by the Students' Legal Aid Society, University of Toronto, in 1974.)

A.　**History of the Legislation:**

Before the Workmen's Compensation Act was passed in 1915 the situation of an injured worker was a sorry one. Once injured, a worker did not automatically receive any compensation. Instead he had to sue his employer in court. Several obstacles made this course of action difficult. The average worker could not afford to go to court to obtain compensation. Once in court the judges were not sympathetic to the worker. Two legal doctrines developed that prevented most workers from recovering compensation in court. First, if the worker was at all responsible for the accident he would not recover any compensation. Secondly, a worker was presumed to assume any risks that were incidental to his type of employment. Thus a railway worker who was crushed by a train would not recover.

With the advent of the industrial revolution more men became injured as industrial jobs increased. Many of these men could not recover from their employers and were forced to go on welfare in order to live. Finally the government decided to remedy this unhappy situation and passed the first Workmen's Compensation Act in 1915. This Act completely removed compensation cases from the control of the courts and substituted a statutory board to direct a new scheme of compensation.

B.　**Who Is Covered by The Workmen's Compensation Act**

There are four ways that a person may be covered by the Act.
1. *Schedule 1:* Schedule 1 covers basically all industrial and heavy labour jobs. Some examples of schedule 1 employees include miners, butchers, stevedores, construction workers, and motel operators.
2. *Schedule 2:* Very few employees are covered by schedule 2. The main employees under schedule 2 are Bell Telephone and railway workers.
3. *Schedule 3:*This schedule contains a list of industrial diseases covered by compensation. If a worker gets one of these diseases, he is covered exactly as he would be if he had an individual accident.

Example: Silicosis is one disease listed under this schedule. If a worker gets silicosis he is entitled to compensation because of schedule 3. He is engaged in mining, a schedule 1 activity. Thus his payments are regulated by schedule 1 type of payments.

A worker should get a copy of the Act, and look under the Regulations to see if he falls under schedule 1, 2, or 3.

4. *Private Coverage:* Two types of people may apply to be covered by compensation even though they are not required to come under the scheme.

The first type of person is the small businessman who may want his employees to come under compensation rather than buy private insurance. The Board is not required to accept these private applications but once they do those employees are covered by the Act. The other type of person that may apply for coverage is the employer. Note that up to this point the discussion has focused on employees. Only employees automatically become eligible for compensation if they fall under schedule 1, 2 or 3. Employers are not covered unless they make a separate special application for coverage.

C. The Effect of Being Covered by the Act

If you are covered by the Act you may not sue your employer if you are injured while at work. Instead, a worker is required to accept immediate benefits and settle any disputes through the machinery set up by the Board. However, if a worker is injured at his job by a person who is not covered by the Act the worker may choose not to accept the compensation provided and can then sue that person.

Example: The worker is a truck driver. While working he is involved in a motor vehicle accident. He has two choices. He may accept compensation benefits. Or, he may refuse the benefits and sue the other person involved in the accident in court.

If a worker accepts compensation benefits the Board then sues for him. If the amount recovered by the Board is more than the amount of compensation the Board has paid to the worker, then the worker will receive the difference.

Example: The truck driver described above accepts benefits and is given a total of $1,000 over a six week period. The Board sues the other driver and wins $8,000. The truck driver will get the additional $7,000 minus the Board's legal costs.

D. Advantages to Being Covered by the Act:

The worker gains the following advantages under the compensation legislation as opposed to his position if he were able to sue his employer in Court:

1. Benefits begin immediately after he is injured. Court cases, on the other hand, take an extremely long time to settle and the worker receives nothing until settlement is achieved.

2. The worker generally will not need to hire a lawyer to make his claim before the Board. Court battles require a lawyer and usually are extremely expensive.

3. The compensation scheme is basically a no-fault system. Thus even if the worker was responsible for the accident he is still able to get money from the Board. However, in a court of law the worker would have to *prove* that his employer's negligence caused the accident.

4. A worker does not have to bring his claim within a specified given time period. He may apply for benefits any time after the accident. In the courts he would have to make his claim within six years of the date of the accident.

5. A worker covered by the compensation Act may apply to have his case reconsidered at any time. If he had sued in court, once he accepted the money settlement his case would be closed forever. It is extremely difficult to assess the long-term effect of certain types of injuries. Back injuries are especially difficult to assess and they are a common injury. If the worker misjudged the severity of the injury and asked for too little money when he was in court he would face the prospect of increasing poverty as his capacity to work decreases.

E. Disadvantages to Being Covered:

There is really only one disadvantage of being covered by the Act and hence not being allowed to bring claim in Court. Under the Act a worker receives no compensation for his "pain and suffering." . . .

ACCESS TO THE LAW QUESTIONNAIRE

1. We are interested in obtaining certain information about organizations and individuals who provide legal information to the general public and/or help with their legal problems. In this context, would you please indicate which of the following categories describes you or your organization:
   —— library
   —— community information centre
   —— social service agency
   —— government public office
   —— legal aid office
   —— police department
   —— individual — please specify occupation:
   —— other: *please specify:*

2. What is the population of the municipality in which you are located;

3. In which province or territory are you located?

4. What is the scope of the service offered by your centre or institution? (Please check all that apply.)
   —— Answering questions using personal knowledge or files
   —— Providing materials for inquirers to use to find an answer to their own questions
   —— Referring inquirers to other people or institutions outside your centre or institution
   —— Providing staff to research an inquiry using resources within your centre or institution
   —— Providing staff to research an inquiry by leaving your centre or institution to use resources at a library or other centre
   —— Other: *please specify*

5. How many inquiries on all subjects does your organization or institution receive each month?

6. Have you a recent description or survey of the people who use your centre or institution? If so, we would appreciate it if you would enclose a copy when you return this questionnaire.

7. Many centres are set up to serve a particular population group, while others aim for very wide coverage. Please indicate which of the following characteristics apply generally to your users:

Age: —— under 20 yrs.
              —— 21 - 60 yrs.
              —— 61 yrs. and over
              —— All ages
Sex: —— female mostly
              —— male mostly
              —— both
Income: —— low income
              —— middle income
              —— high income
              —— all income levels
Occupation: —— student
              —— unemployed
              —— retired
              —— people who do not work outside the home
              —— people employed in blue collar jobs
              —— people employed in white collar jobs
              —— all of the above
              —— other: *please specify*
Location: Most users live within:
              —— 1 mile radius
              —— 2 mile radius
              —— 5 mile radius
              —— 10 mile radius
              —— larger than 10 mile radius of the centre.
              (Please indicate largest area applicable.)

8. How do people find out about your centre? Please indicate all that apply.
              —— local advertising
              —— word of mouth
              —— referrals from other organizations or individuals who were approached first
              —— other: *please specify*

9. The following questions relate to inquiries you receive concerning the law or government-related (i.e. "administrative") problems. Requests for specific statutes and other legal materials are included as well, even if you are not asked for advice or information about a particular problem.
    (a) How many legal/administrative inquiries do you receive each month? If you have recorded statistics, please indicate the period they cover.
    (b) If you keep a record of your legal/administrative inquiries

broken down by subject area, please fill in the section below in column (A).

For the [week ending .....,   ]
[month ending .....,   ] we received
[other period ....., ending .....,   ]

the number of inquiries indicated on the following subjects:

	Column A	Column B
Employment & Unemployment		
Real Estate & Mortgages		
Consumer Protection		
Motor Vehicles		
Operation of Courts		
Immigration & Citizenship		
Separation & Divorce		
Children & Minors		
Other Family Matters		
Criminal		
Taxation		
Minority & Native Rights		
Environmental Law		
Copyright, Trademarks & Patents		
Welfare		
Loans & Debts		
Companies & Business		
Landlord & Tenant		
Legal Terminology		
Estates & Wills		
Contracts		
Other		

(c) If you do not keep a record, we would appreciate it if you could keep track of the legal administrative inquiries you receive for one week, and fill in Column B above.

(d) Do you specialize in any particular legal/administrative area? (For example, in immigration or family law problems.) *Please specify:*

10. (a) Who in your organization first receives inquiries? (For example, switchboard operator, receptionist, reference librarian, etc.)

(b) How does this person handle legal/administrative inquiries or problems? (Please indicate the approximate percentages of such inquiries handled in each specific way.)

—— Immediately refers inquirer to an appropriate outside organization, office, or individual.

—— Gives inquirer answer by using personal knowledge or a "quick answer" information file.

—— Directs inquirer to relevant materials contained in your organization.

—— Refers inquirer to another staff member in your organization.

—— Researches question using materials contained in your organization and gives inquirer answer.

—— Researches question using materials outside your organization and gives inquirer answer.

—— After attempting to find an answer in published materials and failing to find an answer, refers inquirer to an outside organization, office or individual.

—— Other: *Please specify:*

(c) In those cases in which the person receiving a legal/administrative inquiry attempts to find an answer in published materials, what is the average time spent for the search?

—— less than 5 minutes

—— 6 - 10 minutes

—— 11 - 20 minutes

—— 21 - 30 minutes

—— more than 30 minutes

(d) In those cases in which the person receiving a legal/administrative inquiry refers the inquirer to another staff member to whom is the inquirer referred?

(e) Does this staff member have any special training in handling legal/administrative questions and problems? (Including training generally in handling inquiries of all kinds from the public.) *Please specify:*

(f) How does this staff member handle legal/administrative inquiries or problems? (Please indicate the approximate percentages of such inquiries handled in each specific way.)

—— Immediately refers inquirer to an appropriate outside organization, office, or individual.

—— Gives inquirer answer by using personal knowledge or a "quick answer" information file.

—— Directs inquirer to relevant materials contained in your organization.

—— Refers inquirer to another staff member in your organization.

—— Researches question using materials contained in your organization and gives inquirer answer.

—— Researches question using materials outside your organization and gives inquirer answer.

—— After attempting to find an answer in published materials and failing to find an answer, refers inquirer to an outside organization, office or individual.

—— Other: *Please specify:*

(g) In those cases in which this staff member attempts to find an answer in published materials, what is the average time spent for the search?

—— less than 5 minutes

—— 6 - 10 minutes

—— 11 - 20 minutes

—— 21 - 30 minutes

—— more than 30 minutes

(h) In those cases in which this staff member refers the inquirer to another staff member, to whom is the inquirer referred?

(i) Does this third staff member have any special training in handling legal/administrative questions and problems? *Please specify:*

(j) How does this third staff member handle such problems? *Please specify:*

11. To which of the following institutions or individuals do you refer legal/administrative problems and questions? (Please indicate the approximate percentages of such inquiries referred to each.)

—— Police

—— Government departments and officials

—— Lawyers

—— Social agencies

—— Public or academic libraries

—— Law libraries

—— Community information centres

—— Legal aid offices

—— Other: *Please specify:*

12. For legal/administrative problems and questions that are solved or answered by you or your staff, which of the following materials are the most useful? Please check as many as are applicable:

—— Statute citators

—— Statutes and by-laws

—— Regulations

—— Case reports

—— Other government publications

—— Legal textbooks

—— Legal encyclopedias

—— Popular legal handbooks

—— Looseleaf legal services

—— Newspaper clippings

—— Legal dictionaries

—— Legal periodicals

—— Your own "quick answer" information files

—— Other: *Please specify:*

13. What problems do you and your staff have in finding answers to questions involving the law or administration?

14. When the legal/administrative question or problem is one for which you think the answer can be found in published materials like statutes, case reports, legal encyclopedias, legal texts, or looseleaf legal services, which, if any, of the following problems do you have in finding an appropriate answer or solution? (Please indicate more than one if applicable, and put two check marks for frequently-occurring problems.)

—— No published source exists at all which applies to the problem.

—— A source exists, but we do not have it available because we would not use it enough to justify buying it.

—— A source exists, but we do not have it available because, although we would use it frequently, it is too expensive.

—— The only published materials that apply to the problem are too scholarly and complex to be useful for our purposes.

—— The only published materials that apply to the problem are too introductory and superficial to be useful for our purposes.

—— The published materials that apply to the problem are not specific enough to provide information just on the aspect I require.

—— The existing published materials are too difficult to use.

—— There is no published source that applies to Canada.

—— We do not have a published source that applies to Canadian law.

—— Other: *Please specify:*

15. If you find the existing published materials are too difficult to use, please indicate which of the following create the difficulty. (Check as many as apply.)

—— I usually do not know the legal category into which the problem or question falls, and therefore I have difficulty finding the correct statute, book, etc.

—— The published materials have no index.

—— I am unable to find what I want in the published materials because the terminology used in the index is unfamiliar or too technical.

—— The indexes in the published materials are inadequate for other reasons: *Please specify:*

—— The language in the published materials is difficult to understand.

—— The materials are in looseleaf form, and I cannot rely on them because of filing problems.

—— Other: *Please specify:*

16. (a) In your present service, do you think you are dealing with legal and administrative questions and problems successfully?

    —— yes

    —— no

    (b) What are your reasons for your answer to question 16(a)?

17. (a) Have you set up a file to give quick answers to specific questions?

    (b) What percentage of all questions and problems you receive are answered or solved using your quick answer file?

    (c) What percentage of the quick answer file deals with legal/administrative information?

    (d) What percentage of all the legal/administrative questions and problems you receive are answered or solved using your quick answer file?

    (e) Approximately how much staff time was used in setting up your quick answer file and how much staff time is used in maintaining the file?

    (i) Setting up : _____ hours

    (ii) Maintaining : _____ hours per week

18. Which of the following do you have in your institution or centre?

    —— Revised Statutes of Canada

    —— Statutes for your own province

    —— Statutes for other provinces (How many provinces? ——)

    —— Statute Citators

    —— Regulations of Canada

    —— Regulations for your own province

    —— Regulations for other provinces (How many provinces? ——)

    —— Canada Gazette

    —— Gazette for your own province

    —— Gazette for other provinces (How many provinces? ——)

    —— Complete by-laws for your own municipality

    —— Some by-laws for your own municipality

    —— Legal dictionary

    —— Canadian case reports (Please specify which reports)

    —— Legal encyclopedias

    —— The Canadian Abridgment

    —— Canadian loose-leaf services (Please indicate how many binders you have)

less than 5   ——
6 - 10   ——
11 - 25   ——
more than 25   ——
    Legal textbooks (Please indicate the approximate number)
less than 10   ——
11 - 25   ——
26 - 50   ——
more than 50   ——
—— Popular legal handbooks for laymen
—— Legal periodicals
—— Indexes to legal periodicals

19. What suggestions do you have for increasing public access to the
law?

INDEX

WITHDRAWN
FROM STOCK
QMUL LIBRARY